# *Changing Trains in Ulaanbataar*

## *Safe travel and how to avoid it*

*BARRIE CONDON*

# *Copyright*



This is a work of non-fiction. As a recounting of personal experiences, they are naturally told with the bias of single viewpoint.



Isbn: 978-1-914399-75-6



Printed and bound in Great Britain by Clays Ltd, Elcograf S.p.A.



SPARSILE
BOOKS

# Contents

*Adventure is a path. Real adventure—self-determined, self-motivated, often risky—forces you to have first-hand encounters with the world. The world the way it is, not the way you imagine it. Your body will collide with the earth and you will bear witness. In this way you will be compelled to grapple with the limitless kindness and bottomless cruelty of humankind—and perhaps realize that you yourself are capable of both. This will change you. Nothing will ever again be black-and-white.*

*Mark Jenkins*, explorer and author

# *Introduction*

There's no shortage of travel gods.

Apollo and Neptune are the Greek and Roman gods of seafarers; Chimata-no-kami are the two Shinto road gods who protect travellers against ghosts and demons; Ganesha the Hindu travel god removes obstacles from their path; Hecate the Greek god protects them from evil.

Pity I only learned about any of them when researching this book. Perhaps if I'd paid homage and sacrificed a bull or two, they might have stopped me getting into some awful messes.

Being at the wrong place at the wrong time isn't the result of any intelligent design on my part. I never actually seek out trouble. You'd have as much chance of finding me bungee jumping off a bridge in New Zealand as drinking a milkshake on the Moon.

Yet somehow, I've found myself in hurricanes, in a fire at sea, and had a run-in with a South American death squad. I've battled intelligent toilets, been shadowed by SWAT teams just because I wanted to go for a stroll, suffered neurosurgery by pothole and nearly been violently killed by dead cows and rice.

And that's just for starters.

Yet I go to great lengths to avoid problems. For example, I book accommodation well ahead so I have somewhere to stay at night. I found out early that sleeping on beaches and in deserts gets very old very fast. I sensibly consult timetables and do a lot of research months before I even set off.

So why do I get into such difficulties?

It's partly because of all the travelling I've done. I've had a lifetime of it, first as a student then as a sailor then as a scientist and finally as a senior citizen. Each aspect of my life has come with its own danger-laden travel wrinkles.

In the early days not having much money helped. A high limit credit card can get you airlifted out of most places when things go south. Many of my problems arose because money and I were only distantly related.

I'm not complaining about any of my experiences because it's usually those very same dramas that make travel so interesting in the first place. Lying on a beach day after day yields few tales of derring-do. That's why you'll hear nothing of beach holidays in this book, apart from a contretemps with some wild dogs on a beach in Goa.

In fact, beach holidays are my idea of hell and this drives my family wild. For some mysterious reason they consider relaxing by water a good thing. All I see is boredom and a charter flight to heatstroke.

So, this book is for only certain types of readers. Firstly, it provides vicarious tales of danger for armchair travellers (the Covid pandemic made us all into those for a while). Though I'm not one myself, I have a lot of time for such sedate travellers. They have that elusive quality I lack: basic common sense.

This book may also be instructive for people who like to travel but want to do so safely by avoiding everything I talk about here. You know the sort: people who are contented with their lot and don't want to end their lives prematurely. Again, that is a group to be admired because, and I'm generalising unforgivably here, most travellers travel because they are fundamentally discontented. They need its stimulus to feel alive; the same sort of stimulus some get from dangerous sports like rock climbing except with air tickets and the odd complimentary drink.

The final group this book is aimed at is the up-for-it people who like the edginess that travel done improperly can provide.

So, for a travel book, there will be little mention of museums and shopping. We'll talk about restaurants only where the food was bizarre and exotic or just plain alarming.

It's a marvellous world out there and can furnish you with memories that will last a lifetime. Just don't blame me if it all goes pear-shaped. Follow my steps at your own peril.

No kidding!

Before we start, I'd better make it clear that some people's names and those of a couple of ships have been changed so I can body-swerve any libel actions, even though this will inevitably protect the guilty.

I'll leave it up to the travel gods to bring them to justice in their own good time.

## *A Run-in with a Death Squad*

Valparaiso, Chile 1977

I was twenty-three years old and knew it all.

When I went to South America for the first time, the depths of my ignorance led me into a situation that scared the hell out of me. It also led me to make probably the biggest mistake of my life.

All of this was mixed in with over-generous elements of farce. Tragedy and farce: the story of my life. That would have made an alternative title for this book.

My trajectory to South America started when I got fed up with school. Nursery school, infant school, junior school, secondary school, first university degree, masters degree; I had been in one form of education or another for twenty years and I'd had more than enough of it.

One day, wondering what the hell I was going to do next, I was checking a job sheet for graduates and two adverts caught my eye. One was for the Royal Hong Kong Police. This was when HK was still being ruled by the British. Believe it or not, they were willing to fly me, a wet-behind-the-ears graduate, to that faraway exotic city then give me a gun and put me in charge of a squad of ten Chinese coppers who really had seen it all.

That was colonialism for you.

Not only that but the HK police were fabulously corrupt, as indeed was much of HK. If your house caught fire then you had to pay the fire brigade to turn on their water and put it out. Then, when the fire was extinguished, you had to pay them to turn off their hoses before they washed away what was left.

Police officers earned so much from graft they could retire to the south of France when they were only forty. Or, if they'd been really bad, to places like Taiwan which didn't have an extradition treaty with the UK.

God knows, it all sounded tempting but even I knew I'd make a crap policeman. Skinny and of medium height I was physically unprepossessing. My voice was deep but soft. When I tried to shout it was like the faint gurglings of a dyspeptic bullfrog. I had the presence and gravitas of most twenty-three-year-olds. In other words: none at all. Being a child of the freewheeling Swinging Sixties I also had little respect for the law.

As well as my physical and moral limitations there was another reason not to become an HK copper. Once you supped with the Devil, not all paths led to bougainvillea and cocktails in Cap d'Antibe. Some led to floating face down in the water (Hong Kong means *Fragrant Harbour* but fragrant it very definitely wasn't).

Thankfully, I was diverted by the second advert. This caught my eye because it was the only one in colour. On such shiny baubles do the course of our lives sometimes depend.

This one was for the Merchant Navy. It turned out that their old way of recruiting boys straight from school, many without any qualifications at all, wasn't really working any more. In order to become deck and engineering officers, these cadets had to get their 'tickets' by passing exams which then allowed them to move up the ranks. The youngsters they recruited fresh from school just couldn't cut it.

So, one firm (I'd better keep them nameless) hit on the idea of recruiting graduates who by their nature had become professional exam-passers.

The job offered the chance to travel the world with four months holiday a year and a pretty good salary. A no-brainer for an adventurous young man, surely?

I applied and for reasons I still don't understand they gave me a job. They didn't even ask if I could swim.

After only a two-week induction course at Liverpool which consisted mainly of listing all the ways you could die at sea, I was set loose to spread havoc across the fleet. After a couple of voyages on a container ship, about which more later, I was flown out to join a general cargo ship in Baltimore. It was taking cars down to Valparaiso in Chile where it would then load up with apples and take these to Rotterdam.

I was pretty excited. Being flown anywhere back in 1977 was a big deal because it was so extremely expensive. For example, even just a return flight from Glasgow to London then was £160 which would be about £700 in today's money. You can get the same tickets now for as little as £40. Flying across the Atlantic cost an absolute fortune in those days.

So, I felt quite the thing as I joined my refrigerated general cargo ship in Baltimore; we'll call it the *Goneril*. Containerisation, which in my view took all the fun out of the Merchant Navy, was only just coming in. General cargo ships would spend weeks in port, container ships only hours, so I was very pleased to find myself on a ship where big metal boxes did not come as standard.

We set sail down the east coast of the States, across the Caribbean, then through the Panama Canal. From there we paralleled the spine of the Andes as we headed south, occasionally catching sight of their cloud-veiled peaks, all the way down the coast of Peru to Chile.

You might think long sea passages are boring but you'd be wrong. There was much to see that was enchanting. Our big ship knifing through the water disturbed showers of flying fish, their fins iridescent in the sun. They'd skitter in their multitudes across the wave peaks on flights of a hundred feet or more. First thing every morning there'd be scores of them beached on the deck, their glittering colours already lost in the greyness of death. One of my jobs was to brush them overboard.

Porpoises raced us, their sleek grey bodies launching from the waves like missiles from a hidden submarine.

At night the sea would light up with green phosphorescence as our passage excited tiny light-emitting plankton. Behind us the churning of our engines left a line of green light disappearing into the dark.

It wasn't just the sea that could be spectacular. In the air, almost like kites tied to us with a line, albatrosses arced back and forth behind the ship. At night the Milky Way shone down in all its glory and for the first time I saw the stars of the Southern Cross.

It was a trip I much enjoyed. However, if I'd had any appreciation of what lay ahead, I would have spent the entire trip locked in my cabin and whimpering in the foetal position.

Instead, I spent the time doing all the menial jobs on board the ship. I was training to be a deck officer but, rather admirably, the Board of Trade who regulated maritime qualifications took the view that you couldn't command other people to do something unless you'd done it yourself at some point. I was given a whole book containing a long list of tasks I had to get signed off by the mate. So, I crawled through the bilges to measure the water levels, I climbed the mast in a rolling sea to check the stamped-on loading weight of the shackles and I endlessly chipped rust off the deck before repainting it. My hands, pillow soft when I left university, became as calloused as a tuna fisherman's.

After a couple of weeks of this mundane stuff I was gagging for adventure and so was far from displeased when Valparaiso hove into view.

As we drew nearer, the city resolved itself into two distinct parts. Along the narrow shoreline the architecture was

European, or at least the European of the late nineteenth century. It looked prosperous, if a little run down.

The buildings on the hillsides were a different matter. They were basically shacks, most roofed in corrugated iron with walls hammered together from scraps of planking.

That kind of disparity is common in South America, most notably in Rio. Views that the rich might kill for in the developed world, paying top dollar for houses on the hillsides of San Francisco or Vancouver, in Rio and Valparaiso were left to the poor (interestingly the same thing can be found in Port Glasgow and Greenock on the Clyde where council estates command spectacular views of the Highlands across the water).

Perhaps in Valparaiso supplying water and power to such steep landscapes was too expensive even for the upper classes. Perhaps the depredations of the Nazca tectonic plate, jerkily and catastrophically diving under its South American fellow and causing the occasional massive earthquake, made such high living too unsafe. I could imagine a big juddering quake easily scouring these hillsides.

The port itself was a large one. Its harbour sheltered many merchant ships, but it also served as the main port for the country's naval fleet. The grey metallic shapes of military vessels could be seen, berthed cheek by jowl with merchant ships.

Barely a year before, a military coup had brought General Pinochet to power and he was cracking down on all forms of dissent. Terrible, bestial things were happening to civilians on some of the naval ships we berthed next to but my crewmates and I, and the rest of the world for that matter, would know nothing about it until much later.

As we steered gently into the bay, I recognised two frigates and further down the dock I counted six smaller patrol boats and even a submarine.

The docks were chaotic, piles of tarpaulin-covered goods lying around like a pod of beached whales. Around these mounds shambled hundreds of dock workers. Overhead, the long arms of rusty cranes hovered, wooden pallets swinging beneath them. Men took their leisurely time loading these up with crates and boxes. The pallets would then be whisked up high above their heads and out over the water, before descending through the gaping hatches of the waiting merchant ships.

Many of these ramshackle vessels looked suited for calmer waters than the mighty Pacific. On the decks, ill-shaven crew lounged around in grubby singlets, smoking and scratching their behinds and snarling at the dockers who were stowing the cargo in the holds.

The *Goneril* tentatively approached a berth. As heaving lines were thrown ashore, a cracking sound made me glance across at the dock. A crane driver, hauling up too hard, had sheared off a palette side through which the steel cables ran. The wires whipped up and the dockers jumped back as heavy boxes slapped to the ground and burst. A green tidal wave of apples washed over the dock and cascaded into the sea.

The men gesticulated angrily and roared curses up at the crane driver, who stood up so the men could see him through his window and then just shrugged.

They roared and cursed but within seconds they'd drifted back to business.

"Object lesson!" said a voice behind me. It was the third mate. Tall, red headed and with a pan scrubber beard, he stood with hands on hips, radiating disapproval. It'd taken a while to get through his don't-mess-with-me reserve, but we'd eventually wound up drinking together into many a small hour.

I laughed. "Yeah, yeah, don't stand under a loaded palette. Even I can work that out."

"Nah, it's more than that, kid. This is the Wild West. These Latinos, they're worse than the Arabs."

"Yours is not a liberal temperament, is it, Ted?"

Ted dismissed this with a wave. "Couple of weeks here and you'll finally wake up, sunshine. You'll think back to my words of wisdom and realise what a fucking pinko I was."

"Any other sage advice?"

"This is South America. After you've shaken hands with someone, always count your fingers. And do not ever mess with the military. Oh yeah, and always wear a rubber."

"I'll do all that."

"No, you won't."

And he was right.

~~~

During weekdays it was mayhem in the centre of Valparaiso, at least until the crushing midday heat. The few ancient cars made a terrible racket with their horns, supplemented by the shrieking of brakes and the general clattering of trams and ancient buses. Many of these buses seemed fresh from the interior, where steep and unpaved roads had brutally abused their suspensions and mufflers.

Valpo had fallen on hard times since the Panama Canal opened and vessels no longer needed to brave the ferocity of Cape Horn. Passengers and crew no longer sought respite on dry land to sooth shattered nerves and finally manage to keep food down.

Nevertheless, it was still a major port. As well as copper and fruit exported to the rich world in the north, there was more general trade with other South American countries and Pacific Island chains like the Marquesas.

The people were an odd mixture, with many dressed like Europeans and affecting dignified airs. Others were much more poorly dressed. Mediterranean blood seemed generally
~~~

more evident in the better dressed middle-class types, but the rest had the broader, ruddier faces of the altitude-adapted South American Indian.

The streets were grubby, even in what appeared to be the financial district, and the building facades were beginning to crumble. A new coat of paint was needed nearly everywhere.

However, not all of Valpo was run down, as we found later. A shipmate of mine called Paul was also a trainee officer, and we were both taken under the wings of a couple of Chilean naval cadets, keen to get to know us because their navy had essentially been founded by an Englishman, Lord Cochrane. That august gentleman had overhauled what had been a dismal outfit and had redesigned it along British lines, to the Chileans' vast admiration.

The cadets came from wealthy families and took us for a meal to their parents' home in Vina del Mar. After the terrible poverty of the hillside favelas, the wealth there was obscene. It was a place of large hacienda-type houses and extensive manicured lawns. As we drove into it, roads became broader and cars more frequent. Soldiers, lurking all over the rest of the city, were no longer evident.

What I saw next, I just couldn't take in. We'd been driving along the beach road and there on the sand was a plane, a Boeing 707. I didn't recognise it right away because the damn thing was painted red and white to mimic a Coca Cola can. It looked like it'd just taxied in.

I turned wide-eyed to the cadet next to me, an eager, sturdily built young man. He just shrugged.

"Now used as a nightclub," he said. "Very popular with the senior military."

I thought of the shanty towns clinging to the hillsides. The contrast was almost painful.

~~~
~~~

Unloading cars and loading apples was going to take a couple of weeks. That meant we had plenty of time in the city.

Many of the all-male crew were fit young men who had been at sea for weeks. They had just two priorities when going ashore: drink and sex, though not necessarily in that order.

And so, I was out drinking with Dennis, the fifth engineer. Like many Irish he had the gift of the gab and he often had me in stitches with his bullshit. Tall, skinny with hamhocks for fists, he was good to have at your back when things got ugly. Then again, things sometimes only got ugly because of his ready tongue. A young man in his early twenties he was to die just a year later from inhaling his own vomit but, then and there, in the dives of Valpo, he was thrumming with the life force.

The unswept streets around the docks were littered with fruit skins, bits of wrapping paper and beer bottles. Men in grubby clothes and unshaven faces lurked in doorways, staring listlessly at the street. As we turned one corner, a man with a rainbow-banded sombrero, silver jacket and six-foot-long white trousers, walked by on stilts. We stepped back into a urine-wet doorway to avoid his daddy long-legs.

We watched the man stilt away and then looked at each other. Dennis shrugged his shoulders. "South America," he said.

This was a refrain that was to become all too familiar and all too inadequate as time went by. It hid far more than it revealed.

In my nights ashore with Dennis I met a girl, Sandra Rios, who spoke miraculously good English. Petite, curly haired, fizzing with life, she was easy to fall for and I did just that. In her early twenties like me, she was already a widow though she would not say how her husband had died.

Loading was slow and often interrupted when the lorry loads of apples were late. Sometimes I had the whole day off and then Sandra and I would explore the city. She came from the poorer parts of town so that's where we roamed at first, amongst the shacks clinging like ivy to the bare hillsides. We drank coffee and Pisco, a light rum, at open air bars which were little more than sheets of corrugated iron perched on poles. We'd sit hand in hand, watching the people pass by, loud and poor but cheerful.

Several days later I took her to a swanky restaurant, then up the funicular to Artilleria Hill where we spent the night in a small, decent hotel with clean sheets and beautiful views over the endless Pacific.

Not surprisingly this became a pattern. I would wake in some small hotel high on the hills. Reluctantly leaving the beautiful Sandra behind I would dash down the vertiginous cobbled streets, the Andes behind me diffusing the dawn light, racing to get back to my early morning cargo watch.

I was having an adventure, half a world away from home, and life was sweet.

However, to really appreciate sweetness there has to be some bitterness for contrast. And there was a bitterness and darkness all around Valparaiso during those long-gone days.

For a start there were all the soldiers and the checkpoints. Once I asked the Mate why there were so many on the city streets. "South America," he said impatiently, waving my query away.

The ship was filling with boxes of apples and we would soon leave Chile. Late one night I took Sandra to a small hotel, perhaps twenty rooms, not far from the docks. It had been a grand house once upon a time, owned by merchants living off the trade from ships either emerging from the horrors of Cape Horn or girding their loins for the coming passage around it.

Once the Panama Canal had opened and the chandler's trade dried up, big old houses like this couldn't be kept by single families and had become either hotels or bordellos.

The hotel was at the end of a small cul-de-sac. The dark wood entrance was quite imposing but raddled by time and neglect. Beyond it was a small reception desk and behind this slouched a guy, thin like most Chileans. His black trousers were shiny and his white shirt creased. I caught the tang of days-old sweat.

Behind the reception desk was a grand staircase. On the first floor and to the right I saw a large room with a bar, and couples dancing cheek to cheek to scratchy gramophone music.

Our room was large but a little dingy with fly-specked lampshades. Not that it mattered as we had other things on our minds. Parting is such sweet sorrow. And ardent, very ardent.

There was nothing to unpack except each other and our clothes fell like rain. Soon we were making love and I was at the point when nothing could stop me.

Or so I thought.

The door was kicked in with such force that fragments of wood bounced off my bare backside. Two men in battle fatigues, black balaclavas hiding their features, rushed into the room. One of them shoved the muzzle of his assault rifle into my temple.

I stopped.

The soldier shouted at me in Spanish so I didn't have a clue what he wanted. They shouted again, sounding scarily angry.

This galvanised Sandra. Petite though she was, she shoved me off her and leapt out of the bed and grabbed for her handbag.

Unhinged by shock and fear, I wasn't thinking straight. Convinced she was going for a gun, I began to scrabble under the sheets, as though a layer of cotton would shield me from the discharge of a Kalashnikov at point blank range.

Instead of a gun, she pulled a document from her handbag and thrust it at the soldiers. They inspected it carefully and it seemed to pass muster. They both nodded in silent agreement.

Some quality of my whimpering must have given away my nationality because one of the soldiers said, "Oh, excuse us," in English.

And with that they left. Soon we could hear them kicking in other doors.

I didn't know what we should do next. If we tried to make a break for it the soldiers might take it the wrong way and shoot us. So instead, we leaned a chair against the door, its back under the handle, so it wouldn't be so easy to kick in if they came back.

We lay there cuddling fiercely for the rest of the night.

And that, dear reader, is where the farcical element ends. The rest of this chapter is going to be grim and tragic and some historical details will not be for the faint-hearted.

After a while, the sounds of violence abated but Sandra and I stayed where we were until the sun peeped over the Andes. As silently as we could, we removed the chair from the door and tiptoed down the hallway to the stairs. The hotel was deathly quiet and seemed deserted.

We got to the bottom of the stairs but then froze. In front of the reception desk on the uneven floor was a metre-wide pool of blood.

I couldn't understand what had happened. This was 1977 and I knew nothing of South America. The term 'Death Squad' had not even been coined then.

When I got back to the ship, I excitedly told the First Mate what had happened. He just shrugged and said, "That's South America for you."

*Death Squad* didn't enter the lexicon until the 1980s. This was because of Operation Condor, a United States-backed campaign of repression and state-sponsored terror in conjunction with a cabal of right-wing dictatorships throughout Central and South America. This clandestine intergovernmental project resulted in the disappearance and deaths of 60,000 people, as well as turning 400,000 citizens into political prisoners. It began in around 1975 but it would take many years for the Western world to become aware of what was going on and even longer for people to believe it. Murder on such an industrial scale, and in such a place, was just not credible.

Several years previously the democratically elected, though inconveniently socialist, government of Salvadore Allende had fallen in a military coup led by General Augusto Pinochet. Pinochet was widely believed to have been backed by the CIA. Allende had made the mistake of trying to nationalise the Chilean copper industry as he felt that a disproportionate amount of national wealth was leaving the country for the rich north. This had offended some powerful companies in the United States, and Allende had paid for his naivety with his life.

Pinochet's regime killed around 4000 and imprisoned, often with torture, a further 40,000 individuals.

The methods they used against what they considered their more significant opponents were obscenely brutal. To break their spirits and make them docile, captured women were raped and men were castrated. Once they'd supplied whatever information they had, the captives were then 'disappeared'. They were drugged then flown by helicopter far out into the Pacific before being thrown overboard. The sharks got the bodies before they could be washed ashore.

A few years later, when I was working in Southampton in the UK, I met a Chilean political dissident called Jorge who had fled there. He had been captured and tortured by the regime but ultimately released. I told him what had happened in Valpo and, for the first time, I got an explanation more meaningful than a shrug and 'That's South America'. According to Jorge, a death squad must have been tipped off that a dissident was staying or working at the hotel. The fact they had only been interested in Sandra's ID suggested they were looking for a woman.

The blood in the reception area suggested they had found her.

Unfortunately, meeting Jorge and reading about Operation Condor were years in the future. Back then, in Chile, I didn't have a clue what had happened.

And it was that ignorance that led me to making probably the worst mistake of my life.

The time came to leave. The ship was up to the gunwales in apples, our refrigeration system had been connected up to the holds and everything was being chilled down for the long voyage. We were to head back up the west coast of South America, back through the Panama Canal and across the Atlantic to Europe.

My duties as a trainee officer were to shadow the First Mate whenever we entered or left port. This usually just meant being a gofer, taking documents to port officials, or making sure the gangway was retracted and stored. This time, however, he suddenly announced we were going to do a stowaway search. I put this down to the Mate being a driven obsessive. Short, dark-haired and antisocial, if he had a Christian name, I never heard anyone use it.

I reacted to this demand like the spoiled teenager I had been not so very long before. I had previously been on a couple of container ship runs from the west coast of Europe to the west coast of North America, sometimes calling in at eight or nine ports in as many days. Never once had we done a stowaway search.

I assumed that the Mate had bought into the conservative regulations of my rather staid shipping line. An old established firm, we still wore full uniform entering or leaving port and for our three silver service meals a day.

However, I had underestimated the Mate for there was good reason for the stowaway search.

In those days, getting into the States from Western Europe was easy (and vice-versa). There was little need for anyone to stow away and so searches had not been necessary on my previous ship. However, when it came to other parts of the world, stowing away to get to the West was pretty much all there was.

And that was a problem for shipping companies because, under international law, even if they unknowingly brought a stowaway to another country, they were liable for the repatriation costs. The airfare costs in those days, as I have indicated, were huge, especially if you had to pay the return air tickets for their police escort.

Discovering a stowaway while the ship was at sea was very bad news for the captain, who would be held responsible for not finding them before the ship sailed.

On some ships, sailing under flags of convenience, the easiest way to avoid blow-back from the company was obvious: make the stowaway swim home. This still applies today.

My own shipping company, and indeed any ship flying under a British flag, would never have done that, but many other ships were crewed by people little better than pirates. Nobody knows how many die from being thrown overboard, though some extreme examples do emerge. For example, back in 2011, a Ukrainian skipper and first mate were sentenced to life imprisonment for the murder of eight African stowaways who were beaten with iron bars, shot and then and chucked into the sea off Portugal.

There were also at least four incidents off the coast of Somalia in 1984 when Greek captains threw stowaways into the shark-infested waters, one doing this for a dozen in one voyage.

So, stowaway searches weren't bullshit at all. On top of that I later heard that the very ship I was on had done a similar run from Chile in the not-too-distant past. It had been a different crew at the time and they hadn't done a careful search. Three stowaways had made it on board.

Though the officers on the ship were white and British, the crew were black and Barbadian. The Barbadians were rather more sensitive to the political situation in Chile and realised these men were probably fleeing for their lives. They'd found the stowaways and, rather than reporting them to the officers, had kept them hidden and supplied with food and water.

Unfortunately, half way to Panama, the officers had found out. The stowaways were locked up in the hospital (a single cabin) while the captain got in touch with the authorities back in Chile. It so happened that a Chilean naval vessel was coming the other way and arrangements were made to transfer the prisoners at sea.

Somehow the stowaways got hold of a knife. Either they'd brought it on board or someone from the crew had given them one. They refused to leave the hospital, one of them waving the knife around.

In those days, on some ships at least, the captain kept a trusty Webley revolver locked away in his personal safe in case of problems with the crew or, very rarely in those days, pirates.

The captain made it clear that unless the stowaways transferred to the naval ship, they would be shot. I hope he was bluffing but at least the stowaways believed him. The Chilean naval vessel took them back to Chile and, quite possibly, to terrible deaths.

When the Mate told me to accompany him on the stowaway search, I knew nothing about this, or about Allende or Pinochet, or just about anything that was going on in that country at such an awful time.

I was dressed in a filthy white boiler suit, a stout pair of work boots and I carried a torch. Moping like a spoiled brat at having to do the search, and heartsick because I was leaving the (then) love of my life behind, I followed the Mate as we made our way through the holds, shining our lights into any spaces not up to the rafters with apple-stuffed cardboard boxes. The holds were already chilled down and the towering stacks of boxes hid the few lights, so it was cold, dark work.

It was a big ship and I was getting more and more pissed off. After we'd searched the holds and engine room, then the crew's quarters and all the other odd rooms on ships like the paint locker and the bosun's cubbyhole, we started checking the deck.

The ship had a single crane mounted there. This opened the hatches and transferred cargo to the docks in the ports of countries too benighted to have their own cranes. The crane was perched on top of a hollow cylinder of metal about six feet wide and less than that in height. A small oval cut-out in the metal allowed access to the space in the crane base, where the crane rotation mechanism could be serviced.

The Mate came to the oval opening and shone his light in. I turned away in disgust as the man seemed intent on wasting my time. From the docks I could see the rising heights of the favelas. Somewhere up there, in a warm bed, lay the sultry body of...

"Get out of there!" yelled the Mate.

I spun around in surprise. The Mate stepped back from the crane base and put his hands on his hips. He looked furious.

I walked over and shone my torch through the oval. Two pairs of frightened eyes stared back at me.

"Get out!" yelled the Mate again.

Slowly, painfully, like they were being given birth to, the bedraggled men climbed with difficulty through the little oval cut-out. They stood blinking in the sun.

"Trainee, check there's nobody else in there!"

Still young and limber, I climbed through. The crane base was normally kept empty but now there was a crate of Coca Cola bottles that had been filled with water. The only other things there were two cardboard boxes full of apples.

And that, presumably, was what these men had been hoping to live on in the three-week voyage to Rotterdam.

I crawled back out. "It's clear."

"Right," said the Mate. "You guard these two while I get the soldiers."

"What..." I managed to get out but he'd already stridden off.

I turned to look at the stowaways and they turned to look at me.

First, what I saw: two men in their thirties or forties in dirty clothes. They looked like they hadn't washed for a long time. Perhaps they had been hiding in the crane base for days. They looked frightened and they looked desperate.

What they saw: a skinny, wet-behind-the-ears kid who hadn't got a clue what was going on.

I don't think they were impressed.

The rest of the world faded away. I don't remember any sounds. It was like the three of us were in our own little bubble, our own little drama.

The two exchanged glances then began to inch apart. It was clear they were intending to jump me.

I jerked back my torch as if I was going to strike them and bared my teeth.

They flinched then moved back together.

I couldn't believe I'd got away with it. I didn't believe I would get away with it again.

Time passed, maybe only a minute or so, but it seemed like a year. It was only a couple of hundred feet to the gangway and that's where some soldiers should have been mooching. Why was the Mate taking so long rounding them up?

Then again, soldiers, like coppers or firemen, never seem to move quickly.

The two men glanced at each other again and then they began to move apart. This time there was nothing hesitant about it. This time I knew I had a flight on my hands.

Just as it was about to kick off, the Bosun hove into view. As I've said, the crew was Barbadian and they were an affable but dangerous bunch. They were always pleasant and kind to deal with but a few of them also smuggled drugs and guns and so a firm hand was needed to control them. And that's what they got in the form of the Bosun who looked like Mandingo on steroids.

The Mate, it transpired, had belatedly realised he had left me in a delicate situation and had sent the Bosun to back me up.

The Bosun had fists like breeze blocks. He also had a knife slash across his cheek that went down to his chin by way of his mouth. It had made rather a mess of his lips. I had been reliably informed that the man who did the slashing had not survived the experience.

At the sight of the Bosun, all fight left the two men and they cowered and moved back together.

We watched each other. Or rather, I watched the men while they stared at the Bosun.

There was the sound of men coming unhurriedly down the deck. The Mate and four soldiers hove into view. Two of the soldiers ambled up to the men and smashed their rifle butts into their teeth.

The two stowaways dropped to the deck like sacks of potatoes. They were hauled back to their feet and frogmarched away.

Later, my Chilean friend in Southampton told me what might have happened to them. If they had simply been poor guys, economic migrants as we call them nowadays, they would probably have been taken to the local police station, slapped around a bit, then kicked back out onto the streets.

Let's hope!

If, however, they had been politically active trade unionists or academics who had been fleeing the cold, cruel hand of Pinochet then their fate would have been torture and perhaps a horrible death.

The fact is, instead of guarding them I should have hidden the men somewhere better. I knew the ship well and knew where they wouldn't be found.

Unfortunately, the thought never even occurred to me.

Instead, I stood there completely mystified. Why would someone suffer starvation, dehydration, cold and intense discomfort, just to get to Rotterdam of all places?

Later on, I asked the Mate.

He shrugged. "That's South America for you," he said.

## *Offending a Ship's Captain*

### The Container ship Stella Maris in the Atlantic and Pacific Oceans, 1976

Not for nothing is a ship's captain called the Master. Once at sea their powers are enormous to the point where they are within their rights to use deadly force if confronted by mutiny or by pirates. They can sack crew at a moment's notice, they decide what can and cannot be bought in port, they dictate the navigational route. They can even stipulate what meals are served.

With power comes responsibility and theirs is for the health and safety and wellbeing of all passengers and crew.

Though not enforced in law, there is also an unwritten rule that Captains should be the last to leave a sinking ship.

One power they don't have, despite the widespread belief, is to conduct a marriage ceremony. The only exceptions to this are for captains on ships registered in Bermuda or the land-locked Czech Republic.

So that's the situation in law. In practice a lot of the above goes right out of the porthole once a ship sails.

That they might not have the legal right to marry has not stopped some captains. They are also often not the last to leave a sinking ship and, when it comes to the wellbeing of some of their crew then, quite frankly, some of them don't give a damn.

In this chapter I'll provide corroborating evidence, m'lud.

Whichever way you look at it, the captain is pretty much all-powerful at sea and it's always best to keep on his, or occasionally nowadays, her good side.

And that's what I tried really hard to do back in the 1970s but it just didn't work out that way. Partly it was my fault and partly it was the fault of a Captain who I will call McBoag.

McBoag was very much of the old seafarer's school: aloof, bigoted and intellectually challenged (astute readers may sense a subtext here. Though the events in this chapter happened over forty years ago, they're still working away at me and not in a good way).

Tall, thick-set and with a reddened but baby-smooth chin which could only have come from a three-times-a-day shaving habit, McBoag ruled the ship at arm's length, his proxy being the First Mate. Again, to protect the guilty, I'll call him Todd.

Todd was a Yorkshireman who must have trained under Machiavelli. Divide and conquer was his watchword and, as he was the only one in direct communication with the captain, he could sow unease to his heart's content without any comeback.

His tactics were to tell every single crew member that the captain didn't like them. Try to understand how unsettling that was. Your boss at work may not like you, but when you go home at night or at weekends you can leave their malign influence behind. That's not so easy when you're both confined to a tin can a thousand miles from anywhere.

Mind you, that McBoag hated everyone may have been the only truthful thing the Mate ever said.

Todd had other delightful tricks. He would tell one deck officer that one of his colleagues had been saying bad things about him behind his back. He'd say the same thing to the other officer then sit back and watch the fireworks.

Todd was like a chemical catalyst—he accelerated reactions sometimes to the point of explosion without being changed by them himself. He remained exactly the same bastard, come what may.

And a ship is a volatile environment. When we are ashore our life is regulated by thousands of unwritten rules of social behaviour. We don't defecate on the pavement or drive on the right-hand side. We don't kick screaming toddlers or grab the genitals of strangers we fancy.

We stick to all these unwritten rules because everyone else does and because we are, at base, essentially social creatures.

Ashore we live in this consensual social system which is under continual reinforcement. However, when a ship detaches itself from the shore, it loses contact with that consensual bubble of acceptable conduct. A new, much smaller bubble is created. Aberrant behaviour, which would have been suppressed because of the corrective examples of others on shore, starts to emerge.

Think Lord of the Flies, where a group of school boys marooned on a desert island slowly become feral, except played out by adult males (there wasn't a single female in the crews of the forty ships in the fleet at that time).

Under those circumstances, men can go out of control. This might typically first show itself in the flamboyant world of the ship's stewards. With three silver service meals a day and all their cleaning duties, the stewards and cooks made up a significant portion of a ship's crew. I certainly wouldn't claim they were all gay but quite a few were.

On long voyages relationships developed and with it came jealousy. Ashore, if relationship problems arise, you can get out of the house and away down the pub and talk it over with your mates. You can go for a long walk to clear your head. You can get advice or let off steam in a thousand and one ways.

Not so on ship where, after a few days at sea, your tin can has turned into a pressure cooker and some people just go *pop*. On one ship in the British Merchant Navy during my time, a jealous steward crept into the rooms of three other crew members at night and slit their throats.

Enmities build up, sexual or otherwise, and it's all too easy to resort to this ultimate solution at sea. And people often get away with it for a simple reason: murderers on land are faced with a big problem, namely how to dispose of the body.

At sea, not so much.

Suicide has been called the Merchant Navy's darkest secret. No international body keeps a record of global suicides by seafarers so accurate figures are hard to come by. Estimates range from 6% to 15% of deaths at sea being suicide. 'Suspicious deaths' bring this to over 18%. It may even be more than this because some deaths are put down as accidents, an easy thing to do (perhaps to spare the feelings of the relatives) as the body may never be found. In a study looking at the British Merchant Navy the proportion of deaths of seafarers due to being 'lost at sea' was around 4% for those serving on British registered vessels, rising to around 9% for those serving on foreign registered vessels.

Bear in mind that these high percentages are in a profession which is already one of the most dangerous in the world.

Even in well-managed national fleets, such as those of Denmark, Germany and Sweden, death by accident is between 7 and 20 times that of shore-workers. For flags of convenience fleets this is very likely to be much higher, although it is not possible to prove this as central records are not kept.

It's easy to understand why suicide might be so high. Being detached from family and friends and the correcting effects of consensual behaviour means that worries and concerns can grow legs. You lose perspective, things get entirely out of proportion. Jumping over the wall can seem the easy way out.

Neither I nor anyone else has proof to support this, but it seems clear to me that at least some of these 'suicides' are no such thing. If someone is pissing you off, and you have no other way of letting off steam, then why not creep into your enemy's room in the early hours, sandbag the bastard then heave him over the railing?

Set against this already unstable background, we had a Mate who relished turning people against each other. Our pressure cooker turned into a tinderbox, mixed metaphors be damned.

Fights became common on board. The most colourful I remember was when the Third Engineer bottled the Radio Officer. Mind you, the 'Sparks', an embittered Scotsman, was grumpy and spiteful and had it coming in spades.

For the more sensitive of you who may be worried about the outcome, the bottle didn't break but raised a bump the size of a half tennis ball on the sparks's forehead. Sadly, it didn't improve his temperament; you'd need a lobotomy for that.

How did I fare in this emotional maelstrom? What happened to me illustrates how enmities can grow and events spiral out of control on board ship. I was drawn into a feud with the captain that spanned 11,000 kilometres and two oceans.

This was on my first ever trip and it was a tough one. I was on one of the first generation of container ships and it sailed from the west coast of Europe to the west coast of North America. In Europe we had called in at eight ports in as many days. I had become used to the ship's bells awakening me at all sorts of ungodly hours and I hadn't managed to get more than three straight hours of sleep for the past week. That ground me down, as it did everyone else on board.

Finally, we struck out from Europe for a week of uninterrupted sailing across the Atlantic. The day was bright and clear and I was on watch and checking the radar screen when the captain appeared. He usually kept to his cabin so this was a surprise. What was even more unusual was that he started talking to me. I'd been on the ship for several weeks and we hadn't exchanged a single word. In fact, he usually looked through me as though I didn't exist. Understandable, as I was a mere trainee while he was the exalted Captain.

Little did I realise that at that moment we were at the high point of our relationship. Within seconds the downward spiral would begin.

In gruff west of Scotland tones, he asked, "Is that on relative or absolute?"

"Relative, sir," I said.

"What's the difference?" he barked.

Nowadays satellite navigation can tell you where you are to within the width of a ball hair. Radars are so smart they can alert you to even the slightest chance of a collision and write your will for you while they're doing it.

Back then, however, it was much more primitive and all that the radar showed was a monochrome screen full of blurry dots which were usually just wave crests but could be ships. Skill was required to work out which was which.

One recent element of sophistication had been introduced into the world of naval radar. Usually, the ship is always dead centre in the screen and the forward direction is pointing up. This is called *relative* because it shows the sea or coast relative to the moving ship. The new sophistication showed the screen centred on a fixed point, so forward could be in any direction. This was called *absolute* because it was all with respect to a fixed reference point on the Earth.

This may seem fairly straightforward now but it was high-tech juju back in those days. Cadets struggled to grasp it.

McBoag had realised this and used it to torment them by asking them to explain the difference. According to the Mate, he loved to see them flopping around like fish caught in the shallows after the tide has retreated.

What he hadn't anticipated was that I had a degree in physics and was well used to these notions from our studies of Einstein's work on relativity.

So, when McBoag asked me what the difference was between relative and absolute I gave him a full and rather erudite answer, if I do say so myself.

His head jerked back, like he'd unrolled a towel only to find a serpent lurking within. His big bushy brows contorted.

After a few seconds of silence, he offered me some wise words.

"Don't be a cunt all yer life!" he said.

Sound advice, though I'll leave it up to the reader to decide whether it was heeded.

McBoag stalked off to give the lookout a hard time. I remained at the radar, feeling rather surprised. Teachers and lecturers had always been pleased when I gave a good answer.

On my next watch, the Mate appeared and was beaming from ear to ear.

"You've messed up," he said. "The Old Man's really got it in for you now."

"But I was right," I said plaintively.

The Mate shook his head. "Poor old bastard doesn't know the difference between relative and absolute himself. You showed him up good and proper. Silly boy!"

I moved from being hurt to being aggrieved and there was only one more point on that trajectory: anger.

The captain did indeed make me suffer. Through the Mate I was given all sorts of rubbish jobs, such as all the bilge readings. What's worse I was made to do them during breakfast so I missed it. But my main dollop of pain came from the most boring task in the world: chipping and painting.

Sea air isn't a friend to a metal ship. Couple the corrosive effects of salt with the increased reaction rates in the high temperatures of the tropics and it rots the boat faster than a politician sheds his promises.

*Rust bucket* is the pejorative terms for ships where this process has got out of hand. Ships are painted to seal the metal off from the sea air but it can't keep it away for ever. Rust bubbles soon appear in the paint so you need to chip the old paint with a hammer and then scrape it off. Only then can you get at the rust underneath. Then, when you've finally got that off, you have to prime it then paint it again.

I imagine they have power tools and super high-tech paints that offer better protection nowadays, but back then chipping and painting was a never-ending process and all you had was a hammer and a chisel.

Noisy, dirty and a back-breaker in the hot sun. Day after day.

Not really a job for a trainee officer but the captain is God and McBoag could get anyone to do what he wanted.

I cursed that nasty old son-of-a-bitch but, powerless, all I could do was keep my head down and hope he forgot about me.

While this little psychodrama was bubbling away nicely, there were some sights to see.

We sailed through the Sargasso Sea, which is the centre of the Atlantic gyre. This is a clockwise circulating current caused by something called the Coriolis force. Because the Earth is a rotating sphere, a point on the equator is moving at about a thousand miles an hour, while right at the Pole it's not moving at all. This makes the water further North move more slowly than water further South, causing the water of the whole ocean to move in a cartwheel-type manner. Right at the centre of this gyre the water is becalmed, as is anything that floats into it. The centre of the gyre becomes a trap for objects that don't have a means of propulsion.

The Sargasso is to the north-east of the Caribbean and has Bermuda just to its western extremity.

Back in those days what usually floated into the gyre was seaweed and we sailed through great clumps of it. If there'd been much more of the stuff it would have made the Sargasso look like a swamp. The Sea is named after this Sargassum seaweed. Seen from a distance it can look solid and this had spawned ancient tales of lost lands and ships becalmed there for centuries.

Remnants of ships that had been wrecked a hundred years before also eventually made it into the Sea, giving birth to tales of ghostly spectre-crewed galleons.

Nowadays the problem is plastic waste that accumulates in the gyre. Vast floating mats of the stuff have been formed, so dense they are becoming hazards to shipping.

After the Sargasso we sailed through the Caribbean where towering cumulonimbus clouds looked like an ongoing nuclear war was being fought.

Then we made our way through the Panama Canal, which was constructed over one hundred years ago to connect the Atlantic and Pacific through the isthmus of Panama. One of the most difficult feats of engineering, it's 82 kilometres long and requires huge locks to lift ships to a height of 26 metres above sea level so it can take them from one ocean to another. More than 22,000 men perished during its construction, mainly from yellow fever and malaria but also from accidents and from the bites of poisonous snakes and insects.

I watched as tiny locomotives called mules pulled the ships into and out of the locks. Crews of Panamanians came on board to assist in the passage. Black-skinned men, they rested silently by the winches in the sweltering tropical night and literally all I could see of them was the whites of their eyes.

Once through the canal we headed north up the west coast of North America, our first port of call being Los Angeles. Our berth in San Pedro was a couple of miles upriver and so we manoeuvred our 200-metre-long ship very carefully and slowly between rows of berthed ships to reach it.

Usually, we were in port for only a few hours but for some of the bigger ports like LA we were there for a couple of days.

On a general cargo ship the deck officers were heavily involved in loading and unloading, not least making sure the dockers weren't stealing whatever they could lay their hands on, but on a container ship there was little for them to do. The dock side cranes would open the hatches and then pluck the containers from deep within the bowels of the ship before depositing new ones in their place.

That meant we had our evenings free.

And that meant we headed for the bars onshore like iron filings to a magnet.

Long Beach was adjacent to San Pedro. We briefly admired the old Queen Mary ocean liner which had been retired there in 1967, its art deco staterooms made into a fancy hotel, but it did not delay us long.

Late at night, in a bar in Long Beach I met a young lady called Alica. She was from Belize and was studying at a secretarial college in LA. She was tall, slender and very beautiful and eventually agreed to return with me to spend the night back on the ship.

No, I still can't work out why she was so obliging either.

She was a nice girl and perhaps saw it as an act of charity for a poor sailor who hadn't even seen a woman in three weeks.

In the morning I took her down the gangway and to the nearby dock gates for a taxi. One final kiss and she was gone. Ships that pass in the night. Perfect!

I returned to the *Stella Maris*, extremely pleased with myself.

Little did I know that our farewells had been observed.

The Mate, however, was all too eager to tell me when he came knocking at my door.

"You filthy little pig. Now you're for it!"

We weren't supposed to bring women back to the boat, but everyone did if they were lucky. At most it was a misdemeanour, a drop in the ocean compared to the everyday crimes of a life at sea.

"The captain saw you mauling your little jungle-bunny chum. He's fucking livid. Can't stand blacks!" (Sorry for the language but that's how some people talked in those days.)

And indeed, Alica had been black. The idea that McBoag would take against such a kind, gentle girl just because of her skin colour made my blood boil.

"This isn't bleeding South Africa. What's it to him anyway?" I spluttered.

The Mate shrugged, palms up and open, play-acting a liberal nature as easily affronted as mine (like I say, he really was a bastard). "I'm with you, son. The times they are a changin'. But not on this boat and not with this Captain."

"So, what's he going to do, keelhaul me?" Keelhauling was where, for the sake of punishment, ropes were tied to the hands and feet of a sailor who was then dragged under the ship so that his back was scraped off by the barnacles adhering to the ship's bottom. If they didn't drown in the process then their infected wounds usually got them. It hasn't been used on British ships for hundreds of years. That I could even make that joke showed how far things had progressed.

"Oh, he'll get you somehow, count on that. He's made it his mission to make your life miserable. Wish I could help you but..." He shrugged, the gloating expression on his face just begging for me to punch his lights out.

More crap jobs followed. It was all mean and petty but if that was the best McBoag could do then I could handle it.

We called in at the beautiful port of San Francisco. As we unloaded, I watched as an amazing tongue of white cloud drifted in from the Pacific across the surface of the water, gently pushing through the piles of the Golden Gate Bridge before languorously poking far out into San Francisco Bay and enveloping Alcatraz Island.

Next stop was Seattle which at that time was one of the few dedicated container ports. It was so big that we berthed over half a mile from the gates.

I was leaning on the rail looking at the blocky shapes of the container mountains when I heard someone coming up behind me.

It was the Mate and I could tell he was trying to suppress his joy. I had no idea what he wanted but my heart sank.

"Got a job for you," he said.

"Oh yeah."

"An important parcel is being delivered to the dock gates. Go and collect it!"

"And how am I going to get there."

"How do you think? You're the one with the degree."

I pointed out over the harsh landscape of concrete and metal. "It's a container port. Nothing but. You can't go walking through it. At my induction, when they were warning us about all the ways we can get killed in this business, being squished by a straddle-carrier in a container port was in the top ten."

The Mate snorted in contempt. "This is the real world, Sunny Jim, not some namby-pamby course back in Liverpool run by ex-sailors who ran *away* from sea. Get your arse to the gate and in short order!"

And with that, he strode off. I could only see the back of his head but I was sure he was grinning from ear to ear.

I've walked in some wild and dangerous places but this was a whole new level. The banked containers made a form of maze and I would have to skitter through it like a mouse, dodging the straddle-carriers. These were vehicles with the cab high in the air on a platform resting on four very elongated legs. Their sole function was to lift and carry containers between these legs. They rolled in over the top of the containers so there was nowhere on the ground their wheels could not reach if it wasn't covered by a container. That meant there was no safe point to stand.

Even though the operator was in a cab as much as ten metres in the air, so he could see far ahead, the underslung container blocked the view immediately beneath him and also blocked much of the middle distance. In other words, the operator couldn't see anything nearby on the ground. That's why you weren't supposed to walk through container terminals.

My troubles began almost as soon as I was off the gangway. I was quickly surrounded by containers and I realised how easy it would be to lose my way. Even a stack of two of these big metal boxes hid any landmarks. All I had to get me to the gate was my sense of direction.

The maze of containers also took the sounds of the straddle-carriers, from their roaring engines and squeaking wheels and beeping alarms, and bounced it around. It sounded like a whole bunch of them were coming at me from all directions.

I arrived at an intersection in the stacks and gingerly peeked out. Straddle-carriers have two sets of four wheels with black and yellow striped guards at the front and back of each. One of these guards zipped by so closely it almost took my nose off. I watched as the spindly, gangly, ridiculous thing shot by, its driver oblivious to my almost snuffed out existence.

More echoing warning sounds, more of the damned things approaching. I felt panic rising. Even if I tried to retrace my steps, I'd likely get lost and be pursued relentlessly around this maze until finally I was squished like a hedgehog on a motorway.

I took some deep breaths to try to calm myself and waited until another carrier zipped by, then sprinted across the intersection.

More metal alleyways. More pursuit by creatures from the War of the Worlds. It seemed to go on forever and I was sure I had wandered off course. Then between some stacks I saw the sun emerge from behind heavy clouds. It didn't take a sun-sight with a sextant (something with which I was now overly familiar) to work out which direction was south. I'd helped navigate into the port and had noted the bearing of the gate. I'd wandered a bit off course but at least I was more confident about where to head next.

I ducked and dived, bobbed and weaved my way and finally emerged at the gate. Though the Terminator films were still no more than a dream in James Cameron's mind, I'd had a taste of man in the far future being hunted down by remorseless machines.

The guard on the gate was surprised to see me emerge from out of the metal city, red-faced, sweating and shaking .

The parcel was waiting for me. Luckily it wasn't big, no bigger than a stack of four or five books and it was very light. Easy to carry and at least it didn't get in my way of dodging death as I made it back to the ship, racing like a hunted fox from one bank of containers to another while avoiding the prowling daddy long-legs.

By the time I got back to the gangway my uniform was soaking in perspiration. I was unsurprised to find the Mate waiting for me at the top.

"Nice walk?"

I was aching to tell him to go to hell but he was second in command of the ship. He might not be God himself but he was Jesus, although a very unlikely one.

I held out the package but he shook his head. "It's urgent. Captain wants you to deliver it to him personally."

I stumped up the stairs to the Captain's cabin which was on the deck below the bridge. Sometimes Captains bring their own pictures and mementos to personalise the place but not McBoag. It had about as much charm as a public-school dorm.

He was sitting at his desk reading a paperback.

"Your package, Captain," I said and placed it on his desk. The old bastard had hardly ever spoken to me, so I assumed this time would be no different and turned to go.

"Just a moment, Trainee," he said.

I turned back.

Taking his time, he rummaged in his desk drawer and eventually brought out some scissors. The parcel, as usual in those days, was tied with string. He cut this and unwrapped the brown paper, opened the box within and brought out a cylindrical object. He set this down upright on the desk so I could get a good look.

Foot powder!

I was so shocked that my blood didn't even begin to boil. That would come later.

McBoag looked me right in the eye. He gave it a beat, then:

"Fuck off!"

And I did just that, a roaring noise like an approaching typhoon in my ears. Suddenly I was Mr Christian on the

*Bounty*, terrible thoughts of bloody mutiny marauding out of my subconscious.

Unmanned, I ranted and raved to my fellow officers until they all told me to shut up. Student life was behind me, they informed me pompously, and this was the real world.

They were right. I'd thought college lecturers had been bad enough as they hadn't cared whether their students lived or died. But at least they wouldn't have risked their students' lives for the sake of a trifle.

And the Mate, of course, was delighted. It was his mission in life to turn the crew against each other but with the Captain and me he hadn't had to do a damned thing.

He went around smiling like the Cheshire Cat. All his Christmases had come at once.

Like any powerless human from the dawn of time, I dreamed impotent dreams of revenge as we sailed north first to Portland and then to the beautiful Port of Vancouver. Like San Francisco it's in a bay surrounded by hills, although it had the distinctive sight of large, bright yellow pyramids of sulphur waiting for loading on the docks.

One other distinguishing feature of Vancouver was a strip club called No.5 Orange. This was the first of only two strip clubs I have ever been to so I'm not a connoisseur but the one in Vancouver must have been special as it was close to a Ballet School. Some of the girls studying at the school paid for their fees by doing what they did best, namely dancing of a sort, but still with beauty and grace.

So, there were distractions but not enough to subdue my incandescent hatred of McBoag as we left Vancouver and headed south to retrace our steps and revisit the same ports we had visited on the way north.

Little did I guess how quickly I would get revenge, of a sort.

In ten days or so we were back in Los Angeles and again some us hit the bars of Long Beach. Something must have been in the air that night for we all drank heavily, even though we knew we were to head out to sea in the early hours of the morning. When I got back to the ship, I was so drunk I was caroming off the bulkheads as I made my way down the passageway to my cabin.

It seemed like I'd just closed my eyes when the sirens blared, intimating that we were about to leave port. It was my turn to steer the ship so instead of my usual boiler suit I put on my uniform, cap, black jacket and trousers, white shirt and tie.

When I got on deck, I was startled by what I saw. Had all the drink brought on a cotton-eyed blindness? Out of the bridge window all I could see was white. I slipped quickly out into the open air of the port-side bridge wing and found a dense fog diffusing even the harsh dockside lights.

A uniformed stranger was stalking up and down the bridge and this had to be the pilot. A wiry, bearded man, he gave every impression of someone in a hurry, checking his watch every few minutes. Harbour pilots come on board when ships enter and leave docks. They're particularly important when you're berthed well up a river, as their knowledge of the currents and sandbars can be critical.

I wasn't quite sure how useful this knowledge might be when nobody could see a damned thing. It's true we had radar which should bounce off and illuminate the boats berthed along each side of the river, and from this the pilot could at least figure out where the river was, but would that be enough for him to work out exactly where we were in this pea-souper of a fog?

I stepped back onto the bridge just as the pilot turned in his pacing and caught my eye. I was the only other person there but was clearly far too young to be Captain or Mate.

"Where's the Captain?" he asked brusquely

Good question. The captain should always be on the bridge when entering or leaving port. Sometimes the point might be stretched and the Mate might cover, but not when conditions were as bad as this.

Dimly I could just make out a figure on the starboard-side bridge wing. I figured that must be him so I just pointed, trying not to speak in case my drunken slur was obvious.

"Get him!" said the pilot, checking his watch again.

Running my hand along the chart table to give me support, I managed to get out onto the wing. The fog was so thick I had to get within a metre of the figure before I could recognise it.

It was Todd, the Mate. He was leaning over the railing. As I reached him a spout of vomit arced out of his mouth and flopped down onto the dock far below.

"Are you alright?"

He waved me away.

"The pilot's asking for the Captain."

"In his cabin," said Todd thickly. This set something off and he hunched and heaved like a cat with a fur ball. It looked like he was throwing up everything he had eaten for the past year.

I checked to see if I felt any sympathy.

Nope, nothing.

I returned to the pilot. "It's not the Captain."

"Then... get... him!" said the pilot as though I was an idiot.

I staggered down the stairs to the Captain's cabin and knocked respectfully at the door.

Nothing happened.

I knocked again but harder.

"Fug off, ya bastad!" came through the door loud and clear.

Tricky!

I went back up the stairs to the pilot.

"The Captain sends his compliments, sir, but he is at present indisposed." It came out of my mouth more like a speech impediment than a slur.

"Indi... what the hell are you talking about? I'm not taking a 600-foot-long ship out in these conditions without the Captain on the bridge. Get him!" Again, he glanced at his watch.

Piggy-in-the-middle, I went back down the stairs with a heavy tread. I knocked again, and again got dog's abuse.

"Sorry Captain but may I..." and I opened the door before the devil could say anything else. This was the second and last time I ever entered his cabin.

McBoag lay like a beached whale on his bunk, the white blanket rising like the swell of its decomposing, gas-engorged belly.

"The pilot sends his compliments, Captain McBoag, but he insists on your presence on the bridge as visibility is so poor." That, at least was what I tried to say. Articulate enough, but let down by wayward elocution.

A shoe smacked off my forehead. It hurt.

This was accompanied by invective that was obscene but unimaginative.

It later transpired that something had indeed been 'in the air' for the senior staff on board as well as for the juniors who had gone ashore. The Captain, the Mate and the Chief Engineer had earlier on in the evening sat down for a convivial whisky. They had developed a taste for it. When one bottle was finished, they started on another. Then another.

Now I don't know how common this habit had become for them but I'd never before seen evidence of drink in these men. Perhaps it really was just a moment of madness but the upshot was that the Captain was too ill to come up to the bridge.

That was his mistake.

I went back up to the pilot. "The Captain sends his apologies but he really is unwell."

The pilot looked at his watch again. Was he due to perform brain surgery on the President of the United States or something? He looked out at the slumped figure of the Mate and perhaps decided that, useless though the Mate was, a senior officer was technically on the bridge.

So, he decided to go ahead and take us out.

That was his mistake.

I'm guessing here, but he must have had something important to go to that morning. Perhaps if he took the ship to sea and returned on the pilot boat, he could still make it.

However, if he had to wait on standby until the fog cleared then he wasn't going anywhere.

I took my seat by the wheel, ready to follow the pilot's orders. When he ordered us to cast off, I relayed this by walkie-talkie to winch crews at the bow and stern.

Once the crews informed us that the mooring lines were back on board, the pilot said, "Ahead slow, heading 200 degrees." I had a lever I could move which automatically controlled the engine (a recent innovation in those days) and I moved the wheel to 200 degrees.

Looking out of the window was useless so the pilot was hunched over the radar, his face pressed against the visor-like opening in its hood. Green light limned his forehead when he shifted position.

We took it slow and the 600-footer eased its way down the narrow channel.

It wasn't so different from driving a car. The steering wheel was a similar size but instead of accelerator and brake pedals I just had the one lever.

"Heading 210 degrees," said the pilot.

Really, it was all child's pay. Well below the capabilities of a man of my intelligence.

Smug, arrogant and drunk, I fell asleep at the wheel of a 20,000-tonne ship navigating down a narrow river.

And that was my mistake.

"Heading?" The high-pitched shriek of the pilot jerked me back awake

"210 degrees."

"I told you 180! Hard a port!"

I brought the wheel hard over. Big ships aren't mightily responsive, especially at slow speeds but if you turn the wheel hard over the whole ship knows about it.

Later, a crewmate of mine clearing up the lines at the bow told me how he looked up when he felt the course change and nearly soiled himself when the side of an oil tanker come looming out of the fog. He watched slack-jawed as we turned in the nick of time, the metal hulls almost touching.

A few more screamed course changes from the pilot and we were back in the middle of the channel.

The pilot turned to me, his face like thunder. The Mate, puke smeared across the side of his mouth, staggered onto the bridge, holding the bulkhead for support.

And, with a mighty roar, the Captain lurched from the stairway and onto the bridge.

I'm not sure that at any other point in my life have three men all wanted to kill me at exactly the same time.

What should happen next was perfectly clear. The Captain would summarily sack me, as was in his power. I would be told to pack my bags and descend with the pilot onto the pilot launch when we reached the open sea. The pilot launch would take me ashore then, courtesy of the local shipping agent, a taxi would take me to LAX. A plane would then fly me back to the UK where I would be officially dismissed. I would be jobless and disgraced.

And, God alone knows, I deserved that and more.

But on the bridge that night something funny happened. Rather than a hanging trial what we had was a good old-fashioned Mexican stand-off. The Captain, the pilot and myself were like in that scene in the Sergio Leone film *The Good, The Bad and The Ugly* where Clint Eastwood, Eli Wallach and Lee Van Cleef stand regarding each other across a Mexican graveyard, waiting to see who will draw first.

It all went silent as we made our calculations.

The Captain had me bang to rights and he dearly wanted to see me sacked. I'd been drunk on duty. Unfortunately, he'd been drunk as well and had twice refused the pilot's demands to come to the bridge. If I went down then so would he.

The pilot clearly had come to the impression that we were both scumbags and I'm not saying he was wide of the mark on this. He'd have been happy to see us both sacked. Sadly, he'd made the decision to take the ship out in dangerous conditions without a functioning senior officer present. He was in trouble too.

As I dimly began to realise all this, I could imagine an Enrico Morricone theme tune rising in the background.

Three careers teetered on a knife edge. The fact was they'd invested considerably more time and sweat in theirs than I had in mine.

The silence hung like the fog on the port. Then, without a word being spoken, the pilot turned back to look in the radar hood and the Captain strode away to the little galley off the bridge to brew tea.

It was as though nothing had happened. This, despite the fact that if we'd hit that oil tanker, and if it had been even partly loaded, I could have taken out most of the Port of Los Angeles in a cataclysmic conflagration.

The Captain and I never exchanged a single word after that. Other than the odd perfunctory order, the Mate also kept his mouth shut and left me out of his elaborate schemes to undermine crew moral.

I had done something terrible and yet had got away with it scot free. Not only that but things were actually better afterwards. There were just too many sleeping dogs around and everyone was keen to let them lie.

~~~

So, the guilty escaped punishment. The take-home message from this is that things that happen when you travel are, like in life itself, rarely fair. Sometimes they work in your favour and sometimes they don't.

I recently heard that McBoag had passed away. His obituary had been written by someone who was clearly struggling to find something positive to say about him.

After I'd read it, I checked myself for signs of sympathy.

Nope, nothing.
~~~

# *What Does 'Worse Things Happen at Sea' Actually Mean?*

Various locales, 1976–78

In case you're not picking up on the subtext, the last two chapters are essentially describing what a terrible sailor I was. They've also been a bit of a *mea culpa* as well as an apology to my shipmates and to my shipping line.

Too late in the day, perhaps, as both the line and some of my shipmates have sailed over the bar. That's the rather affecting expression used when seafarers pass away. The bar is the sandbar often found at the mouth of a river. Once you cross over that you are sailing out into the deep blue sea.

This final chapter on my seafaring days is a miscellany of some of the scary things that happened during my time at sea. One of those experiences, namely that of apartheid in South Africa, is thankfully now just the stuff of history books. The rest, however, are still common experiences and will provide a lifetime of tales to bore friends and acquaintances if they ever happen to you.

If you survive them, of course.

These are things to do if you want to avoid a safe and quiet life.

## Sail the Atlantic in a Winter Storm

I'm not afraid of storms for I'm learning how to sail my ship. Amy: from Louisa May Alcott's *Little Women*.

The woman's an idiot!

The container ship *Stella Maris* on the western Europe/western North America run. Some 20,000 tonnes and two hundred metres long, in its day it was one of the biggest container ships around. When loaded up, the containers were stacked three high on deck and five deep in the holds.

It was an awesome beast when you looked up at it from the dock.

Containerisation was just coming in so this was a newish ship with all the latest mod-cons in the crew accommodation. Even lowly trainees like myself had en-suite cabins to ourselves. The canteen with its factory condition chairs and tables, new silverware and table cloths took it almost up to high-end restaurant standard.

With uniformed stewards serving us three meals a day we could have been on the maiden voyage of the *Titanic.*

The whole reference frame has changed since. The meals seemed high class because the food available in British restaurants was so limited back then. Prawn cocktail was considered sophisticated and well-done steaks were the height of fine dining, at least in the provinces.

Ship sizes have also changed. Recently, the container ship *Ever Given* blocked the Suez Canal. Twice as long as the *Stella Maris*, it has nearly ten times the gross tonnage. On the *Ever Given* it must feel like you're sailing around on a moon.

However, back in the old days, the *Stella Maris* gave every appearance of being so substantial, so solid, so well-geared in all its functions, that I felt a deep sense of security as I walked up the gangway to join this, my first ship. If I'd read the above quote from *Little Women* at that point I might even have nodded sagely in agreement.

As I arrived, the huge towering dockside cranes were lowering the massive 40-foot-long containers into the ship's holds and officers and crew were bustling around in preparation for its imminent departure.

Tilbury cringed under a lowering gunmetal grey winter sky. Across the Thames was Gravesend, so called because bodies thrown into the water upriver in London usually washed up there. The name alone was morbid and Dickensian and redolent of cold, wet cemeteries.

So, of course I was made up with the idea of leaving this all behind for the Caribbean heat.

After we cast off, we made our stately and apparently implacable way down the river and out into the English Channel, then south and then west into the Atlantic. Here the weather deteriorated but still the ship was stable. Being new it had all the latest design features, including a bulbous bow. This is a protrusion that looks like a stubby penis thrusting out just under the water line, though more shamelessly into the open air when the ship is unloaded. It reduces the slamming effect of waves.

A common feature on modern ships, it is also where the bodies of whales wind up after strikes. With eyes on opposite sides of their heads, they have a panoramic view of everything except what's dead ahead of them.

If they hit hard enough the sharp bow slices them almost in two, and the carcass slithers down until it lies draped decorously over the top of the bulbous section.

It usually takes a crane to pull them off, something container ships don't possess so removal is delayed until the next port, the whale lolling across the bulbous bow like a hideous hunting trophy.

The bulbous bow and many other features of the *Stella Maris* all served to reduce the effects of the moving ocean but it didn't eliminate them. This soon became apparent as we entered open water. Depending on the direction of the wind and water a boat can move back and forth about all three axes. It can pitch (up and down as the boat meets waves head on), roll (where the water is coming at you from the side) and the final, less easy to understand but the most insidious and nauseating effect, yaw (where the bow of the ship moves to one side, while the stern moves to the other. In other words, it's like you're swivelling).

Yawing is supposed to be the best for producing sea sickness, though I wouldn't know as I have never been travel sick in my life. This made me more unusual than you might think amongst sailors and most did succumb if the weather got really brutal.

One Chief Engineer I worked with got sick on every single trip. Imagine the poor man working down in the oily, stinky and, especially in the tropics, abominably hot engine room and always being sea sick as well. Is there a better definition of hell? Brave guy to put up with that!

The problem on this trip was that we were heading into big waves coming right at us. They were fleeing a faraway storm which was battering the east coast of the States. Pitching was therefore the main problem. We would hit a large wave, the boat would rise, then it would dive down on the other side of the crest.

Waves can be separated into 'sea' and 'swell'. The former are the little wind-blown waves that produce the white tops, sometimes called white horses, at their crests. The Beaufort scale attempts to classify these waves. Force 0 is sea like a mirror, 1 is ripples without crests. Force 4, a moderate breeze, has small waves with fairly frequent white horses.

Up to this point the numbers owe more to 'sea' than 'swell'. The little wavelets, blown by gusts of wind, travel at different speeds. Some catch up with others and add to their height. So, as they move away from the centre of the storm, more and more waves add together to form this much higher swell. It also produces 1-in-7 waves. We've all seen these on the beach where around one in seven waves is higher and more powerful than the others.

That, however, is just the average. This constructive interference effect does not regularly produce one high wave in seven.

At Force 7 the wave height is five metres, a moderate gale. The water heaps up and white foam from the crests is blown in streaks along the direction of the wind. At Force 10 (on land trees would be uprooted by such a strong wind) we're now in a proper gale with very high waves and overhanging crests; the wind blows this spray so far that the entire surface of the sea looks white.

And a Force 10, with a peak wave height of fifteen metres was what we were heading into. The slowly rising swell was our first real sign of things to come.

The up and down movement didn't bother me too much except when it came to trying to sleep. In my single bunk I rattled around like a pea in a whistle. No matter how many pillows I used to wedge myself in, I still couldn't stop the movement. Because of the 1-in-7 effect, the movements were too irregular to allow me much sleep.

Little sleep, night after night, weakens a man. Like the rest of the crew, I became hollow-eyed and slow to respond. A greasy feeling settled in my guts, making it difficult to eat.

For several days as the storm approached, the crew got wearier and greyer and pukier. Walking around the ship, even inside the superstructure, became increasingly hazardous. Woe betide anyone walking down the stairs who didn't have a firm hand on the stair rail!

The evening when it all got very ugly indeed, I was on the 8 to 12 watch and I had a grandstand view of what was happening as we ploughed into the storm. The bridge was about 150 metres back from the bow. As we reached each wave I'd watch as the bow rose, the whole ship tilting upward until I could see only sky ahead.

That wasn't so bad. It was when we came off the crest then smashed down into the next trough that all the action happened.

Above the bulbous nose, the bow flared out, presenting a huge area to smash down into the next wavefront. The effect was to pulverise vast amounts of water into spray. This would blast back over the bow, across the banks of containers and smash into the bridge window like a fist.

It was like riding a rollercoaster, except nobody was squealing with delight.

At least from the bridge I could see what was happening. As we headed into each trough, I would grasp the handrail around the map table and manage to keep on my feet. Anything movable had long since been stowed away because otherwise it would have disappeared, ricocheting from one bulkhead to another. Crockery in the galley had been placed in storm racks a metre deep but the rocking made them shiver and they rattled like an army of skeletons. Even stowed-away objects weren't entirely secured, there was always some margin for movement.

As for the cargo, who knew? The containers were locked so we rarely knew for sure what was in them. Some might be chock full of carefully stacked boxes so they'd be okay. It was the stuff that was packed loosely that was suffering, and we could hear things rattling and banging all over the ship.

All these noises had a certain regularity, though not enough to dance to. First, there was a sliding sound as everything rolled backwards when the bow rose up the wall of water. Then another sliding sound as we topped the wave and fell towards the trough and everything rolled forward. Then numerous thuds as we hit the trough and the movement of everything was suddenly arrested.

And the surface of the sea, as advertised by the Gale Force Scale, was white with the blown spray. That's a disturbing sight all by itself.

Normally we'd have a lookout stationed out on one of the bridge wings but, with the blow-back of water from the impacting bow, they'd have been smashed to the deck or even pitched overboard. So, we had him inside, peering myopically out of the spray-smeared windows.

The radar was also pretty useless. The big waves were reflecting it like crazy. A super-tanker could have been a couple of wavelengths away and we wouldn't have known until we ploughed right into it.

And the waves got bigger and bigger, looming over us and making this big ship look like a toy.

Worst of all, we knew there would be no respite. It would be days before this ride stopped.

As night wore on and the waves got higher and higher, and the noises grew more and more cacophonous, it began to dawn on me that things were getting very serious indeed.

The worst of it were the 1-in-7s. Those occasional bigger waves are a boon where you're surfing, but not when your surfboard is a 200-metre-long boat and there's no shore nearby where you can rest up and lick your wounds.

And there was no coastguard to rescue us. If the hull was breached in one of the impacts and we started to take on water then nobody would be able to rescue us in these high seas, even if another ship was nearby, which was very unlikely.

We were on our own and at the mercy of an uncaring sea.

Sick, weary from the battering and dizzy from the continuous irregular movement, I watched each mountainous corpse-grey wave as it reared up before us like a phantom from a tomb. Each time I was convinced it would wash right over us, scouring the deck, or smash us to pieces or capsize us. Each time this big heavy ship rose up the approaching crest, the wave never quite breaking on us, until we arced free, then dived down the other side.

Each time we hit the bottom I was almost knocked from my feet despite clutching the handrail. Down below nobody was getting any sleep. Some, I suspected, were saying their prayers.

In those days, before satellite navigation, you had no idea where you were until you took a sun-sight or saw land. There was also no way to tell how fast we were actually travelling. We were full speed ahead but I doubt we were making much progress. We had to keep full ahead for if we turned aside, we'd have been capsized.

Up and down, up and down, hour after hour, it felt like I was being battered by a pile-driver.

I must have taken my eyes away from the window but a fist of spray hammering into it brought them back.

I heard the lookout say, "Jesus!"

And there, coming out of the maelstrom ahead of us was the most dreadful 1-in-7 I had ever seen. It towered over us, the gale raking the crest and blowing the spray out into taloned fingers. The bow began to rise up its terrible slope, the deck tipping to an impossible angle. It seemed inevitable it would turn us head over tail and drown us all.

Over by the window, the lookout started praying.

My feet slipped from under me and I hung from the rail like a curtain.

The ship kept rising and I was sure we weren't going to make it. If the wave broke over us then the bridge window wouldn't hold. It would disintegrate into flying glass and the water would surge in, battering us against the bulkhead, or washing us out and overboard to freeze or drown.

But then, joy of joys, the bow found air and we lifted clear and the ship began to tilt down. We'd crash into the trough but at least we'd live.

I was giving a whoop of joy but this froze in my mouth. Instead of a big trough, close up behind the big wave was another 1-in-7. I watched goggle-eyed and powerless as our bow drove right into it just below the crest.

With a terrible bang the impact stopped the 20,000-tonne ship dead in its tracks.

I slammed against the chart table and was winded by the handrail. A mixture of spray and water came swarming at us over the tops of the containers like a rampaging devil army. I don't know how the glass of the bridge withstood the impact.

I then heard a noise that I'll take to my grave. With the bow embedded near the top of one wave, and with the stern still hanging on the top of another, the midships of the ship was suddenly out of the water and unsupported. Loaded boats are designed always to be supported by water. Without it, the ship's back can break instantly and the two parts plummet to the ocean floor four miles below.

The whole ship moaned like it was in pain. This cry of despair seemed to go on forever but it could only have been a few seconds. Then the stern began to fall and the water of the next wave once again cupped the ship's gravid belly and we all lived to tell the tale.

The rest of the night was bad but that double 1-in-7er marked the worst point. By morning the waves were appreciably smaller. Within a few days we were in the Caribbean and the storm was just a memory.

But it left marks. For a start, the stupendous impact had given the stacks of plates in their storm racks in the galley enough energy to rise out of their metre deep wells and fly out in a geyser of ceramics. Next morning the galley was three inches deep in broken crockery.

And that wasn't the only crockery that didn't survive. Some bright spark of a loading manager had assigned a consignment of Wedgewood crockery to the front row of the above-deck container stack. Steel containers that had started out as forty feet long, emerged from the storm one foot shorter. The contents, of course, had completely disintegrated.

When we got to San Pedro, all the deck officers took a walk down the dock to get a good look at the bow. The smooth, stylishly flared bow looked like the forehead of a dowager, its surface marked by horizontal and vertical wrinkles. These showed the once-invisible strengthening beams that kept the bow in one piece. The impact had driven the plates of the bow hard back against them.

Whoever installed those strengtheners, I thank you!

If the ship's back had broken, we'd have sunk like a stone. Indeed, even today ships can disappear very suddenly before they can get out a distress call. It usually happens to bulk carriers with heavy loads of ore. The theory is that they too break their backs in heavy seas. For them, the only way is down and with such velocity they will strike the ocean floor far below at fifty or sixty kilometres per hour.

Bear in mind that this all happened to me when I had thought myself safe on a big modern ship. Storms at sea are one reason why I'd never go on the ocean in a dinky little sailboat.

Here's another reason.

## Sail Across the Atlantic in a Sailboat

I'm up for most things. I've crossed the Atlantic many times in a ship so why would I never do it in a boat?

First, let's define our terms: what is the difference between a ship and a boat?

Perhaps the most important difference is size. A ship can carry a boat but a boat can't carry a ship. This is true and indeed we once carried a commercial hydrofoil ferry across the Atlantic strapped to the top of some containers.

That's about the clearest definition you can get but even that doesn't pass muster. A yacht can carry a dingy so does that make it a ship?

Other definitions involve propulsion systems, design, cargo, where they sail, professionalism of crew and navigational systems. All these definitions come with handy holes you could drive a coach and horses through.

Even so, professional sailors delight in scorning landlubbers who call ships boats. Then, almost within the same breath, when talking to another professional seaman they'll refer to what they do as 'working on the boats'.

As with so much talk about the sea, there's more than a tincture of bullshit.

Size, in this matter, is everything. My willingness to cross an ocean is directly related to the size of the vessel. The idea of being caught in a bad storm mid-ocean in anything less than a hundred metres long and ten thousand tonnes in weight fills me with dread.

If a yacht gets caught in a bad storm, then it is entering a world of fear. Imagine yourself at the bottom of a grey-walled trough, a breaking wave towering over you and coming down to smash you to smithereens.

But there's another reason the sheer vulnerability of yachts and small boats in mid-ocean would stop me ever going on one.

We were approaching the Sargasso Sea from the east and, as usual, the sea was pretty calm with waves of little more than a metre high (Beaufort scale 3 or 4). I was on the bridge wing acting as lookout and was leaning on the rail idly staring at the water below. Suddenly, a broken mast, the wreckage of a hull and an orange lifebuoy went by below me. It was clearly what was left of a yacht so I yelled to the Mate who was on the bridge. We were doing the usual twenty knots so the wreckage was already behind us when we started to turn.

The procedure was the same as for a man overboard. Ships are heavy and impossible to stop in their tracks (with rare exceptions, see the section above). Some super-tankers take kilometres to stop if they're travelling at full speed. So, the ship can't just stop and reverse because by then the current will have swept the man or wreckage far away.

So, instead a Williamson turn is adopted. The ship is turned through a figure of 8 so that it will in theory wind up back where it started. That can be done quickly and effectively, though even then the current will have had time to take the target elsewhere.

So that's what we did. The sea was quite calm and I was on a bridge wing ten metres above the ocean and could see for many kilometres. I was confident we would spot the wreckage, particularly because of the bright orange lifebuoy.

But we never saw any of it again.

That's the problem with even small waves, never mind the bigger swells. They hide things from someone looking, unless the observer is really close and is looking at that exact point in the ocean at the exact moment the wreckage is topping a crest.

The message is that if you fall overboard or your yacht goes down and you are clinging to a piece of wreckage, you are very unlikely to be picked up even if there is a big ship in the vicinity.

Many is the time after crossing the Atlantic that we've pulled into port and I've walked down the dock to inspect the bow only to find smears of paint. Somewhere in mid-ocean we'd struck something man-made. We hadn't seen it coming, we hadn't heard it hit, and we hadn't seen it left behind in our wake.

Perhaps these were just packing cases washed overboard from a ship in a storm. Or perhaps it was a yacht with people on board.

Let's try to keep this in perspective, though. If you're in a yacht your chances of being hit and killed by a big ship are pretty small. It is far overshadowed by the biggest yacht-related cause of death: having too much to drink, falling overboard and drowning.

Which is ironic, because they only way you would get me on a yacht is to pour a bottle of whisky down my throat.

## Be Suspected of Miscegenation

We were picking up apples again, this time taking them from Cape Town in South Africa back to Rotterdam. As we sailed in, Table Mountain was framed by a blue sky of crisp, clean air.

Even as I was admiring the view, just off to port Nelson Mandela was biding his time in the prison on Robben Island.

But, of course, in those days I'd never heard of him and I didn't even notice the prison as we sailed into Table Bay.

Terrible things were going on, just like they had been back in Valparaiso when we'd docked next to Chilean naval ships. On board those, torture and murder were happening just a stone's throw away but we'd been entirely oblivious.

The difference now was that while Pinochet's repression may have been hidden, in South Africa apartheid was something even a dope like me couldn't avoid noticing.

The first dead giveaway came soon after we docked. The *Goneril*, my refrigerated cargo ship, always had white officers and stewards, but the rest of the crew were Barbadian. As

I have indicated before, they were all nice chaps but they did, in some cases, smuggle drugs and guns. They also had a tendency to go with ladies of the night.

Whichever port we called in at, a day before one of the Barbadians would go to the radio operator to call ahead to arrange female company. When we arrived, a horde would be waiting.

So, in Cape Town, I was unsurprised to see a large number of rather substantial black women come sashaying down the dock towards the ship. However, what happened next was something I'd never expected to witness.

Being a general cargo dock, goods were loaded onto wooden pallets and these were lifted into ships' holds via rickety old cranes. A long line of these loomed over the dock.

In South Africa, crane drivers were white. From their elevated viewpoint all they could see were some black prostitutes heading towards a ship where white men like me, dressed in our summer white uniforms, were poncing around on the bridge.

Miscegenation, or the banning of marriage or even just sexual relations between the races, had been in force in South Africa since the time of the Dutch East India Company back in the seventeenth century. Specifically, it banned marriage between whites and full-blooded black slave women. However, it wasn't just a bi-polar black/ white thing. For a time, fine distinctions were made between 'coloured' or mixed-race women. Whites could freely consort with them until 1949, when a more hard-line approach was taken, banning whites from marrying anyone who was non-white. In 1950 an act was passed banning sexual relation between the races altogether.

The women were half way down the dock when it all kicked off. Jumping to the erroneous conclusion that the black women were there to service the white officers, the crane drivers suddenly swung their empty palettes over the heads of the women then dropped them down. As the first came smacking down onto the dock with a mighty crash, the targeted woman barely leapt aside just in time.

All the women began dodging to avoid the sudden squall of heavy palettes crashing down from the sky. The dock began to sound like a war zone.

The women ran the gauntlet. Luckily, even without cargo on them, palettes could be manoeuvred either quickly or accurately but not both at the same time, so nobody was killed.

The noise and screaming had brought all our crew on deck to watch the terrible spectacle. Everyone was deeply shocked and soon there was a clamour for the captain to call the police.

However, the crane drivers beat us to it. Within minutes the police were on board with a view to convicting us under the miscegenation laws. That the dockers had tried to kill the women was of no interest to them.

Things cooled down when the coppers went below to the crew's quarters and saw only black men, with the women already making themselves at home in their cabins. This seemed to mollify them and they left us alone from that point on.

South Africa then was like a car accident: you just couldn't look away. Maybe I should have kept to my cabin and read the Bible but going ashore whenever I had the opportunity was something I could never resist.

I managed to get ashore by myself and, after a hard day gawping at Cape Town and riding the cable car up Table Mountain (and finding myself eye to eye with rats the size of tom cats called dassies. These inhabit the rock and clouds at the top and luckily don't seem very aggressive), I repaired to a bar for refreshment.

It was an old-style panelled bar, with only men as customers, all of them white except for a single black barman. Behind the bar a tinny transistor radio was playing, the barman filling glasses as he danced around in time. He was a tall, strapping fellow. He was smiling and open faced, while the whites were mean and surly

As I sat there drinking my beer and reflecting on this strange country, the owner of the bar arrived. A big burly white guy, he weaved a little like he'd already had a skinful. He started shouting at the black man in Afrikaans (a language from Dutch vernacular and German, both the opposite of romantic. For example, any language that calls nipples 'breast warts' has missed something somewhere). He pointed angrily at the transistor radio. The black man turned it off but the owner wasn't placated.

Dutch is a brutal sounding language at the best of times but whatever the owner said next it went beyond even that. When he pointed at the exit it was clear he was sacking the black guy.

The black guy seemed to take it on the chin and came out from behind the bar and made to leave. However, when he got to the door, he hesitated then came back and went behind the bar.

The owner roared with rage. The black pointed at the radio, I'm guessing it was his, and then made to take it.

The owner attacked him, punching him about the head and neck. The owner wasn't small, but the black was bigger. Even so, he didn't fight back, just crouched down, arms looped over his head to deflect the blows.

These rained down for what seemed like an eternity. Around me I could hear the white customers laughing appreciatively at the spectacle.

Perhaps I should have intervened but, on the other hand, I'm not totally stupid.

Then, as quickly as it had started, the owner's storm of rage dissipated. He said something that still sounded brutal, such is Afrikaans, but it was like feather pillows compared to what had gone before. He bent down and almost gently pulled the barman upright. He put an arm around his shoulder and led him over to the beer taps. The black poured a beer and gave it to him.

And then it was as if nothing had happened. The black went back to serving and the owner went over to sit at a table with some of the customers. They all had a good laugh.

I reflected that I'd been to some fucked-up places in my time but South Africa had won the prize.

Later on, some of us hired a car and we drove around, far enough to see the dreadful townships where the blacks lived. Cape Town itself could fool you into thinking it was a typical modern Western city but, in some ways, it was more like a medieval castle. It was only able to look gracious and dignified because it was supported by a huge hinterland of serfs living in mire and misery.

In my life, tragedy and farce are often too close together for comfort. I'd seen plenty of the former in South Africa so I should have realised that the latter would not be far away.

What happened next was an experience that lurks in my dreams, scaring me wide awake forty years later, groaning and cringing in mortification in the early hours of the morning.

We were about to leave port. To get the full embarrassing context you need to know how I was dressed when this happened. It was summer so we were wearing uniform whites. That means short-sleeved white shirts, white peaked caps, white shorts, white shoes and knee-length white socks.

In other words, I was dressed like a dick personified. Even the biggest, hairiest-arsed sailor looked unmanned in this outfit.

As usual I was shadowing the Mate. He was nice enough but intense and so was rather peremptory in his orders.

"Get rid of the black whores!" he said then strode off.

Easy said but not so easily done.

I looked down at my summering Little Lord Fauntleroy outfit and my heart felt heavy as lead. After the trouble with the police the West Indian crew had kept their women out of sight in their cabins. However, when they'd arrived, I'd seen enough of them to realise these women were battle-hardened by dreadful lives into the toughest of warriors.

And I was going to have to deal with them. If I'd been wearing military fatigues with a gun in each hand I might have got somewhere. Armed with only my Summer Whites, I anticipated a less satisfactory outcome.

Already sweating, I descended the stairs. Unlike the officers' cabins that were above decks with portholes and views, the black crew lived in the bowels of the ship without any natural light. Also, unlike the officers, they lived two to a cabin.

The crew's quarters normally didn't smell any different, except for the ganga fumes. However, now they smelled all too human; of sweaty bodies toiling lustily to climax.

In other words, it smelled like a knocking shop.

The reason was plain enough. The cabins had bunks for the two crewmen. Now each bunk and crewman were supplemented by two women in various states of dishabille.

As I appeared in the first doorway, the women's blank incurious eyes swivelled slowly to regard me.

"Bazza!" said Menzies, a young and at present naked crewman. I hadn't noticed him at first, submerged as he was by women.

"Hi there, Menzies," I said and tried for the placatory, "The Captain sends his compliments and says that it is time for your lady friends to leave the ship."

The women did speak some English but it was approximate. In any case, the dope tangled up the feet of their comprehension and it took quite a while for the truth to dawn. When it did the effect was galvanising.

Their English may not have been good but, when it came to international invective, they were Shakespearean. Being a poor black prostitute in an apartheid-cursed country must have dug a deep well full to the brim with bitterness. Standing before them, a skinny white guy dressed in poncy summer uniform, I personified all that they detested.

Their brutal, Dutch inflected delivery brought a chorus of women from the other cabins. The verbal cannonade thundered at me like it was 1812 all over again. The word raasclaat featured, even though the word was of Jamaican origin. If you want to know what that means then look it up because I'm not going to tell you.

I withered before their contempt and hatred.

Even now, over forty years later, the memory makes me groan with embarrassment.

Like I've said, the Barbadian crew were nice guys and eventually they took pity on me and took it upon themselves to bundle the protesting women off the ship.

I went to my cabin and had a long lie down.

~~~

So, all in all I didn't like South Africa. I hear it's much better nowadays.

I still won't be going back.
~~~

Cross the line on a ship

*Griffins, slimy pollywogs, dirty tadpoles*
Names sailors use for those who have never crossed the equator.

Forty years ago, off the coast of Peru, we were due to cross the line. This would be my first time entering the southern hemisphere and I wasn't looking forward to it.

Terrible things were supposed to happen at Crossing the Line ceremonies. So fearsome had these ceremonies been in the past that most navies outlawed them. Originally, and benignly, the ceremony had been used to boost morale on long cruises to the southern hemisphere. However, due to man's innate sadism, but also supposedly to ensure new crew members were tough enough to handle life at sea, these initiations had become ordeals.

Treats included being blindfolded, whipped, ducked in tubs of salt water, lathered in pitch and paint. Some of the newbies were thrown into the sea, some dragged through the surf behind the boat. In the US navy pollywogs were electrocuted.

'Sump and rump' involved noxious liquids being smeared on the cock and balls and anus.

No surprise that sailors sometimes died. In the US navy even today, they have 'Wog Day' with pollywogs being subpoenaed to appear before King Neptune and his Court. Pollywogs can be pilloried and pelted with rotten fruit, made to eat hot sauce and raw eggs. They can be whipped with fire hoses, locked in a 'water coffin' full of green dye.

Tellingly, the ceremony is usually preceded by a beauty contest of men dressed as women.

If that's not an upwelling from the Jungian subconscious, then I don't know what is.

Of course, I was perturbed that something like this might happen to me. So, when I was asked by the wild-eyed and wild-haired Third Engineer if I'd crossed the equator before I was as dismissive as a Noel Coward put-down. "Oh yaah! Went down to Cape Town on the *Stella Maris*."

The 3/E clapped his hands in triumph. "That's a locked run, mate. west Coast of Europe to west Coast of North America. Try again!"

"Anyway, been through the Panama Canal loads of times."

"That's a few degrees north of the line. Gotcha!"

And he literally danced away in jubilation.

I'm not the bravest of men, but I had cause for alarm. These guys and civil behaviour weren't even on nodding acquaintance. Whenever we called in at a British port, police cars would be waiting. Some crewmen regarded getting on a deep-sea boat as a way of letting things cool down after some crime or other; that somehow the coppers would just give up. Clearly this didn't always work.

Going to sea in the first place suggests at least an adventurous spirit. In my experience this is usually associated with a decrease in inhibitions. Sometimes lairy, louche and with poor impulse control there was no limit to the things seafarers could get up to.

Plus, there was the matter of resentment. Hiring graduates was something new and we were rare and privileged. Traditionally trained staff were still coming in as cadets on less than half our income and with half our leave time. How could that do anything but make them resentful?

Now they'd have the chance to get back at me.

I'm no Clint Eastwood and I couldn't stop myself acting nervous. A few of the crew took pity on me and assured me that such barbaric behaviour was a thing of the past.

They lied.

I was sleeping peacefully in my bunk after coming off watch when a bunch of the ruffians burst in, stripped me naked and dragged me out on deck where they tied me to a crane cable. Over what seemed like an eternity they smeared me in sump oil and kitchen waste they'd been saving for over a week.

At the end of the ceremony, they hit me with a high-pressure salt water hose. I was so filthy I might even have welcomed that but the blast of salt so shrivelled my eyeballs that they dropped out my skull.

At least it felt that way.

Nowadays, for allowing such behaviour, the bosses of the shipping line would have been manacled and put on a charter flight to the Court of Human Rights in the Hague.

Those were different times, however, and I just accepted what had happened. It did me no harm and I turned out perfectly normal, as all my friends and family would no doubt attest.

In my dreams, at least.

## Self-medicate at Sea

Self-medication is a big thing in the Merchant Navy because it is usually the only thing. Unless you are on a cruise ship or a massive Russian fishing factory ship, then the nearest doctor may be a thousand kilometres away.

There is another alternative, namely relying on your totally unqualified crewmates to diagnose and treat you. We're talking big trust issues there.

So, you have no real choice but to do it yourself. You are not entirely alone, however, as there is usually a green-covered book called *The Ship Captain's Medical Guide* on board.

This handy book instructs you how to treat everything from a splinter in your pinky, to your whole arm being torn off in a winch accident. Knife, gunshot and sucking chest wounds also feature.

Also, on board there may even be a 'hospital' room or at least a cupboard containing sewing gear and antibiotics and a few other medications to treat conditions such as angina and constipation.

Usually, one of the mates is designated as a sort of medical officer, but when presented with the typical and rather unsavoury complaints sailors suffer from at sea, the mates don't want to know.

This is precisely what happened when I rocked up to the Mate's cabin and described my symptoms.

I'm not sure exactly what I was expecting. Concern maybe, sympathy possibly.

Instead, the Mate shoved the hospital key unceremoniously into my hand and told me to bog off and sort it out myself.

What was I suffering from? After a couple of weeks in a South American port, followed by a few days at sea to let the condition mature and develop, the skin over my abdomen had become extremely itchy. It was so bad I couldn't sleep and I scratched my stomach raw.

On closer inspection I noticed rows of little red dots across my skin. The dots were separated by a centimetre or so and went from my ribs almost down to my groin.

This latter detail is probably what had left the Mate so deeply uninterested in my condition.

So, I went to the hospital and consulted *The Guide*. It was not a very large book, at least in those days, but my condition was common enough to have sufficient prominence that I could find it easily.

I had scabies.

These tiny insects burrow under the skin and take up residence to lay their eggs. The red dots were the skin's allergic reaction to their presence.

This was all news to me and most unwelcome at that.

I was at least relieved my problem was so readily identifiable and commonplace. Even better, there was a simple cure. According to *The Guide* I had to run a deep bath with water as hot as I could bear. I was to lie immersed for ten minutes, topping up with more hot water as necessary.

The heat would bring the nasty little critters to the surface of my skin and then I was to jump out of the bath and smear an ointment called benzyl-benzoate all over myself.

This would kill the mites.

Sounded straightforward, so I did just that. We were still sailing through the tropics so getting into a boiling hot bath wasn't ideal but it was better than this agony of scratching.

I lay there sweltering until I could bear it no longer. I leapt out and smeared the ointment all over my body including my eyes and the inside of my foreskin.

It was so soothing.

For around twenty seconds.

Then my eyes and genitals caught fire.

I roared like a lion. The pain was excruciating and I was blinded. Feeling like my skin was covered in napalm, I groped my way out of the hospital and onto the deck. We were doing twenty knots so there was a decent cooling breeze. I stood there, arms and legs outstretched like a naked, crucified Christ, the racing air balm to my molten skin.

Of course, I hadn't read the small print on the ointment bottle. It turns out you're not supposed to smear the stuff on your eyes or under your foreskin.

Live and learn.

Our sojourn in that port had two other outcomes.

Firstly, the hospital became very much in demand. The port had been suffering from a biblical surfeit of the clap. So much so that even though well-stocked for such an eventuality, the hospital came close to running out of antibiotics.

So many of the crew were affected that when we got to the next European port, the shipping company had to lay on a bus to take them all to the nearest clap clinic.

Secondly, the *Ship Captain's Guide* got me interested in medicine and made me wonder if there was anything a physicist could contribute. That made me find out about medical physics and its role in radiotherapy and nuclear medicine and (later) MRI. Ultimately, I would make my career in this. In time I rose to become a consultant scientist in the NHS and an honorary professor at the University of Glasgow.

And all because of a few dozen South American mites.

## Stall the Engine of a 20,000-tonne ship

If you haven't always driven an automatic car, then you must have stalled a manual car at some point. Well, I managed to do that on a great big merchant ship.

The Zeebrugge dock was a little dog-leg affair. We were berthed at the top of the long bit. When the time came to leave, we cast off, with me doing the steering (would the shipping line never learn?).

We were taking it gently because ahead of us, at the bend in the dog-leg, was an ammunition ship. Artillery shells were being unloaded, a long line of dockers carefully passing each shell from hand to hand.

The pilot seemed very nervous, stalking into the wheelhouse then immediately back out on the wing to get a better look. The slower it travels, the less responsive a big ship is, so if we were to start turning into the other bit of the dog-leg, we had to do it in plenty of time.

The pilot ordered a course change and I complied immediately. Problem was, the ship hardly responded at all because of our slow speed. Rather than turning away we were still heading straight for the ammunition ship.

"Full astern!" the pilot shouted in alarm.

As well as steering I had the engine controls. You'll have seen these in old movies. You have a brass handle you can move back and forth between the extremes marked 'Full Ahead' and 'Full Astern'.

In those old movies these controls were connected to a similar-looking lever in the engine room. As the lever moved, the chief engineer would note where it wound up then he would issue commands to the other engineers. They in turn would work their magic on the engine.

But this was a brand-new ship with the latest technology. Rather than my lever just telling the engineer what we wanted, it controlled the engine directly.

I was fresh on the ship and nobody had bothered to tell me (teaching in the fleet was... inconsistent) that you had to take the engine steadily through intermediate states rather than jamming it full astern because this would stall the engine.

And that is exactly what happened. The engine cut out and we continued to drift sedately but inexorably towards the ammo ship.

Along with the engine, everything went quiet on the bridge.

Then: "Full astern, full astern!" screamed the pilot.

But try as I might I could go no fuller asterner as the lever was already as far back as it would go.

I didn't have a clue what to do. I mean, how do you go about restarting a ship's massive engine? There's no big crank handle to turn.

A friend of mine, another trainee, had been at the bow when we cast off. As the engine cut out, the crew there rushed to the railings. As they did so our flared bow moved over the ammo ship, casting it into shadow.

My pal said that he found himself looking directly down on a docker who stood there, looking directly back up at him while holding an artillery shell out before him like it was a sacrificial offering to a vengeful god.

Meanwhile, the Chief Engineer and his men had been working feverishly to restart the engine. And thank God they succeeded, bringing the ship to a halt just before the lower edge of our bow sliced into the ammo ship.

I wasn't a good sailor, as you may have gathered, but just this once it wasn't my fault. Rather than assign a particular mate to training me, they all just seemed to assume that one of the others was doing it.

As a result, critical information just wasn't passed on. This is why such incidents weren't uncommon and I got caught out again in Vancouver Harbour.

Again, I was steering and after we cast off, we travelled about a mile  across the harbour, the pilot giving me headings and me assiduously following them.

Finally, a little perplexed, he said, "I don't think the steering is responding."

And he was right.

It turned out that there was a button, hidden on the opposite side of the steering wheel cabinet where it pressed against the bulkhead. This had to be switched on to engage the steering gear. Usually, it was always left on and so I had been steering happily in and out of a dozen or more ports. However, for some reason, someone must have turned it off and not told anyone. I'd been moving the wheel and absolutely nothing had been happening.

Again, a big heavy ship, moving through a busy port without any steering could have had apocalyptic consequences.

Nobody had told me the button even existed.

Zeebrugge, San Pedro and Vancouver: a hat-trick of near misses by just one trainee.

The thing is, the shipping line I worked for was one of the better ones, registered under the British flag and complying with an extensive (though clearly patchy) Board of Trade training programme. Many ships then, and even more now, sail under flags of convenience where training may be almost non-existent.

The only surprise is that there aren't many more disasters.

## Get Caught in a Fire at Sea

Balmy tropical breezes wafting out over us from the Panamanian jungle did little to disguise the stench. At anchor all around us bobbed small fishing boats. Bunting hung over the decks of these boats but the little triangular flags were all coloured grey, like at a really mournful party.

And indeed, it had certainly been no party for the sharks, for the little triangular pennants had once been their fins. The sharks had been caught, their fins cut off, then they had been left to sink or flounder or whatever fin-less sharks do until they quickly died.

Shark conservation is a big thing nowadays but, like many sailors, I really couldn't give a toss. If a sailor was caught by a shark, he'd have been treated no less gently.

These rotting fins drying on their lines stank to high heaven. Indeed, the Mate had taken care to anchor upwind from the fishing boats. Unfortunately, several more had later appeared and parked upwind of us.

If you'd given the perfume a name it would be 'Fishy Charnel House'.

Not that it deterred other sharks in these waters. Fish were attracted to the detritus flung overboard from the anchored ships and the sharks were attracted to that. You could see their sinuous but evil shapes gliding hither and thither just below the surface.

Evening was coming on and so were the lights of Panama City. We were anchored several miles offshore waiting for the shipping company to make up its mind what the hell we were going to do next. We'd come from Rotterdam, empty after unloading Cape apples there, then had headed across the Atlantic and through the Panama Canal. It seemed that whatever contract we had been chasing had fallen through and so we wound up becalmed and awaiting instructions.

The anchorage off Panama City is a full one because the canal is busy and so there is a queue of ships. The usual wait may be no more than a few hours, or even overnight. For us it looked like it would be much longer.

On our way across the Caribbean, we'd stopped off in Barbados and the officers had got hammered on Mount Gay rum while the crew was changed. The new Barbadian crew had been on board for only a few days and were unfamiliar with the ship, as would soon become all too evident.

I believe alcohol is banned on cargo ships now but it definitely wasn't in those days. Indeed, we had our own bar where beers and spirits were sold duty-free and we made very good use of it. Being at anchor, there was no cargo loading and no navigation so, apart from the watch, we had nothing to do in the evenings but drink and stare mournfully at wicked Panama City twinkling in the distance.

So near but so far.

With little to do one evening, after a few drinks in the bar, I thought I'd have an early night. I was sharing a cabin with another trainee called Paul. We'd had several months of cheek-by-jowl living and had become good friends but there was one aspect of my behaviour that Paul could not abide.

I had the top bunk and, in the small hours, would have nightmares about the container ship I had sailed on previously. I dreamed I was caught deep in the hold and a container was being lowered on top of me. I'd reach up my hands and they'd whack into the ceiling just above my bunk.

I'd panic, thinking it was the descending container, and twist to the side to avoid it. This made me fall off my bunk.

Paul often slept with his arm over the side and I'd smack down onto it as I fell. This annoyed him.

However, that night in the Panama City anchorage, it wasn't a nightmare that awoke me but something much more real.

I woke up suddenly and smelled smoke. Then I heard the voices that must have woken me in the first place. They were outside in the corridor.

"It's in the engine room," said one urgently.

"Jesus Christ! We've just bunkered."

What this meant was we had just taken on 4000 gallons of fuel oil. If the fire was in the engine room, then the ship could easily turn into a bomb.

I rolled off the bunk and smacked down onto Paul's carelessly positioned arm.

"Fuck off, ya bastard!" he murmured.

Good suggestion. Unfortunately, I was stuck on board a burning ship and the only place to go to was the shark-infested waters of the anchorage.

This was not the time for finely reasoned argument. I hauled my foot back and kicked him.

"Wha...."

"We're on fire! Wake up for God's sake!"

And that's just what he did. We both struggled into our work boots and boiler suits just as the fire alarm finally warbled into life.

Fire on board a ship is a terrible thing. Not only is there nowhere to retreat to, but the fire brigade is an awfully long way away and fire engines don't do well in the ocean.

Fire drills are practised every week and everyone has a clearly defined role. Mine, as was so often the case, was to shadow the Mate and be his gofer. I made my way up to the bridge, which would be the centre of operations.

Just as I got there all the lights on the ship went out. The anxious Mate quickly paced out onto the bridge wing and leaned over to look at something.

"The navigation lights are gone too!" he said wonderingly.

More bad news. It was a moonless night, we had no lights at all, and this was a busy anchorage with ships coming in and out all night long. Something very big might at any moment plough right through us and only become aware of our existence when they heard the sound of metal tearing into metal.

Our lives hung in the balance. The odds were mounting but not in a good way.

"Get the breathing gear out of the foc's'le!" commanded the Mate.

I've never been good with direct orders but I wasn't going to get bolshy now. I took the key and made my way down to the deck.

In the old days, the foc's'le was where the crew slept but nowadays it was just a metal hut full of assorted gear. As I got near, I had to stop in surprise. A bunch of dark shapes were moving around like moths. I brought up my torch and there were the Barbadian crew.

They were milling around but in a cooler, more leisurely West Indian sort of way. They had only come on board a few days before and I realised they hadn't had a fire drill so had no clue what to do.

"We abandoning ship?" I heard one of them ask.

"Not yet," I said, though it sounded like a good idea provided we could get the lifeboats away. I wished I'd thought to ask the Mate but had been too sleepy, drunk and shocked to think of it.

The fo'c'sle door was padlocked and I quickly unlocked it. As I did so I heard heavy boots. It was a couple of the engineers and as soon as I creaked open the heavy metal door they were inside and dragging out the breathing apparatus.

They headed off back to the superstructure and I followed. Inside, at the entrance to the engine room all the engineers were clustered round and talking in whispers. I saw my pal Dennis, the Fifth Engineer. The tall, thin, fearless Irishman glanced across at me. I didn't like the look in his eyes one little bit.

I hurried back up to the bridge to find out what the Mate had in store for me next. He was on the bridge wing staring around anxiously, a flare pistol in his hand. If he caught sight of a ship coming towards us, a flare was the only warning he could give them.

Before I could raise my concerns, he fixed me with a Captain Bligh look and said, "Check the crew's quarters! Make sure nobody's lying there overcome with smoke!"

The chance for heroism had rarely ever presented itself but here was my John Wayne moment. I clumped off back down the stairs.

The crew's quarters were deep down and the smoke got worse and worse, the beam of my torch diffusing like a drunkard's good intentions.

The first cabin was empty, so was the second but the third was locked. I banged on the door. "Anyone in there?"

No answer.

John Wayne made kicking in doors look easy but I knew it wasn't like that. I'd once kicked open a toilet door in a pub. It was a stag do and the groom had disappeared in there and not come back. It took a lot of kicks, and I nearly broke my foot, but I did knock it off its hinges. Rather than choking on his own vomit, I found the groom fast asleep on the bog.

So, I knew there could be no messing about with this cabin door. I braced myself against a bulkhead, brought my foot up and booted it just next to the lock. It made a hell of a noise but only gave a smidgeon.

Boot, boot, boot. I was raising a hell of a racket. Then, just as the lock gave way and the door swung open, a voice by my shoulder asked, "Hey, man! Why you kicking my door in?"

I turned around to find a bemused West Indian looking at me.

Yet again, my chance at heroism had been thwarted.

I checked the rest of the crew's quarters but they were empty. When I got back on deck it looked like the air above London during the Blitz. Instead of searchlight batteries trying to pick out Nazi bombers, the crew was clustered round the bow and stern waving their torches to fend off approaching ships.

It was a tricky time but then suddenly the lights started to flicker uneasily before coming back on, though dimmer than usual.

The true heroes of the evening were Dennis and a trainee engineer called Donald. Donald was a good foot shorter than Dennis so they made quite a pair. As far as I could understand, the Chief, First, Second, Third and Fourth Engineers had made the lowly Fifth and Trainee Engineer go down into the engine room and put out the fire.

It turned out the problem was that a gauge showing the pressure of the engine's lubricating oil had been faulty and had been removed. Unfortunately, it had not been replaced. When the engine was started up as part of some periodic test, lubricating oil had spurted onto the engine manifold. Lubricating oil is designed to lubricate, not burn. However, as with any oil, it will burn if hot enough.

Dennis and Donald had climbed down the steep oily stairs in their clunky breathing apparatus amongst the smoke and flame and put out the fire.

They'd then turned on an auxiliary generator. Nowadays, generators can be started with a switch remotely but not back then. I imagine they struggled away with a hand crank in the hot smoke-filled engine room. Don't ask me for any more detail, I'm not an engineer.

Whatever they did I was extremely grateful to them.

Next day we made it to dock in Panama City for repairs. We were there for a couple of weeks in that sinful place. We were buzzing with life after being reprieved from a fiery death. I'm going to draw a discrete veil over what happened next. Imagine the worst and you won't be far wrong.

One thing of historical note did happen during that time, though. The bad parts of town were jumping with American servicemen. Then suddenly they weren't.

Something similar happened on the Canal Zone TV station. It was run by the American military and all the announcers were officers in uniform. Then, overnight, they all changed into civvies.

This was because we happened to be there during the signing of the Torrijos-Carter Treaty which was the starting gun on the handover of the canal from the US to the Panamanians. Unrest in Panama had been ongoing with some civilians and US military being killed. Even after the treaty had been signed it was over twenty years before the Panamanians gained full control.

In other words, the sudden disappearance of military uniforms was only symbolic and US helicopter gunships still flew over the canal zone. Nevertheless, the fear was that the Panamanians would take this as a sign of retreat, spurring them on to a full-scale takeover. Violence, it seemed, was in the air.

But then Panama always had been a tinderbox. The military dictatorship, aided and abetted by the US, had tortured and killed dissidents over many years. In return General Noriega (called Pineapple Face because it had been so badly scarred by smallpox) later supplied the Nicaraguan contras with guns and other support.

Following accusations that Noriega had murdered a previous leader and decapitated an opposition politician, a Civic Crusade was mounted which was met with brutal repression, leaving six hundred dead.

Even the US was to become fed up with Noriega and in 1989 they invaded the place. This included the torching of the El Chorrillo favela. Estimates of the number of civilians killed was put at 4000 by the US Attorney General.

Whichever way you looked at it, Panama City was a wild town.

~~~

Before leaving behind my old sailor's stories, I need to redress an imbalance of my own making. My tales have concentrated on the hazards of life at sea and have involved sailors who
~~~

were criminals, psychopaths and incompetents (mainly me in the latter case).

Not all merchant seamen are like that. The great majority are kind, thoughtful and dependable and there were no police cars waiting for *them* when they returned home. It must be said, however, that it takes an adventurous nature to take up this dangerous profession. That alone makes merchant sailors an admirable breed.

The merchant navy is also very much the forgotten service and this has always been the case. If you're ever in London and leaving Tower Hill underground station to go to the Tower of London, instead of going straight ahead, turn right. You'll come across a small grassy area surrounded by bronze panels now blackened by age and pollution. On these are engraved the names of British merchant vessels lost due to enemy action. Under each of these are listed the crew members who have no grave but the sea.

This area, towered over by Neptune on the marble edifice of the Port of London Authority, contains the Mercantile Marine War Memorial designed by Sir Edwin Lutyens to commemorate the 3,300 British and Empire vessels sunk and the 17,000 merchant sailors who died in the First World War. This was added to with the Merchant Seamen's Memorial by Sir Edward Maufe to commemorate the 4,786 ships lost and the 32,000 merchant sailors who died in World War II.

During WWII the casualty rate in the merchant marine was around 25%, a much higher figure than almost any of the armed services yet this was rarely recognised with awards for bravery.

So poor was the recognition by government of the role of these sailors, risking life and limb and at the mercy of the U-boat packs hunting them, that Lloyds of London privately produced its own Medal for Bravery.

Even today's sailors get little recognition. Comfortable lives across the globe depend on the transport of goods from one country to another. From knickers to neo-natal ventilators, from ottomans to oil, 90% of world trade is carried by shipping. Around 50,000 merchant ships are operating, crewed by 1.6 million seafarers.

These men, and increasingly women, sacrifice much to keep us thriving.

Life at sea may be good for the young but at some point they marry and settle down. I recall only too well the empty, haunted looks of men as they left their home port. Their babies and young children would be unrecognisable when they returned perhaps six months later. That was a price I was unwilling to pay and was one of the reasons I left the profession.

These men and women keep us all alive as they ply their dangerous trade in far-flung countries or out on the deep blue sea.

Out of sight, out of mind.

## *Travelling with Someone who has no Fear of Death*

Lima, Peru 2015

Craggy Andean peaks fell away as the plane descended towards a desert city. Even though the desert was yellow and dusty and bone dry, dense white clouds partially covered the city and stretched out into the deep blue waters of the Pacific.

*The strangest, saddest city thou can'st see... For Lima has taken the white veil; and there is a higher horror in this whiteness of her woe.*

That was Herman Melville's take on Lima in his book *Moby Dick*. As usual, he pretty much got it right.

Lima is famed for this shroud. Other writers have compared its colour to the belly of a dead whale. The dry dusty air of the Atacama Desert meets the damp Pacific wind and squeezes out the water vapour. This clings to the shoreline from April to October and can make the city a very depressing place.

Lima was a bad location to build a city right from the start. Back in the sixteenth century the conquistador Pizarro, who founded it, arrived in January at the height of the southern hemisphere summer. By the time the fog descended in April, the construction of the city was already underway. The *conquistador* wasn't around to realise his mistake because he'd already left to wreak havoc throughout the rest of South America.

The proximity of the Atacama Desert means Lima is the second driest city on earth after Cairo; just another of its charms.

I was on a mission and travelling to Peru with my old mate Nick. Nick is a study in contrasts. Well-built, always conservatively dressed and with a deep resonant voice, he exudes such gravitas and empathy that people immediately trust him. He had been a deputy head of a school and tasked with dealing with disturbed and disadvantaged children from poverty-stricken areas in the west of Scotland.

However, beneath the sober exterior, Nick is off-the-wall and out-to-lunch. He has a considerable reputation as a paranormal investigator and researcher and for many years was President of the Scottish Society of Psychical Research.

Though individual spirits of the deceased speak to Nick, the dead share a collective consciousness which spiritualists call the world of Spirit. Spirit woke him up one night and told him he had to quit his job and go to Sao Paulo, a place he had never heard of and had to look up on Google.

In the event, his education authority was reluctant to let him go so Nick did not heed the instruction. Exactly one year later, Spirit woke him again and told him to stop messing about. Spirit reckoned it had taught him all it could in the UK and that's why he needed to go to South America.

Nick promptly resigned and prepared for his trip into the unknown. Not being a seasoned traveller, what was being suggested by Spirit was quite a tall order. So, he asked me if I would go with him. I'm seasoned enough, though some might say I'm just as off-the-wall and out-to-lunch.

Forty years had passed since my merchant navy days. I'd taken up a career in Medical physics, researching new diagnoses and treatments. Though Nick had been bending my ears for decades, and despite reading books on the paranormal, I hadn't come across compelling evidence to believe in Spiritualism.

And so we made quite a pair. The believer and the sceptic, yin and yang. A complementarity made in heaven, though I don't believe in that either.

I always jump at any half-baked excuse to go travelling, more so now that I'm retired. The idea of two old fools blundering around South America on a mystical quest was appealing.

Unfortunately, I hadn't budgeted for one aspect of Nick's belief system. Nick has had so much communication with Spirit that he no longer had any fear of death. That was something we definitely didn't have in common.

So, we found ourselves gliding down onto the baking tarmac of a South American runway. It soon became apparent that they did things differently in Peru.

After passport control our luggage clumped down on the carousel. So far so good. Then there was a moment of disorientation as we were wheeling our suitcases out of Customs only to find our way blocked by more barriers and a gargantuan X-ray machine.

Am I leaving or arriving? I wondered.

Peru not only produces about as much cocaine as Columbia, but it's also considered the cocaine distribution centre of the world. That's why your hold luggage is X-rayed when you arrive and not just when you leave.

Luckily both of us had gone to considerable lengths not to fill our suitcases with cocaine.

We emerged from the airport into thudding tropical heat and taxi drivers yelling for our attention. Taking a taxi into town was like rafting through a maelstrom. Abused cars of every description jostled for space on the gridlocked streets. As we left the airport behind, and between bursts of frantic motion, lots of little vans lay momentarily becalmed. Multi-coloured with symbols and pictures garishly daubed on their sides, inside they were crammed with placid, nut-brown faces.

Mopeds and small motorcycles darted in and out amongst the cars and vans like wasps attacking lumbering steers. Several times we drew quick breaths as imminent collisions were narrowly averted.

When the maelstrom wasn't churning, logjams of traffic impeded the way and the taxi inched down streets of half-finished concrete buildings. Diminutive native Indian men and women wound their way through the stalled traffic selling newspapers, sweets and ice creams. The men wore bright striped ponchos, the women billowing skirts and red cardigans with rainbow trim. Red hats with upturned brims perched precariously on the bobbing heads.

I spotted a little girl, barely taller than a car tyre. She was wearing the same outfit and following her mother through the dense traffic. Just then the traffic jerked forward and I had to look away, giving a little prayer of thanks when there were no crunching sounds or screams.

Lima is a city on the edge, physically and metaphorically. Its precarious nature was revealed as we drove down the coast road. Metal netting covered hillsides that in places became cliffs. It looked at first like they were strung with fishing nets containing a bounty of muddy fish. Closer inspection revealed the hillsides were made of mango-sized grey cobbles bound together by dirt.

Peru is a major league earthquake zone. The Nazca tectonic plate dives under the South American plate, nudging it up. That's how the Andes formed in the first place. But the Nazca plate doesn't just dive down smoothly. It sticks, pressure builds and then it slips and the earth trembles. Over 100,000 people died in an earthquake in Peru less than fifty years ago.

The cobbles are held together by dried mud. The netting stops the usual erosion that would make the cobbles fall down onto sunbathers on the beach below. In an earthquake it seems to me likely the dirt will turn to slurry and the cobbles collapse. The hillsides will fall, taking all the expensive hotels and condominiums down with them into the Pacific.

Parts of the hillside had already slipped through the net so the beaches below are a mass of cobbles. I wound down the window and heard the cacophony of sea-tossed cobbles crashing together.

Even if you do miss this evidence of boisterous tectonics, you'll find more in each hotel room. There's a sign, a big white letter S set against a green background. In my room the sign was under a lintel. It said: ZONA SECURA EN CASOS DE SISMOS. Basically, the idea is that you should cower under this as the rest of the hotel falls down around your ears. It seemed more aspirational than offering any actual safety.

Tired after a very long flight from the UK, we retired to our rooms for a night of disturbed sleep.

And that's when Nick had his first visitation.

He woke in what at first seemed complete darkness but he sensed a presence. As is his wont in such circumstances, he said "Welcome friend."

Nothing much seemed to happen for a while but then he saw something, some faint movement at the extremity of his vision. Whatever the thing was, it was up there, high in the room and pulsing. As his eyes adapted, he saw what looked like a purple jellyfish the size of a human head. It was expanding and contracting as though it was breathing.

The jellyfish wafted slowly across the room at ceiling height and down in an arc, before stopping and reversing direction. It gently drifted back and forth like this until Nick, for whom these sorts of things happen all the time and perturb him not in the least, fell asleep.

He recounted it all to me the next day and, naturally enough, I told him to bugger off.

~~~

We had a couple of days in Lima to decompress before our flight up into the Andes. Nick had asked Spirit if he could visit the famous Machu Picchu en route to Sao Paulo and had been given permission. So, we were heading to this ancient city perched high in the clouds.

With time to kill we set off to explore Lima and that's where I first realised that travelling with Nick would never be less than interesting.

The main feature of Lima's city centre is a series of plazas linked by lanes where pedestrians can walk freely. In the lanes, the shops and buildings are modest with a modern appearance, but in the Plazas the old Spanish colonial style becomes more evident. Here, elegant arched colonnades support four-storey buildings. Unusual and ornate dark wood structures project from the upper floors, allowing people to sit behind glass and look down on the squares below. 'Moorish style' was how the guidebook described them.

The sun had burned back the white veil of fog and raw heat scorched down from the vast blue sky. Occasionally a furnace-like desert wind found its way through the streets and breathed hotly on our cheeks.

We found a bench in the main square called the *Plaza de Armas*. Office workers with briefcases were heading home from the ministries, but the rush hour, such as it was, was already on the wane. A few native Indians were trying to sell guidebooks and maps to the sparse number of tourists. Old churches filled one side of the square, a palace filled another
~~~

and orange-coloured buildings with the Moorish balconies took up the other two.

Old as the square was there was evidence of more modern concerns. I spotted an ancient Mercedes Benz water cannon truck parked in a corner and almost hidden in the shadows, its two brass nozzles sticking out from the roof of the cab and looking like the devil's horns.

Checking around more closely, I became aware of uniformed figures lurking in the shade. Some toted assault rifles, others had riot shields and helmets hanging on straps from their arms and shoulders. This was a bit of a jolt but then I noticed how relaxed the men appeared. Bad things clearly happened here but probably not right now.

"We're not in Kansas anymore," I said.

"What?" Nick replied.

I pointed to the lurking figures. I figured it was all down to that Pizarro chap. This square wasn't just the centre of old Lima, it was the centre of the Spaniards' whole conquest of South America. It would be a natural place for demonstrations even today.

As nothing seemed about to kick off soon, I relaxed and we both sat there, enjoying the sun, and not looking for trouble.

At least I wasn't.

A uniformed figure came walking by. I couldn't recognise the uniform, but it wasn't the utilitarian battle fatigues of the soldiers. It was blue and neat, probably that of a plain old copper.

"Excuse me," said Nick loudly and rather suddenly, "but do you speak English?"

The man halted and turned. He was in his forties with wide brown eyes and a slight stoop. He had small flashes on his collar and on his shoulder were absurdly tiny but somehow stylish gold-tasselled epaulets.

"A little." The man sounded like whatever Nick had to say, he'd heard it all before.

"My friend and I were wondering where we could obtain some *ayahuasca*."

I froze. Had Nick really just asked a copper in something approaching a narco state where he could get hold of a powerful hallucinogenic drug? I looked at the copper's hands, which were still down at his sides and not yet reaching for a holster.

Then I realised the man didn't have a gun at all, at least not one in view.

"Not good for you, gentlemen. It can make you very ill. Can kill you." The man's forefinger swept back and forth in admonishment.

"But, even so. Where could we find any?"

I turned to my dear old friend. "Shut... the... fuck... up!" I whispered carefully, enunciating every word as clearly as I could.

Nick waved this notion away.

The copper seemed to be considering. "The mountains, of course," he said. "Cuzco, naturally. Are you going there?"

"Yes, we are."

"Everyone does. But I would suggest something else to take, something alcoholic. *Chica de Jora* or even *pisco*. It is a light rum. *Gran Pisco* is the strongest. Or, if you must have something with narcotic effects, *Mate de Coca*, a tea made from coca leaves, is legal here. At least it will not kill you the way *ayahuasca* can. Most importantly gentlemen, it won't get you in jail the way cocaine will, although it is made from the same leaves."

Nick nodded appreciatively. "Thank you, that was very helpful, and can I ask, are you a policeman?"

The man shook his head. "No, I am here to help the tourists. It would be more than my job is worth to point out that you don't have to go all the way up the mountains and that you can find what you are looking for right around the corner. Good day and enjoy your time in Peru."

As the man walked away, Nick turned to me, arms wide, point apparently made.

"Are you out of your frigging mind? Don't do stuff like that! If that'd been a copper we'd have been banged up for years."

Nick chuckled. "Relax, I'm betting ayahuasca isn't illegal here. Besides, Spirit wouldn't bring us all the way here just to do that to us. You're a terrible old worrier. You have much to learn." And he gave a dismissive laugh at my naivety.

Not in Kansas anymore? I wasn't even on the same planet.

~~~

Later, we walked along the cliff top at Miraflores, which is about as upmarket as Lima gets. Shopping malls are built into the cliff and are overshadowed by high-rise apartments. Westwards, all one can see are the endless waters of the Pacific, its surface lifted by swells that had travelled half way around the globe.

As we strolled along, traffic wardens on Segways, those weird two wheeled self-balancing scooters, whizzed by. New at the time, these were surprising sights in a country that was poor by Western standards. However, there's money in Peru, not just from mining but from the trickle-down effects of the drug money. The first places it trickles down to are the banks and the malls of Miraflores.

It also trickles down to the Shining Path guerrillas. Maoists, they almost sent the country spiralling down into civil war back in the 1980s. There aren't many of them left but they still wage violent campaigns against virtually any form of modern industry in the Andes.
~~~

I was still obsessing about our encounter with the tourist information guy. "So, what was that about? If that had been a real copper we could have wound up in jail. This is a narco state that's in denial."

Nick waved this away, his confidence impenetrable. "Spirit told me to come here, that it would provide. I mean seriously, do you think it would go to all that trouble just to have me wind up in jail?"

I'm usually quick with comebacks but this statement cleaned me out.

"You can't be serious," was the best I could manage. "The guidebooks say..."

He held up a hand to quell my whining. "Don't bother with guidebooks, they're for wimps."

"What the hell are you talking about?"

"Spirit... will...provide." Nick can speak with such gravitas that it sounds like his words are chiselled into stone.

"Have you or your Spirit chum made any actual plans?"

"Nope, I haven't. As for Spirit—I'm sure it has plans which will be revealed in due course."

We were due to spend over a month in South America. As this trip was at Nick's behest, I figured he'd arranged everything. I had assumed he'd at least corresponded with fellow believers in South America, had set up some meetings, had at least the faintest concept of what he was doing.

A number of assumptions and all apparently false. Instead, we were stumbling into the unknown without benefit of a map.

The story of my life and, incidentally, 'Without Benefit of a Map' might have made another alternative title for this book.

"Let's just sit here a second," I said. It was a bench with a breathtaking view over the blue ocean. I hauled out my own guidebook and dug out the bit about ayahuasca.

And, just this once, Nick was right. Distilled from the leaves and stalks of the ayahuasca vine, it is called the 'teacher plant' by many of South America's indigenous peoples and is considered a gateway to the spiritual world. Indeed, *aya* means soul and *huasca* means vine.

*Vine of the soul* made it sound pretty appealing.

It has such cultural and spiritual significance that it's not banned in some South American countries (though, note, it very definitely is in the UK and US).

This is despite it not being a gentle drug like marijuana. For a start, it is a nasty purgative. It also beats you up emotionally and spiritually. Occasionally it kills and the Web is full of tales of Westerners who've fallen foul of it, either because it stresses the heart or through induced paranoia. Panic and anxiety drive the subject to suicide. This is why takers need to be supervised by a shaman. Indeed, even the redoubtable Nick would later come to be affected. Several days after taking the drug Nick acknowledged an unprecedented urge to throw himself from a seventh-floor window.

And it didn't necessarily sound like the drug of choice for pensioners like Nick and myself. Not only that, but we would be taking it in the high Andes and far from decent medical attention.

However, that was a problem for another day. We had to get up into the Andes first.

~~~

Tickets and timetables are vital for travellers but sometimes they lie.

It was the Peruvian Indian families I felt most sorry for. Short of stature and wearing brightly coloured clothing they seemed confused and out of place in this gleaming modern airport. Perhaps on their first ever flight, they stood disconsolately as staff explained the concept of 'bumping'.
~~~

The children looked like someone had snatched away their Christmas presents.

I couldn't hold back. "I mean for Christ's sake!"

"'God grant me the serenity to accept the things I cannot change,'" said Nick gently.

"Oh, please!" I said. "I mean, you do understand how this might really mess us up? You've read our travel itinerary, right?"

Nick nodded his head in affirmation but then laughed and said, "No."

"This is *so* not funny. There are no roads to this godforsaken place that *you* wanted us to go to. If we miss the train connection then what?"

"We'll find somewhere to stay until we catch the next one."

"The High Andes isn't Bournemouth. There are no handy B&Bs. Who knows what it's going to be like up *there*?" I pointed out the window at the faraway peaks.

At the check-in desk voices were suddenly raised. I couldn't help noticing that Peruvians of Hispanic origin, as well as being quite a bit taller than their Indian compatriots, tended to be more aggressive and vociferous. They did not take kindly to being bumped.

"How common is this overbooking thing?" Nick asked. "I mean, it seems to be happening to a sizable chunk of the passengers."

I looked at the guidebook and found a tiny panel of text I'd missed. "Endemic, apparently."

We sat for hours. In the end the airline offered us a $50 voucher towards a future flight on an airline we wouldn't have touched with a bargepole.

So, we were bumped to a later flight, and then in turn delayed due to bad weather at our destination. When we finally took off the flight was rather unusual because instead of climbing and descending, it was more a matter of climbing and then landing. Cusco at nearly 11,000 feet sounds like it should be the highest airport in the world but I was surprised to find there are a dozen higher in the Himalayas, one at an incredible 14,000 feet. La Paz at 13,000 feet takes the prize for the highest in South America.

By the time we finally came into land over Cuzco the sun was already beginning to set. To my surprise, as we came in for our final approach, the airstrip was at the end of a narrow valley with hillsides looming on both sides.

"Behold the Navel of the Universe," Nick intoned.

"What?"

"This I do know about so we don't need your precious guidebook. Cuzco was the centre of the Inca Empire. Everything sprang from here."

It didn't look much like it to me. In the dusk I saw swathes of corrugated iron covering tattered rows of half-built homes washing like waves over the hills surrounding the town. "And when did they start building it? Yesterday?"

The plane thumped down and the pilot gave reverse thrust a serious workout. The engines sounded like they were about to explode. I couldn't help pushing myself back in the seat as the plane charged towards the centre of town, coming to a halt with what seemed like only metres to spare. The passengers gave a ragged cheer.

When the cabin crew opened the doors, the air that came rushing in was far colder than in Lima and felt heavy with the smell of the drizzle I could see misting down outside. By the time we got to the terminal and collected our suitcases, night had fallen on the city centre which, bizarrely, was right outside the terminal building. It was like landing at Heathrow then stepping out into Trafalgar Square.

We wandered around the terminal trying to locate what we were looking for. We finally found the little stall tucked away in an alcove.

"There are no seats left on the train." No doubt used to dealing with many foreign tourists, the clerk's English was good.

"Our flight was delayed," said Nick.

The young woman, dressed in a neat black suit, shrugged her slender shoulders. "It usually is. The weather up here is bad and needs to lift otherwise..." She indicated the hills, buildings, roads, cars and buses that might otherwise form impediments to a smooth landing.

I didn't like the look of Cuzco and didn't fancy staying for the night. "Is there any other way we can get to *Aquas Calientes* tonight?"

It was evident this was a conversational path the woman had been down many times before. "There are no roads to there, only rail. The road ends at *Ollantaytambo*. But it is possible there are still some train tickets for *Aquas Calientes* available from there."

"And how do we get to Ollatam...?"

"*Combi* or taxi but..." she looked at her watch "... *combi* won't get you there in time for the last train. But taxi is expensive."

The idea of taking one of those crammed little *combi* buses, vans basically, which transformed the Indians who used them into brightly coloured sardines was not, in any case, appealing.

"And where can we get a taxi?"

She pointed and we hurried out. The rain was getting heavier now as we shuffled through imprecating taxi drivers. "Look for the one with the least damaged vehicle," I muttered. It took a while, but finally we found one that was unmarked except for a long scrape down the driver's side.

As I climbed into the back seat, I became aware of Nick's heavy breathing. Then I felt a catch in my own breath as though I hadn't quite managed to grab a full lungful of air.

"Do you feel that?" I said. "Eleven thousand feet."

Nick nodded and put a hand to his chest. "We should take it easy." He tapped the driver on the shoulder. "Ollantaytambo. How much to get there?"

The man turned and came out with what I suspected was one of his few words of English: "Eighty."

Nick screwed up his eyes but clearly it wasn't enough to do the trick. "How much is that in Sterling?"

"About thirty quid. It's quite a way so that's not bad." I nodded at the taxi driver. "Okay."

The taxi started off through the rain-slicked streets and soon we were climbing on a twisting road. As we left the vicinity of the airport, finished buildings gave way to more makeshift efforts. Corrugated iron shacks and roofless concrete shells had been put down randomly beside the road. Where roofs and windows were absent, they were supplemented by tarpaulin and even newsprint. Dogs picked through vast mounds of garbage by the road. I could only imagine how many rats must be crawling around.

Small, garishly clothed children, standing stock still amongst the rubbish and the dogs and the rats, expressionlessly regarded our taxi as it passed by. Gaudily coloured tuc-tucs, or mototaxis as they are called in Peru, weaved fearlessly in and out of the crazy traffic. Once we whizzed by an ancient wooden tram labouring up a hill and I finally noticed the rails in the fractured, rubbish-strewn road.

Dodging rubbish piles and dogs and people, as well as oncoming cars and lorries straying onto our side of the road, our taxi would also sometimes veer alarmingly onto the wrong side. All this time pedestrians would, without thought, step out into the path of the traffic. Our driver didn't seem surprised or perturbed by any of this, though he was constantly swerving.

Having gained some height, the road now levelled a little but the shacks continued up the steep slopes of a hill to one side. The place wasn't so much 'navel of world' as 'favelas in the clouds'.

Perhaps the most dispiriting thing of all was the people. They stood in groups on street corners as though they had nowhere to go, their colourful clothing wet with rain.

We left the meagre street lighting of Cuzco behind and plunged into darkness as we drove through grim little towns and villages clinging to existence in the High Andes. Of the mountains and ancient Inca ruins we saw nothing in the black night and the rain. Once, we passed a newly crashed truck on a bend, the driver standing gesticulating to drivers with a torch beside his overturned behemoth, its exhaust system like shining metal genitals wantonly displayed.

The taxi driver gave no heed to the crash and simply drove by without even looking.

I began to fret. "How big is Olla... whatever the hell it's called? Suppose there are no tickets left. Where do we stay for the night? Do we kip down in the rain with the rubbish and the rats?"

Nick smiled at me. "Wimp," he said and laughed.

"Look, I've done my share of sleeping rough on beaches on the Med and deserts in the States or whatever. But I'm not a young man anymore and neither are you. It's cold and it's dark and we're surrounded by poor, desperate people who may be tempted to rob and kill us."

Nick snorted derisively. I blew out a breath with annoyance and again had the sensation of not quite getting back enough air on the next intake.

The road now dipped down towards a sparse group of lights. "Ollantaytambo," announced the driver with a hint of triumph.

He dropped us off at a cabin around which milled a few westerners with backpacks. There was a brief altercation when the taxi driver rejected our eighty sols and said: "Dollars, *dollars*," which would have more than doubled the fare. There was something perfunctory about his anger and he quickly settled for twenty sols extra to the eighty arranged and disappeared back into the night.

We trudged up to the ticket desk, our suitcase wheels making heavy weather over the cobbles. The westerners ahead of us in the queue were dispersing and didn't look happy.

"Two tickets for *Aquas Calientes*, please."

"For when?" The man was middle-aged and wore a nicely pressed uniform.

"Well, now."

The man smiled. "I am very sorry, sir, but the train is full tonight. Tomorrow, at seven, there are seats, but not now."

I bit my lip. Coming into town we had seen only three small guest houses and had noted groups of tourists hanging around disconsolately at their entrances.

"Is there anywhere we can stay tonight?"

The man nodded his head sadly. "It may be difficult. We are very busy, more than is usual at this time of year. Many Germans. Perhaps in Germany they show something on TV about *Machu Picchu* and everyone wants to come. It happens."

He turned to another man further back in the cabin who was typing on a PC with a boxy old-style screen and said something to him in Spanish. The man shook his head.

The ticket master turned back. "My friend's mother owns a hotel just up the road. He says there are no rooms. Perhaps... perhaps you could find a room in one of the guest houses up there." He pointed back up the road the taxi had brought us down and then to the right into the darkness.

Showing him perhaps more ill grace than the man deserved, we bought tickets for the morning train and trailed our suitcases back up the narrow street, wheels clicking angrily over the cobbles. Even in the time we had arrived, the traffic situation had got worse as people tried to catch the last train. Barely wide enough for much more than a single car, the road was hemmed in by stalls filling the pavements on either side and spilling onto the road, forcing pedestrians to step well out into the traffic. Taxis and *combis* were now locked in a stand-off, unable to pass but not yielding their positions. Soon we passed our taxi and the driver waved at us wearily.

"Maybe we should get this taxi back to Cuzco," I suggested.

"We have the tickets for the first train and we'd never get back here in time. Don't worry, we'll sort something out."

I wasn't reassured and cursed myself for not thinking this through. We should have stayed in Cuzco, rat hole thought it had appeared to be, because at least it was big and there would be plenty of places to stay. This mad dash through the mountains had been crazy. I began to wonder if the altitude was getting to me.

The stallholders were already packing up their trinkets and baubles. Jewellery, hats, T-shirts, plates, mugs and pictures all sported the same vibrantly coloured zigzags and parallel lines, like a 60s acid dream. The stallholders were mainly brightly dressed native women but behind them, lounging against walls, were altogether more darkly and poorly dressed men. They smoked cigarettes and peered grimly out at the world from under battered, faded hats. As we passed, their eyes followed us.

We passed two well-lit guest houses, each time stopping to ask for rooms. The proprietors were polite and apologetic. The directions the station master gave us would take us off this narrow road that was at least busy and lit and onto a side road little better than a dirt track. Far along we could make out occasional porch lights, like a sparsely strung pearl necklace leading away into Stygian night. The heavy clouds that had delayed our flight were still smothering the moon and stars.

I looked down this track to nowhere, then back at the road that led to the station. The men behind the stalls were still looking at us. What happened if we started down this dark road and they came after us?

"I'm not sure about this."

"Only two hundred metres, that's what the guy said. Come on!"

And with that Nick was off, struggling to keep his case upright on the hardened, undulating surface of impacted dirt. I quickly fished out my phone to provide some illumination and hurried to keep up. At least Nick was solidly built and would give any robbers pause for thought.

The silence was shattered by a nearby dog barking angrily and my suddenly numbed legs almost gave way. I fumbled the light around at a raggedy wooden fence and it cast shadows on the fierce eyes and sharp teeth raging behind it.

From the distance came a forlorn whistle. The last train was leaving.

I looked back the way we'd come. Light from a car passing along the main street splashed across the dirt track, for a second illuminating a couple of black objects near the sides. Were they moving or was it just the light?

"Come on," I said urgently and picked up the pace. Within a few metres I'd passed Nick, whose strides were slowing due to his breathlessness.

My suitcase tilted and bucked over the uneven ground and it felt like I was dragging a live animal behind me. To my dismay, a low battery warning appeared on the screen of my phone. More dogs started up their rabid barking and I broke into a stumbling run.

"Not so fast!" Nick called out.

I passed by a single-storey derelict building showing dark holes where windows must once have been. Black runes of graffiti were plastered across the adobe wall. Barely had I passed this wall when I was hit by the weighty, rancid smell of a maturing mass of organic rubbish. I glanced back again and this time was sure I saw shadows moving behind Nick's bulky silhouette.

At least now the first inhabited house was close, its little porch light illuminating a veranda. A couple of plant pots made it look like a homely oasis in the threatening darkness. I dragged my case up the two wooden steps and through an open door. The little reception desk was unmanned, but through a door to the right I saw a man sitting watching TV in a little lounge. Mixed race, middle-aged and with the same lined face as the men back on the main street, he seemed surprised at my dramatic entrance, his hand holding a brown cigarette frozen halfway to his mouth.

"Sorry for all the noise, but I wondered if you had rooms for the night."

The man opened his mouth, but just then Nick strolled up behind me.

The man blinked. "English?"

"Scottish actually," I said. The man looked puzzled. "British." This didn't seem to help either.

"Yes, English," Nick interjected.

The man nodded: this clearly explained everything. He waved the hand holding the cigarette. "One room only. One bed. One night. No more. Busy!"

"Double bed?" asked Nick.

The man shook his head a little, but it seemed to be from incomprehension. "I show you!"

He got slowly to his feet and shuffled by us and through an archway to the left of the reception desk. He touched a switch and weak light illuminated a short corridor with two doors on either side. The walls were yellowing and bare.

At the end door on the right, he stopped and turned the handle. As he was pushing it open a shout came from within.

"*Lo siento!*" he said and closed it again quickly. Turning, he tried the door on the other side. This time there were no protests. The man turned on the light to reveal a small room with a double bed, a chair, a mirror on the wall and a little bedside table. A door led to a small shower room with a toilet. This was a pleasant surprise as I had been expecting to have to do my business in the fields. The washbasin was a large slab of dark granite with a concavity for the water. The man turned the tap and hot, steamy water sputtered out. "Volcanic. Very hot!"

"How much?" asked Nick, looking round the room disapprovingly.

"Hundred dollars."

"For this?" said Nick, aghast.

"We'll take it," I said quickly.

"This is a bit steep, isn't it?"

"I don't care. I'm not going back out there tonight. You can if you want to."

Nick seemed to be considering this. I noticed how drained he was, not his usual bumptious self at all. His brow was creased and his eyes were beginning to droop.

"OK," Nick said, "but you'd better not snore."

*Good luck with that!* I thought. When I've travelled on group tours and had to share bedrooms, more than once I've awoken in the early hours with a stranger's hands around my throat. And not in a good way.

Bone weary, I was desperate to climb into bed and get some sleep but not before taking precautions. Perhaps the men who had been following us down the road would barge in or, even worse, would be allowed in with the proprietor's blessings. I wouldn't have put it passed the man. A hundred bucks for this!

To forestall our throats being cut in the middle of the night and both of us subsequently waking up dead, I jammed a chair under the door knob. Then I took the guidebook from my case and balanced it against the door so even the slightest movement would send it slapping down.

I had a cursory wash using only the cold tap lest magma come spurting out of the 'volcanic' one.

When I got back, I saw how little Nick had achieved in all this time. He'd only managed to open his bag and was now kneeling down and pawing through the contents. With rising alarm, I realised he was slowly and methodically unpacking.

"We're only here for one night. In fact," I checked my watch, "five hours of one night. You don't need to unpack."

Nick glanced up at me but his eyes were blank and he proceeded with his sloth-like unpacking. Having carefully extracted two piles of socks, he then seemed nonplussed when he realised there was nowhere to put them. Dazed, he looked round the room and his eyes fastened on the bedside table. Getting to his feet, and staggering slightly, he deposited them there then turned back to the case.

Weary beyond belief, I could almost feel my blood pressure surging and, for a second, I felt quite giddy. "For God's sakes let it be!"

But still Nick was methodically unpacking and it was only when the little table was full of underclothes and socks that he halted. There was no wardrobe to hang his shirts and trousers in, and now no surfaces left to lay them on except for the moth-eaten, filthy carpet.

Stymied, Nick stood still with two carefully folded shirts in his hand. He swayed slightly even though we'd had nothing to drink.

At last, he seemed to bow to the inevitable and put his shirts carefully back in the suitcase. "I'm a bit hot," he mumbled. "I hope you don't mind."

"Don't mind what?"

Nick didn't answer as his backside thumped down on the bed and I found myself thrust upwards on the swell of the mattress and then rolling down into the trough created by his bulk. I put a hand out to stop himself and it smacked against his back.

"Sorry!" I said but then grimaced at the wetness. Nick was dripping in sweat even in this cold Andean night.

"S'okay. Goodnight." Quickly as that he was asleep and his snoring began.

I realised the light was still on and I was summoning what was left of my strength to get up to turn it off when I saw a switch by the bed. I touched it and the room went mercifully dark.

It was only then I noticed what I had missed in my weariness. The room didn't have a window so the darkness was absolute. Great value!

I closed my eyes and listened for sounds of desperate Indians with sharp knives tip-toeing down the corridor to our door. With them would be more Hispanic types, like Mexican baddies from old Hollywood Westerns, wiping their glistening brows with filthy bandanas as they gently clicked the hammers back on their Colts. And far away, a dusky senorita, her heart lost to the gringo with the clear blue eyes...

A snore like the discharge of a shotgun jerked me back awake. My eyes blinked open, but instead of complete darkness what I saw sent a shock through my body and drove all breath away.

I had come on this trip as a lark, just one more excuse for travel. I was here as a professional sceptic with someone who believed in the full panoply of the paranormal from spirit orbs to UFOs, from poltergeists to banshees. I was here to cast a cold, appraising scientific eye over the paranormal.

But somewhere, in some Jungian deep had been a fear that I might see something I couldn't explain. If I really saw a ghost, what would I do (other than wet myself, of course)?

And now I had opened my eyes to the very thing I feared. It was hanging balefully above the bottom of the bed.

The apparition pulsed and then pulsed again. I blinked, but the sight remained. An orb the size of a human head hovered there inflating and deflating in deathly silence. It resembled nothing more than a large purple jellyfish pulsing in unknowable currents.

I lay transfixed as the purple glowing bulk descended in a stately arc to the left. I felt a jolt of fear lest it drop below the level of Nick's obscuring bulk and then, unobserved, it might do anything, perhaps fly under the bed and come at me from my other side.

I gulped and blinked again. Immediately the thing stopped and rose back along its invisible arc. It sailed slowly overhead and started to descend to my side of the bed. My scrotum shrank as though grasped by ice-cold hands.

This couldn't be happening!

Its motion kept reversing, this strange back and forth sidling seemed predatory. It was scoping out its prey, waiting to pounce.

Very occasionally in life something happens that whips the foundations of your belief system from under your feet, leaving only a terrible void. I clutched at the bedclothes lest I fell.

I watched as the pulsing purple globe swung back and forth; I was paralysed like a mouse before a cobra, waiting for it to strike.

What would it do next? I very slowly reached out and turned on the light.

## *Never Trust Your Guts in South America*

The High Andes, Peru 2015

The alarm on my watch nagged us awake at 6 a.m. We'd not slept well and Nick was showing clear signs of altitude sickness. He was still sweating and, even though he was only getting dressed, he had to keep stopping to catch his breath.

I wasn't feeling so great myself but I tried a brief wash. Forgetting the warnings of the proprietor the night before, I managed to scald the edge of one hand in the Vulcan's piss that erupted from the tap.

We'd arrived in the dark and hadn't been able to see anything of the land around. As we now emerged into the sunlight, my feeble breath was taken away by the encircling mountains shouldering their way to the clouds.

In the dark I had peopled the place with phantoms and danger but now it all looked rather lovely. Cloud or mist clung to the upper slopes and the mountain air felt nicely chilled against my hot skin. Little houses were dotted amongst fields of corn and beans.

Then I noticed regularities amongst the scattered rocks on the vertiginous slopes.

"Inca fortresses and food stores and terraces to grow food," said Nick, who must have followed my gaze. "Tough work building stuff like that on the sides of mountains. They must have been hardy people."

On the walk back to the station, the early morning light had dissolved the horrors of the night before. I wondered how many had sprung from my overactive imagination, and how many from altitude sickness.

All the stalls on the main road down to the train station were already open and laden with clothes and trinkets and looking as though someone with a very tiny brush had tried to cover them in fluorescent lines and dots. Even in the sunlight they seemed as bright as neon signs at night. The stalls had locked the traffic solid again and heated exchanges between drivers rang out as they tried to negotiate any kind of movement. Tourists and Indians carrying an assortment of bags wound their way through the cars, buses, stalls and insistent stallholders.

A blue train with yellow flashes was already at the station. Guards and heavy metal gates barred the way. Indian passengers were bunched up in an unruly queue to the side, but westerners were being waved straight through.

When we got to the platform, I could see a fierce river paralleling the rail track on the other side. Cacti and yucca plants and palms covered its banks.

On the platform side of the track the station hotel, its dark wood giving it a strangely Alpine air, was disgorging expensively dressed travellers. Staff in grey uniforms were directing them to their carriages.

We found our seats and appraised the river, which was called the Urubamba. I imagined the angry water, dark brown and turbulent, scything its way over eons through the hard rock of the Andes. The only thing I knew about it was that a famous British geologist called John Walter Gregory had drowned in it when his boat overturned. The only mystery was why he'd thought he could sail on it in the first place.

The train nudged our backs, then juddered into forward motion and we watched as the platform slid away behind us. Clapboard huts with corrugated metal roofs came into view beside the tracks. Brightly painted in greens and blues and yellows, they became more and more sparse as the train left the little town behind. Terraced fields slipped by and, through the observation windows built into the roof of the carriage, I watched sharp ridged mountains move in a stately dance as the train wound its slow way along the rocky valley floor.

The train never reached more than thirty miles an hour, although the gradient was always gently down. Beside us the river grew fiercer and fiercer.

The vegetation was changing as we lost altitude from the corn and yucca and cactus of the high desert to the vines and moss of the tropical jungle. Just one thousand feet separated *Ollantaytambo* from *Aquas Calientes* but their ecosystems were entirely different.

The mood in the carriage was happy, the scenery wonderful. People laughed and cameras clicked. The mist burned away and the sun shone down on verdant mountainsides.

"Again, last night," said Nick apropos of nothing, "I was visited by that spirit orb. The one that looked like a big purple jellyfish. It was in the early hours."

"What did you do?"

"What I always do with visitations. I said, 'Welcome friend, come closer!'"

I'd seen enough of Nick's fearlessness not to doubt this for a second. If anyone was resistant to night horrors it was him. "And did it? Come closer, that is."

"No. It just moved back and forth. I tried to get a photo but the flash drove it away."

I've been listening to him tell me these things for years. What it usually came down to was anecdotal evidence and, from a scientific point of view, that's the weakest of all. Humans are poor observers—even scientists, although we are trained not to be. We come at everything with assumptions and preconceptions. Too often we see what we want to see and we ignore what we don't, or at least try to explain it away.

It's like the tales of South Sea islanders in the days of sail. Isolated, with hundreds or even thousands of miles of empty Pacific between them and the nearest habitable islands, the only boats they had seen were the outrigger canoes they used themselves.

Then, one day, a British warship or a Nantucket whaler would sail into view. With no reference frame to judge this colossally unnatural construct by, they simply ignored it. Some couldn't see it, even though it was crowding out their empty horizon.

Criticising anecdotal evidence gets you nowhere with true believers like Nick. They simply reply that you weren't there so how would you know if it was true or not. And they're right.

But, this time, I had him!

"Oh yeah, I know, the big purple jellyfish. Saw it last night as well."

Nick turned in surprise. "You saw it!"

"Yup, saw it pulsing away to its heart's content."

I looked back out of the window, acting casual.

"So, what happened then?"

Nick knows me too well to bother lying to him. "Scared the shit out of me."

"But it didn't mean you any harm."

"I know."

He was managing to look confused and surprised at the same time. It was nice to turn the tables for once.

"So, you believe in the paranormal now? At least when it comes to spirit globes?"

I looked abashed, giving it a beat, leading him on. Then: "Not a chance!"

"What?"

"It wasn't some spirit jellyfish. It was just a light fitting."

"Yeah?"

"I'm telling you. I found the light switch by the bed and turned it on. The light flared into life exactly where the jellyfish had been but there was nothing there except the lightshade. I turned the light off, waited until my eyes adapted to the darkness of that windowless little room and the jellyfish came back. I turned the light back on and got exactly the same thing."

"But it was pulsing, swelling like lungs inflating. You don't see plastic light fittings doing that."

Although I was retired, it's easy to slip back into lecturer mode, like sliding your fingers back into an old pair of leather gloves. "There's a little smoke detector light built into the fitting. Maybe it's a standard thing in this country because you also saw it in the hotel back in Lima. As the light slowly pulsed it looked like it was the fitting that was moving but it wasn't."

"But the whole thing moved, from one side of the room to the other."

I was enjoying this more than I should. "It wasn't the light that was moving, it was our eyes. The room was completely dark, so there were no other reference points. We were tired and as our eyes started to drift it was as if the fitting was moving."

Nick gave me a wide smile. "Yeah, I know all that. I was just testing you."

"Waddya mean?"

"I saw it last night as well when I woke to go for a pee. As I was passing on the way to the bathroom I reached out and touched it. I was expecting ectoplasm but got glass instead. Looks like we were both fooled, for a while at least."

The train's already stately progress dribbled away as it came to a halt on a gentle incline. Here, for the first time since we'd left the station, a second set of track lines appeared.

We were at one of the few passing places on the long route through the mountains.

As we watched, a couple of figures, each carrying a bunch of newly picked flowers, appeared on the track. First came a young Indian woman in a purple checked smock, jeans and blue wellington boots. Secured to her back by a shawl was a little baby girl with a top knot who peeked shyly out at us.

"How cute!" said an American lady opposite us.

Shambling behind them came the bent figure of an old woman in a skirt and with an ancient trilby perched on her head. In profile she looked like a question mark wearing a hat. Her jaw, long since emptied of teeth, worked constantly up and down like a concertina, collapsing inward as it closed.

"Poor woman, what a life she must lead!" said the American.

I didn't even like to contemplate what kind of existence these people could eke out in such a remote place and caged in by these steep mountains.

The two women held up the flowers but nobody was buying. A couple of seats down, a German lady was putting fruit into a little polythene bag. She reached up and opened a sliding section at the top of a window then lowered the bag down to them.

The younger women reached up and the baby smiled. A sigh of approval went through the carriage.

Bent though she was, the old woman struck quickly, knocking the bag out of the young woman's hand and sending the contents bouncing over the track. Moving as fast as her bent frame would allow, she snatched the fruit from the ground while using her contorted body to block the woman with the baby.

There was a collective intake of breath, the passengers going from pity to disgust in a heartbeat.

"That was so unfair." The American lady couldn't seem to believe what had just happened. "What an evil old woman. Someone should do something!" She clutched at her throat.

"Welcome to the High Andes," said her husband, gloomily.

The two women stepped back quickly off the track and a train coming slowly from the other direction cut them off from view. Even before it had passed, our own train began to move so by the time we could look back the two women and the baby had disappeared from view.

Though the sudden shadow had passed, the happy chatter of the passengers didn't resume.

"The skull beneath the skin," I said.

"You're such a drama queen," said Nick.

The nearer we got to *Aquas Calientes* the more brutal the river became. Over countless years, huge boulders had tumbled down from the steep mountainsides but had not been able to check the water's fierce flow. Instead, it impacted on the rocks in explosive bursts that gave the river the most uneven appearance of any water I had ever seen. It was like a liquid minefield in perpetual detonation.

The mountains were no longer just steep but literally vertical. Hydraulically brutalised by this dreadful river, a gorge at least a thousand feet deep had been hollowed out. Tropical plants, the like of which I usually saw only under glass in botanical gardens, now hung from the sheer rock in vast green curtains. As we came around a bend, a little further downriver I saw ramshackle buildings hanging precariously over the torrent.

"I guess this is it," I said.

We were definitely slowing now but, just before we reached the station platform, I looked down and saw something that made me feel physically sick. On the gravelly slope below the tracks that led down into the river, a couple of Indian children were playing what looked like tag. They scrambled and chased each other over the slippery gravel, at times sliding down the slope towards the churning river's spiteful embrace. One misstep and they'd be dead in an instant. Visions of shattered skulls and bones broken like matchwood came unbidden to my mind and I had to look away.

*Aquas Calientes* is a small river town surrounded by vertical mountains. It's the staging post for Machu Picchu so there are always plenty of tourists there. One river running through it is the scary, brutal Urubamba, the other the tamer Vicanota. Little bridges strung with fairy lights cross the latter and give the place a magical appearance at night.

It's famous for its hot baths (hence the town's name) though these are sometimes washed away in floods.

There are no roads out. There are no cars, only a fleet of buses to take tourists up to Machu Picchu. The big blue and yellow locomotives and carriages, resting between their infrequent runs, park in the middle of the street.

Power comes from a hydroelectric plant which has in the past been damaged by landslides.

Landslides, or to be more precise, rockfalls were my main worry when I saw our hotel for the first time. It sheltered—although cowered might be a better word—beneath a rock overhang several hundred feet above. The reason this had formed was because a big column of rock beneath it had fallen away at some point in the past.

"Sleeping here will be literally like waiting for the hammer to come down," I said nervously.

Nick, of course, was having none of it. Again, why would Spirit have led him to South America just to let him be squished beneath thousands of tonnes of rock. The idea was ridiculous.

We went to our rooms, me to dump my suitcase, him to laboriously unpack.

That evening we set out for something to eat and drink. It would have been much better if we'd starved.

I had already had something of a run-in with Peruvian food. I like food and I like variety and that can get me into big trouble when it comes to exotic fare. I can't help ordering it. Back in Lima we had been to an upmarket restaurant at the Huaca Juliana, a huge 1500-year-old clay brick pyramid surrounded by a plaza.

Excavations had shown that the Incas who built it had slaughtered four poor young girls and buried them in the foundations for luck. The Inca were a blood-thirsty bunch.

I had ordered stewed beef heart, a national delicacy. I chewed and chewed and chewed. 'National delicacy' made it sound like it should be... oh, I don't know... delicate, but it most certainly wasn't.

Nick meanwhile was making short work of his *ceviche*, a lightly pickled fish dish, though this one was dotted with odd looking white, yellow and even purple things, some the size of olives. According to the menu these were kernels of corn of different varieties, none of them resembling the corn we get in the UK. They also tasted strongly of corn, a charge you can't level at the UK variety.

I gave up gnawing on my bit of inner tube, surreptitiously fished the unyielding flesh out of my mouth and put it on the side of my plate. The ball of tissue blossomed like a flower and kept unfolding until it had flattened out again.

"Maybe the dead girls worked," said Nick between mouthfuls.

"What do you mean?"

He waved a fork at the flattened Inca pyramid that overlooked the restaurant. Made of millions of thin white bricks, it rose in seven large flat stages into the deep red tropical dusk. "Despite the earthquakes, it's lasted over fifteen hundred years. Blood of maidens: better than a preservation order."

And now here we were eating more Peruvian food on a balcony overlooking the sleepier of the two rivers in *Aquas Calientes*. From where we sat, we could see a series of little bridges over which people walked and cycled. One of the bridges carried the train tracks.

"Damn!" said Nick. "I forgot to take all this stuff on the train so I'm well behind." With that he took out a multi-compartment pill dispenser and flipped back the lid to reveal their variegated contents.

"What is that?"

Nick shrugged. "It's for helping me know what pills to take and when. One compartment for morning, one for evening, each day for a month."

"How many different pills do you take? It looks like a jumbo pack of misshapen Smarties."

"Well, I don't know what they're all called. Just the usual meaningless bunch of polysyllables the drug companies use, but I think these yellow ones are for my diabetes, the blue and white ones for my blood pressure... oh yes and these white ones are for my blood pressure as well. I think these little ones here are statins to degunk my blood vessels and these reddish ones are for my allergies and these..."

"My God! I had no idea you were so sick. You look so... robust."

Nick shrugged. "I feel fine. I wouldn't bother with this stuff but my wife insists I take them." A thought suddenly occurred to him. "But we're not even on the same continent right now. I think I'll give it all a miss."

"Whoa," I said, deeply alarmed. "The last thing I need is you stroking out on me or having a heart attack." I decided not to mention that if he should need mouth-to-mouth resuscitation then, quite frankly, he was a goner.

"I don't even believe in these things. I only take them to humour her."

I could see there was no point arguing so I went back to my food. The deep-fried guinea pig, jointed and with torso split, lay before me on the plate. Two protruding teeth identified the lump that had been its head, though thankfully its eyes had been gummed shut by batter. It's said the Peruvians consume sixty-five million of these rodents each year. High protein, low fat, take up less room than cattle, the big surprise is that we don't eat them back in the UK.

Less of a surprise is that the meat tastes like chicken.

Nick meanwhile was wiring into a beef saltado which seemed to consist of beef boiled in soy sauce.

It was a reasonably cool evening but I noticed he was sweating.

"You still feeling breathless?"

"Yes. You?"

"Occasionally but it's not as bad as it was. We're a thousand feet or more lower than Cuzco so things should have got a bit better. Hang on a second!" I fumbled my iPhone out of my pocket. I peered at the screen then grinned. "Wi-fi here! Well, I'll be damned!"

Nick looked around. "I suppose it's for all the tourists."

I consulted Wikipedia, checking the section on altitude sickness. "Have you got a headache?"

"Why do you ask?"

"Humour me!"

"Yes, well more a sort of muzzy one than real pain."

"Fatigue, pins and needles?"

"I definitely feel knackered." He wiggled the fingers of his right hand. "Now you mention it, I do have some tingling in my thumb and forefinger. I'd put it down to sitting awkwardly on that long flight. Maybe pinched a nerve. Anyway, what are you getting at?"

I waved him for silence. "OK, that all sounds like your bog-standard altitude sickness so far, except for the fever. But this breathlessness: is it only when you're walking upstairs or up a hill, or do you get it even when you're lying down?"

Nick nodded reluctantly. "When I woke up this morning, I thought I was suffocating, but it eased a little."

I shook my head. "Fever, shortness of breath even on resting, you've got more than the usual altitude sickness. You've got pulmonary oedema. It's even got its own acronym: HAPE. High altitude pulmonary oedema. You must be particularly susceptible because it normally doesn't show until a couple of thousand feet higher than this."

"Where are you getting this from?"

"Wikipedia."

"Ah, so it must be true."

"Jesus! HAPE can progress rapidly and can often be fatal."

"What's the cure?"

"*Get down to sea level! Do not pass Go!* OK, I'm paraphrasing, but that's basically it."

Nick took a sip of his Pisco sour. Here they were served with a frothy egg white top and a dash of yellow something-or-other to resemble the yolk. They were delicious but were, as it would turn out, our biggest mistake.

I checked my watch. "The last train's at six. If we hurry, we might still catch it. There won't be any tickets but if we tell them it's an emergency..."

Nick chuckled.

"Err... have you been listening to what I've been saying?"

"I'll be fine. Take your time finishing your dinner!"

"You... could... die"

"I won't."

"How do you know? Wait a minute! Let me guess! Spirit wouldn't have led you all the way here just to wipe you out with a case of raging mountain sickness."

Nick shrugged.

I leaned as far forward as the table would allow. "Please! Let's go!"

He shook his head.

"OK, but let's get you to a doctor." I said it firmly but then glanced round nervously, wondering if they had such a thing as a doctor in this one-horse town that didn't even seem to have a horse.

Nick smiled. "I'll take my chances. And even if I were to succumb, a better world awaits." He studied my reaction with evident amusement.

"You are out of your mind! And you on all those pills. You're obviously not a well man even at the best of times."

A Hispanic looking waiter wandered over. His face looked like it had been on the losing side of a number of knife fights. He asked if we had finished with the food we'd both been ignoring for several minutes.

"My companion hasn't finished his," said Nick. The waiter turned to leave but Nick stopped him. "Tell me," he said, "do you happen to know where we might find some ayahuasca?"

~~~

Awaking in my bed the following morning I became aware, faintly through the enveloping blankets of heavy sleep, of a pressure in my lower abdomen. This wasn't entirely unusual.

What happened next definitely was.

I was out of bed quickly, but not quickly enough.

Belatedly, I remembered the advice of a much-travelled friend when told of our upcoming trip: *In South America never trust a fart!*
~~~

This had never happened to me before, at least since I emerged from nappies. Absolutely mortified, I cleaned up my mess.

By the time I finished I had to get up anyway so I headed down for a tentative breakfast. Nick was already there and for that I was grateful. I needed a father confessor and he's always been good at that.

"You'll never guess..." I did a double-take. "My God, you look awful!"

Nick nodded sadly. His face was the colour of putty and sheened with sweat and the skin around his eyes was swollen. To my alarm, I noticed the fine tremor in his hand holding the fork.

"We've got to get you out of here," I said earnestly.

Nick shook his heavy head. "I'll be fine. Bit of a stomach upset, that's all."

"And altitude sickness and pulmonary oedema plus your diabetes and whatever the hell else is wrong with you."

"Nothing to a man like me," said Nick gamely. I couldn't tell if he was being ironic or if he really meant it. "But I think I'll be giving those pisco sours a miss in future. I'm thinking it was the beaten egg white they used to top it. Raw eggs in a country like this..." He swung his fork in a wide arc.

I had to agree. "Maybe you should give food a miss for a while. What is that you're eating anyway?"

"Just the same as they had in that hotel in Lima. It seems to be the Peruvian breakfast thing. Scrambled egg and cold slices of processed meat. Oh, and white rolls and fruit."

"Well, I'm going to give it a miss, anyway."

"Why? How are *your* guts?"

"Same as yours by the sound of it."

"Even so, you should definitely eat something. The waiter from last night was pretty clear we shouldn't eat after midday if we're doing ayahuasca. Unless you get something down you now, you'll never last."

The thought of the arrangements for the coming evening just added to my sense of impending doom. Maybe I *should* try to eat something.

~~~

Scrambled eggs still churning in my guts, I returned to my room and checked the parts of the sheets I had scrubbed clean. I'd done a good enough job; the sheets were changed and washed every day anyway but at least the maids who collected them wouldn't realise what had happened. I couldn't have coped with the look of disgust and disappointment in their eyes.

I'd been inspecting the sheet closely when something else caught my eye. I realised that the sheet, at first sight a nice clean white, was actually shadowed here and there with traces of faded stains that had clearly survived multiple washes.

At last, the penny dropped and I made the belated association between what my friend had said and these hotel sheets and their historic evidence of soiling.

I thought of all the tourists who'd had similar accidents on the same linen. Perhaps tens, perhaps scores, perhaps hundreds.

The scrambled eggs danced in my stomach.

~~~

Hordes of tourists, like an infestation of locusts, climbed amongst the ancient ruins in their garish, multi-coloured rain gear. Surrounding the flat top of this mountain, a ring of even higher zeniths pierced the wispy clouds with their jagged spines.

Machu Picchu is one of the few tourist destinations that live up to the hype (FYI the Taj Mahal, the Pyramids of Cairo and the view of Rio from Christ the Redeemer also deliver). We had time to kill before our next meeting with the knife-scarred bandit waiter from the night before and this was the obvious place to go.

Despite the cooling drizzle Nick looked unaccountably hot, almost like he'd slugged his way up the mountain rather than riding comfortably in a bus around the many hairpin bends.

We'd been wandering around for a while. According to Nick, psychic power oozed from every rock. The whispering of numberless faint and long dead voices tickled his consciousness.

The Crystal City some mystics called it, some because mica and quartz in the rock can make it glint in sunlight. Others because they considered it a metaphor: crystals grow from seeds that are the templates for the form they subsequently take. This city in the clouds was the template from which the world itself had been shaped.

"Can you feel it?" Nick asked.

His electric blue rain poncho over his backpack made him look like a gaily dressed hunchback. "Feel what?"

"The power, of course. Thousands of years of it."

"This place is only five hundred years old."

Nick waved this pedantry away. "But what was here before? Why did they build all the way up here in the first place? Because this is a well of ancient energies."

"Good or bad?"

"Light swirls through dark, like milk through coffee."

"Surely it should be black as pitch, what with all the human sacrifices the Inca were so keen on? You make it sound like some good could come from such barbaric rituals."

Nick shook his head. "Spirit would never agree with something like that. But for the Inca... well, perhaps they erroneously saw it as the only way of opening the path to the Next World."

We were on the side of the site where it fell vertically to the river, and where several terraces were cut into the mountain. As we watched, a group of workers walked out along them. Where once their ancestors might have tended beans and corn and peppers, now they scythed grass. As they worked, it was like a curtain had opened and centuries had slipped away. We both stood motionless, watching.

The worker on the lower terrace suddenly stepped back as though to get a better view of his efforts and I gasped as the man's foot came within inches of the edge. One more incautious step and he would plummet fifteen hundred feet to the valley below.

Unnerved, we turned away from the valley view and back to the site itself. Here, even more terraces had produced most of the food but now only a few llamas grazed on them, surrounded by hordes of camera-clicking tourists. At the other end of the site ruined houses and turrets were all that remained of where people had lived and worked and worshiped. Beyond this rose two vegetation shrouded and bullet-shaped peaks.

Nick waved his arm, encompassing this city in the clouds. "Why did the Inca build this place? What does your scientific view say?"

He may not have read his guidebook but I had. "There are various theories: that it was built for the Inca emperor Pachacuti, or was a temple for priestesses, the Virgins of the Sun, though recent evidence suggests this unlikely. Another theory is that it was a holiday home for the royal family.

Or that, like Stonehenge, it had some function as an astronomical calendar with alignments between certain buildings and the surrounding peaks corresponding to equinoxes and solstices."

"They're all wrong," said Nick emphatically. "*Look* at it! Not with the eyes of science but with your soul. Look at the magnificence!"

"Enlighten me!"

Nick gave it a few seconds, then: "It was built to house a God," he said simply.

Portentous or not, I suspected he was right.

## *Taking Drugs: Just Say No*

Aquas Calientes, Peru 2015

I'd had some close calls with drugs. Once at university and on LSD, a girlfriend had had to physically restrain me from crawling out of a third-floor window to get a closer look at the brightly coloured roses in the quadrangle below.

Another time, I'd been taking downers (barbiturates) while visiting an abandoned gold mine in the Rockies that was far away from the nearest road. Trying to get back to the nearest town afterwards meant walking over a rocky stream bed but my balance had gone and I kept falling, feeling neither the ice-cold stream water nor the repeated impacts of the rocks on my flesh and bones. The next morning it looked like I'd spent the night in a tumble drier.

Another time I'd been flying out to join a ship in Hamburg and was changing planes at another German airport. It was back in the 1970s, at the time of the Baader Meinhoff gang of terrorists who planted bombs and kidnapped and killed. I landed soon after a major outrage and the whole airport was locked down with tanks on the tarmac. Everyone was being searched and I suddenly realised I'd left a lump of cannabis in one of the pockets of my jacket. I just managed to drop it to the floor and boot it clear before I was frisked.

I'd long since stopped taking most drugs, still indulging only in alcohol and pills for high blood pressure. Now, in South America, I was an anxious pensioner with an ailing have-a-go friend for company who regarded death as a promotion. The idea of taking a high-powered narcotic somewhere many hours from the nearest medical help wasn't sitting too well with me. Nevertheless, I was up for it.

Even though we hadn't had to climb to get there, the day on Machu Picchu had drained us even further. Both of us were suffering badly from diarrhoea and Nick's altitude sickness was making him look sicker and sicker.

After a quiet day of recovery, the evening came and it was time to leave for our mysterious appointment. The piratical looking waiter who Nick had accosted about ayahuasca had arranged to take us to a shaman.

Nick and I met in the lounge of our hotel and made our way down the steps to the street. Unable to resist the same morbid urge, we both turned back to look up at the spectacle of the jagged, menacing overhang a few hundred feet directly above the hotel. Well aware of Peruvian tectonics, I had contemplated refusing even to enter the hotel when we had first arrived. If I'd been travelling alone that is exactly what I would have done. In the end I'd kept quiet as the unbreakable Nick would have ribbed me mercilessly.

We regarded the looming rocky cudgel. "Let's hope that's not a metaphor," said Nick.

We turned and plodded up the steep, car-free narrow street that paralleled the smaller river feeding down into the brutally roiling waters of the Urubamba. We wound our way around and between two parked blue and yellow trains.

On either side of the path upwards were little stalls selling shawls and tee-shirts and handbags and blankets, all with the strong colours in parallel bands that seemed to be the basis of the local designs. Across these were emblazoned zigzags and diamond shapes and circles.

Still heading up we passed the restaurant of the night before and saw the same waiter lounging against the wall of the next-door bar. He was dragging on a cigarette and seemed lost in thought.

I looked round carefully. "At least there's no police I can see. I guess that leaves our waiter friend free to lead us further up the canyon to somewhere quieter where he can slit our throats in peace."

But Nick was already stumping towards the man. He reached out a hand. "Good evening, my friend."

The waiter hastily threw away his cigarette and shook the proffered hand. "It is good to see you again, *senors*. I have arranged *everything*. Follow me!"

With this he turned and started off up the street with the deceptively slow and easy style of all the people from this steep little town. Soon we were both puffing to keep up.

But at least we didn't have far to go. The waiter turned into a large bar. As we followed him in, I could just make out in the gloom that the walls were covered with Bob Marley posters and clumsily hand-painted pictures of marijuana plants. Ancient leather armchairs, collapsed inward with age like the cheeks of a centenarian, littered the floor and, far at the back, I could make out a ramshackle bar. The place was deserted. Reggae music thumped away in the background.

"Choice!" I said under my breath.

The waiter had already got to the bar and was tapping with a coin. By the time we caught up, a figure was coming out from behind a curtain. Before the curtain closed again, I glimpsed what looked like a small kitchen. Sitting at the kitchen table was a petite Indian woman breastfeeding a baby.

The man who emerged was whipcord thin with a goatee and long greasy hair tied back in a ponytail. He looked European or perhaps American.

Whatever he was, he spoke good Spanish because there was a rapid-fire exchange with the waiter who then turned back to us. "Alejandro will look after you now. He know everyone."

"Thank you, my friend. This is for your trouble." Nick in his usual magnanimous way pressed a ten-dollar bill into the man's hand, a sum I regarded as outrageous for someone who had most definitely not arranged *everything*. The waiter disappeared in a burst of profuse gratitude.

This left Alejandro grinning at us. "You want a drink?" The accent certainly wasn't American.

"That's a surprise," said Nick grandly and slowly which was the way he talked to anyone who was foreign. "I thought one could not drink before taking ayahuasca."

The man did a double-take. "Oh no. You no take ayahuasca tonight. There is much preparation. And Zorro, he must agree."

"Zorro?" I asked in surprise.

"Zorro the shaman," said Alejandro patiently. "His name mean fox. Because he is a wise old fox."

"So can we meet this Zorro?" Nick asked.

"That is why you are here. I phone my brother."

"Zorro is your brother?"

"No." Alejandro was beginning to look exasperated. "He take you to him."

"I think I'll have a beer after all," I cut in quickly. Alcohol may not solve all these complications but I would care less about them.

"This is like pass the parcel," I said a few minutes later as we waited for the next intermediary to arrive. The beer at least was nice and cool.

"They're sizing us up. Making sure we are worthy."

"FYI: we're not. Not that it matters. You realise that after they rob us, all they have to do is chuck us into that nasty river and we'll be red mist in an instant. No bodies, no forensics."

Nick looked at me wearily. "Spirit is telling us to go with these men. There is no sign of malevolence in their auras."

"I'm vastly reassured."

We'd been too busy bickering to notice the guy enter until he was almost behind us. We turned to see a tall, dark-skinned man. Dull eyes stared out from an emaciated face. They didn't seem to be able to focus properly.

"My brother, Raoul" said Alejandro who had appeared right on time from the room in the back. "He take you."

"Thank you, Raoul," said Nick grandly.

"He speak no English but he know where to go."

"Thank you for your help, Alejandro," said Nick, using both hands to shake the man's outstretched right. "Please take this for your trouble." I was aghast to see a twenty-dollar bill change hands.

When we emerged from the bar, I was surprised to find how dark it had become. Deep within this gorge, the sun disappeared quickly behind the mountains. Raoul shuffled ahead, his gait unsteady. We turned back down the sloping main street, now lit with strings of little lights, but then we quickly turned into one of the smaller alleyways. Illumination from the lights soon faded and I had to pick my way with care over the broken paving.

We came to a bridge over the smaller river that at this time of year was not much more than a stream. Down its path we could see the many other little bridges that forded it. Some were illuminated with the same drooping lines of bulbs, barely brighter than Christmas lights, but it gave the scene a certain charm.

Across the bridge now we turned onto a well-trodden dirt path along the bank. After fifty metres we turned back suddenly onto a little dog-leg path. Raoul pushed his way through overhanging vegetation. As we followed, a broad two-storey building was revealed. There was no door at the front so Raoul made his way to a rickety gate at the side that opened onto a little alley lined with old wooden crates and several overflowing rubbish bins. A dog suddenly barked, but I had no idea where the sound came from.

Raoul hissed angrily and the barking stopped instantly. He chapped at a door and we waited in silence. All I could hear was the faraway roar of the ever-raging Urubamba.

Time passed as Raoul stood motionless, a man used to long waits. Even Nick had begun to shuffle impatiently when the door opened and a sweet little Indian girl was revealed. She smiled and nodded at Raoul and he nodded back. She opened the door wide and we all trooped in.

My expectations had not been high so I was startled to find a large open space which rose through both floors of what I belatedly realised was a hotel. Ancient but well upholstered and comfortable chairs and sofas covered the ground floor. A wooden balcony ran around the first floor and behind this were the doors to several rooms. A large plant with aspirations of being a tree rose up almost to the level of the balcony. So verdant was this plant that I looked for its source of light and then realised that the roof above was glass.

On the faded white walls of the ground floor hung posters of mystical landscapes showing lush vegetation and mountains and eagles. A picture of a fox was rendered in exquisite detail but with an intensity of colour that could only come from a psychedelic vision. Rather than the tatty, slinking vermin I was used to, this fox stared out at me with serenity and fearlessness.

By the time we had all sat down, the girl had vanished, but she soon returned with bowls of nuts and cups of tea infused by sprigs of plants I didn't recognise. A cautious sniff yielded an aroma of dried sage and suggested a herby bitterness. I decided to give it a miss.

Raoul, yet to say a single word, lit a cigarette and leaned back in his chair. Nick reached into his pocket and gave the man ten dollars, but he made no attempt to leave.

As the minutes stretched, nobody seemed inclined to break the silence.

The door to what looked like a kitchen opened and a little Indian man came out. No more than five feet tall he wore the sort of multi-coloured woollen hat I'd seen on the trinket stalls for the tourists. He beamed with pleasure, revealing deeply etched laughter lines around eyes that hinted at an older age than the vitality of his movements suggested.

He plumped himself down on a chair facing the three of us and, laughing, held out both arms. "Welcome!" he said in clear English.

"And thank you for allowing us to meet you like this," replied Nick in his stately, ponderous way. "We are deeply honoured.

We made our introductions. That Nick had been summoned here by Spirit, caused not a moment's consternation with Zorro. Indeed, he seemed to think it was the most natural thing in the world. It appeared Zorro was quite famous as a shaman and claimed he had even been to London to lecture at the Society of Psychical Research.

As Nick and he swapped their unconventional credentials I wondered what measures Zorro would take to ensure we were fit to take the drug. It certainly killed people now and again. Even more frequently, it cracked open the skulls of the more psychologically fragile and let the devils out. In response to the bad publicity such fatalities and mental injuries had generated, many shamans had taken to running potential clients through a safety checklist to eliminate those who might be vulnerable.

That's what I had been expecting but I was to be disappointed.

"And you must prepare," Zorro said emphatically. "You must empty your bodies of toxins for the next twenty-four hours. No red meat, no pork, no alcohol. Avoid salty food. No sex.

"And you must be healthy. If you have heart problems then ayahuasca can kill you. Are you healthy, Barrie?"

"Yes," I said, though hesitantly. Not many men get into their sixties without any health niggles.

Zorro nodded. "And you, Nick?"

Nick opened his hands wide. "Fit as a fiddle."

Somewhere, far away, little fairies were dying in droves.

And that appeared to be Zorro's 'checklist' completed. It suggested that, when it came to health and safety, Zorro was trusting rather than rigorous. One look at Nick could tell you he was not a well man.

The sick man in question raised his eyebrows, a thought apparently coming to him. "Is it true ayahuasca can sometimes make you vomit? Not that I'm worried. I ask simply out of interest."

"Oh, no," said Zorro firmly and I was very relieved as I hate puking.

"No," continued the little man. "It *always* makes you vomit!" He nodded slowly. "And usually you shit yourself as well!"

I like to believe I'm up for pretty much anything, as I think this book proves, but right here was a deal-breaker. My guts had been producing boiling hot ordure in vast quantities all by themselves. Taking something that would make it even worse was just not on, unless Zorro was happy for his hotel to be pebble-dashed with crap.

So, like one of those 1960s newshounds who'd set up a sex sting on some luckless politician, I basically made my excuses and left. Everyone at an ayahuasca ceremony, even the shaman, must take the drug so I wouldn't even be allowed to stay as an observer.

And that was all the preparation that Nick was going to be given.

The next day I tried to talk Nick out of going ahead with the ceremony.

"Come on, mate! You're not in good health. You've got a serious case of altitude sickness, your bowels, by your own admission, are in a mess *and* you take more drugs than Keith Richards. You're a wreck, man! And have you ever thought where we are?" I indicated the looming mountains.

Nick looked unperturbed.

I tried to lay it out. "You don't start taking the damn stuff until nine at night. There is no road out of here. It doesn't have an airport. The only way out is by train and the first one isn't until six in the morning. Even after you catch that you're still at least three hours from the nearest hospital. In other words, the dope can play merry hell with your body for twelve whole hours before you could get any medical attention."

Nick gave me a patronising smile. "Lighten up! Shame we can't have any alcohol. I could murder a beer. What do you reckon, should I risk it?"

"No!"

"Twenty-four hours is a long time without a cold beer in this climate."

"Funny you should say that, but I had a look on my phone. Preparing yourself for this stuff is supposed to take two whole days at least, two weeks preferably. Zorro's got you on a fast track so that's strike one for his credibility. Plus, shamans are supposed to probe to establish the health of their clients. Some even take them through lengthy checklists. Zorro just asked one question and then bought your 'hale and healthy' bullshit wholesale."

But, of course, none of this worked. We parted and I watched him toiling his way back up the road to Zorro's hotel and wondering if he'd come back in one piece.

~~~

When I saw Nick again afterwards, I questioned him and took extensive notes. I include his account as you may find it educative, particularly if you're thinking of taking ayahuasca yourself.

Nick was led into a special room set aside for the purpose. There was a single table, a jumble of paraphernalia on its weathered surface. The shaman retrieved a roll-up cigarette from the table. It was much thicker than the emaciated objects you might see old men smoking outside a UK pub. Lighting it from the single candle on the table, he came towards the two participants puffing out smoke. He blew this over each of them and then walked round the whole room until it was filled with a faint haze. Whatever was in it smelled heavy and sweet, like pipe tobacco marinated in honey.

"Mapacho tobacco," said a Swedish guy who Nick had never seen before but who was the only other one participating. He was with Zorro for a couple of months to train to be a shaman himself. "To the Indians it is sacred."

The Swede had taken ayahuasca around forty times and had reassuringly told Nick, 'You might feel as if you're dying.'

Zorro was still exhaling the fumes but now wafting it over himself and the other two with what looked like a large and splendid eagle feather.

The shaman kept returning to the table, which Nick realised might be some sort of altar. Looking more closely he saw what he presumed to be power objects including various animal skulls.

There were three mats arranged around the room. Nick sat down and made himself as comfortable as possible.
~~~

Zorro left them for a second then bustled back in with three small red plastic pails just like those used for making sandcastles on beaches. The shaman laid one pail by each mattress.

"That'll be for the vomit, presumably," said Nick.

"Yes. Place it close by so you can reach it quickly."

"The bucket seems rather... small." It had been many years since Nick had thrown up but he recalled the vomit being both copious and projected with almost explosive force. If you did that with this little toy it'd bounce right back at you.

"But you haven't eaten anything since midday, Nick, so there should be little to produce."

"And it always makes you sick?"

Zorro smiled down at him radiantly. "Purging is a vital part of the ceremony. You must eliminate all the bad from within you."

"Bad what?"

"Spirits, emotions, desires, negative energies. You must clear yourself to allow the spirit guides to enter you."

"Through my stomach?"

"Indeed." This was from the Swede. Tall, slender, bespectacled, he was now unpacking a large knapsack. Out came a personalised vomit pot decorated in the Peruvian style of zigzags over parallel bands of colour, then a long thin cylinder which turned out to be a supplementary rolled up mattress. A thermos, paper tissues, a water bottle and a set of large crystals were aligned ceremoniously to the right of a blow-up pillow that was the final item out of the main body of the bag. A torch with a red transparent strip taped over the bulb was extracted from a little side pocket.

"It looks like you're preparing for a Moon shot," said Nick.

"I have done this many times before," replied the Swede, whose rather complicated name Nick had already forgotten.

"One must prepare. No meat for two weeks, vegetables only. And for that period too, no drink and no sex."

Zorro now pointed at the door through which they had entered. "You can leave if your legs become sore and you want to stretch them. Also, some people like to look at the stars through the window in the roof above the lounge. You can do this but only for a few minutes at most. This is a circle." He pointed to the three mattresses. "And I can keep the evil from entering it, but I cannot protect you when you move outside."

"Then surely we shouldn't leave at all?"

"That is indeed what I would prefer, Nick, but these spirits do not strike like snakes. They must stalk you and their power takes time to build. If your guides move you to look at the stars then do so."

He looked at each of them. "You are ready?"

They both nodded and Zorro squatted down in front of the Swede. "What is your intention, friend?" he asked the Swede.

"There are still doors, doors the spirit guide would not let me through. Aggression is my problem, the guide said, from a separation many years ago. I have thought much of this over the last month and I feel at peace. I am ready, Zorro, for the next stage."

Zorro nodded and shuffled over to Nick. "And you, my friend?"

"Spirit says there are things to teach me and it is easier to do this in South America than in the UK. It told me to come here for deeper insights into this world and the world beyond."

Zorro nodded. "Like with all drugs, the more you believe, the greater the effect. This is a psychoactive drug. It will affect your consciousness. Psychoactive drugs swell the emotions. If you start with negative thoughts then things might go badly. You do understand?"

Zorro stood and went to the altar and picked up a bunch of thin, pointed and well-dried leaves. They were tied tightly at the stems but the leaves themselves spread out like a feather duster. Sitting down cross-legged on his mattress he began to chant, shaking the leaves in a rattly, scratchy accompaniment.

As the ceremony droned on Nick found his eyelids getting heavy. His upset stomach had interrupted his sleep the night before and he wasn't feeling well. The breathlessness and spells of dizziness were slowly abating but he was still sweating profusely even now in the relative cool of the evening. He was glad that the one thing he had thought to bring was a large bottle of water.

Perhaps sensing he was losing his audience, Zorro made them join in the chanting to call Mother Earth close and help with their understanding.

More smoke, more chanting. Nick found himself drifting into the strange, dissociative state he sometimes entered before his best mediumistic readings. Some small, far distant part of himself watched as his mind slowly emptied. Then his eyes closed.

Perhaps he fell asleep for he did not see the potion being prepared. It was only the sudden ending of the chanting that made him open his eyes to see a chipped China cup half full of fluid held before them. Zorro was holding it up to his mouth.

"Drink this slowly."

Nick took the cup in both hands. "Spirit guide me," he said and raised the cup above his head. Lowering it, he took a gentle sip.

Nasty! Harsh like the taste of old coffee grounds though the liquid was smooth. Underlying the bitterness was a sharp herbal tang.

"Can't I drink it down in one go?" he asked.

Zorro, still smiling, shook his head and moved on to the Swede.

Nick persevered. It was like taking the spartan medicines of his youth that were unsweetened by sugar.

He felt the urge to vomit rising swiftly and had to stop for a second. Purging was an important part of the ceremony, he knew, but if he brought the ayahuasca back up now then surely it would have had no time to take effect? His sips became even more cautious.

After a long struggle he managed to finish it. He put the container down beside him and wiped his mouth with the back of his hand. He gave a sudden, bilious burp.

"Excuse me," he said, but nobody seemed to be listening.

Again, the fugue state crept over him and he entered a timeless realm of being whose surface was untroubled by the ripples of thought. Far away across eternity Zorro began chanting again and lit more cigarettes and, circling round the room, waved his eagle feather. Finally, he sat down so they were all sitting cross-legged. Nick was vaguely aware that the Swede's head had dropped to his chest.

Nick realised that the windows of the room, previously showing only the darkness of the night, were now being lit by what looked like neon lights.

Then, far away, like a long dormant volcano easing back into life, tiny vibrations disturbed the peace of the little room. Straining his senses, Nick searched for their source and was surprised to find that these signs of alarm came not from without but from within.

It had been so long that, when he finally understood the full import of what was about to happen next, he had to scrabble quickly for his little bucket. His stomach heaved and a gob of brown fluid flopped down into the pot.

Zorro sat back quickly, a look of surprise on his face. "Such power!" he said. "It was like someone hit me on the chest. You are a remarkable man, Nick."

Nick peered in puzzlement at the little puddle of puke and reflected that this was high praise indeed. Another little spasm pulsed through his innards and another liquid eructation politely emerged. This was not the volcanic vomiting from food poisoning. All in all, it was a much more gentlemanly way to be sick.

Just then, in one smooth motion, Zorro reached for his own bucket, threw up into it and set it back down. Casual but business-like, the process had taken only a couple of seconds.

Something seemed to be wrong with Nick's vision and he tried to blink it away but to no effect. Zorro was outlined by a thin line of vivid scarlet. The line was so fine and bright it was almost painful to behold. Looking away for a second, Nick became aware that everything in the room had an outline. The colours were different but intense. As he looked more closely, he realised that each object was full of shimmering rainbow dots.

That's when he understood that all the zigzags and dot patterns in all the tourist mementos he had seen in Peru were based on these hallucinations. The jumbled native bric-a-brac that showed parallel lines and lightning strikes motifs, the little dots, and all in intense colours. The Indians have been taking ayahuasca for thousands of years. It had informed their whole culture and their artwork.

Then from all the dots and squiggles black rods emerged and curved back to form an arched backdrop. Within this he saw what looked like robotic spiders striding purposely towards him. As they approached these morphed into something more like animated clay figurines and their movements, restricted by their blocky little forms, were so toy-like and comical he felt no fear. They looked like Lego men stumping along.

But as they drew closer, he realised he had been mistaken. Though their heads and torsos were block-like, each corner was slightly rounded. Their skins were pale but for fluorescent purple flashes on their heads and arms and their stubby four fingered hands seemed to be wearing purple gloves.

The foremost being came to stand beside him. Naked, without visible genitals but with flat raised disks for nipples, it waved a hand in greeting. "Welcome, Nick," it said in a voice like a breeze tamed by numberless jungle fronds to the gentlest of whispers. "We have been waiting for you."

In such momentous circumstances Nick felt he had to be polite. "I am very honoured to meet you. What is your name, my friend?"

"They call me by many names and none, Nick. I am your guide."

The little figure turned on its thick legs and pointed to the left. "This way, my friend."

The way led through deepest jungle but, amongst the verdant, glistening foliage, there were little doors and windows.

And everywhere vines twisted around each other in frozen vegetal love. Their colours were legion, though never green, and their long lengths were embossed with intense, intricate patterns.

Waiting for them was small car, although it was little more than a hollowed out rectangular block with a steering wheel and a wheel at each corner. It was a jaunty yellow colour but for the wheels which were red. A Noddy car, in other words.

"This is like something I played with as a child."

Suddenly before them was a glass door with a silver handle. "What's behind the doors, my friend?"

Keeping a steady pace and without looking back, the guide, whose slightly blurred form had somehow taken on the appearance of a Venetian-style harlequin figure, said, "Knowledge. Opportunities not taken. Commitments, real commitments, not made to Spiritualism. But you cannot progress further until you are cleansed."

And Nick found himself back in the darkened room. Dimly he could make out the Swede still sitting cross-legged and slack-jawed on his mattresses, his eyes firmly shut. Zorro meanwhile was on his back and rolling from side to side and giggling.

"Zorro," said Nick and then, more loudly: "Zorro!"

The shaman sat upright and smiled. "Yes, Nick?"

"My spirit guide... says I must take more ayahuasca, to get through the door and progress further."

"Of course." Zorro rose smoothly to his feet and went to the little altar. He came back with another mug of liquid and, once he had given it to Nick, he went back again and got another cigarette and his eagle feather and started to circle the room, chanting and smoking and wafting away.

The second helping of drug tasted no better than the first, but the vomiting that followed was hardly troubling. Three or four times he expelled little gobbets of puke yet the little pail still wasn't yet full.

At one point Zorro suddenly looked startled and shuffled over to check that Nick was okay. He said he had seen a burst of white light appear from Nick's chest.

"I've only seen that happen once before," Zorro said earnestly. "And the man died."

Nick, of course, was unfazed by this and lay back. He closed his eyes and did not open them until he again heard the guide's voice.

"Wake up, Nick! We must go."

Nick opened his eyes to what had now become a kaleidoscope of every imaginable shade of green and many others besides. The edges of every leaf and frond had all the colours of the rainbow radiating away like ripples in a pond.

With a start he realised how silent the jungle had been before because now he was almost deafened by the thunderous roar of teeming life in all its myriad forms. He felt the weight of infinite existence heavy on his shoulders. He gulped for air.

Nick noticed the Noddy car had gone but did not think to ask why.

The harlequin was back and Nick decided to test him. "Are you the person I am to learn from?" he asked.

"Indeed. I'm here to tell you that you're only playing at all this. We asked you to go full on, but instead you only devoted yourself part-time."

That was fair enough but you could say that about any practitioner of anything. Did this creature really know him at all? Nick tried another test. "What is it like to work with me as a medium?"

"You are like a raft, surging in heavy waters. Spirits are trying to clamber aboard but are kept being washed off."

Nick could get his head (what was left of it) around this but it was hardly definitive.

They were making their way through little breaks in the tracery of vines that now covered everything with their serpentine convolutions. Each vine was like a thread in a blanket that had been thrown over the jungle.

Finally, Nick found himself in some sort of celestial café with a round table at which sat Peruvian gods. As Nick walked in, they turned, the room going silent. He felt like a gunfighter walking into a western saloon.

But then the vivid hallucinations slowly shaded back into reality. And that was the end, more or less. All in all, it was a bit of an anti-climax.

Nick left the hotel tired but at least he was physically and psychologically in one piece, though that strange shifting vegetal world lurked at the periphery of his vision for days.

The good thing was that he didn't die from altitude sickness, the ill-effects slowly dissipating until by the time it came to leave Peru and head off to Brazil, he was almost back to normal.

Our guts, however, would not return to equilibrium until we finally got back to the UK.

Nick's verdict on the ayahuasca? That it had been a simple hallucinogenic and that he had not sensed Spirit within it. As far as he was concerned all he had seen had more likely come from his subconscious and he hadn't been told anything he didn't already know.

Even though I had not taken the ayahuasca, the brutal civil war in my guts, the altitude and the strangeness of the High Andes worked on me in other ways. At least that's my excuse for why I behaved like an idiot when we flew over the Amazon towards our next stop in Brazil.

The sun was going down on the opposite side of the plane and the ground on my side was dark. Occasional lights showed some godforsaken habitation with access to a diesel generator. How many didn't even have that, I wondered. For a moment I felt dizzy at the thought of being surrounded by hundreds of miles of dark, teeming jungle without any light at all.

Taking a sip of my whisky I looked again out of the window and saw the blazing hemisphere of a nuclear explosion rising above the Amazon.

I gulped in shock and the drink slid from my hand, bounced once on the little seat table, then tipped its icy contents onto my lap.

I hardly felt it.

I jammed my eyes shut.

I tried to still my thudding heart. As though playing dead and surrounded by Kalashnikov wielding psychos, I ever-so-slowly cracked open an eye.

Surprisingly, no blast wave blew the plane like a fluttering, shotgunned pigeon from the sky.

I fixed on the explosion. At six miles below us, I estimated it must be many miles in diameter. Detonated deep in the wilderness there would still be casualties. For a few lonely Indians a burning death god would have risen in their midst.

I felt Nick leaning over him. "What's so interesting?"

"That! What the hell is that?"

"What? All I can see is the moon."

And I knew immediately he was right. Like with the ghostly purple jellyfish, my eyes had been deceived: the horizon was not where I'd thought it had been. It wasn't the darkness of the jungle that I'd been looking down on, instead it had really been the darkness of space. Rather than an atom bomb detonating, what I was seeing was the moon rising over the horizon. Its rays of light, coming to me obliquely through many thicknesses of atmosphere were fractured, its colours shifted to blazing red.

I'd been fascinated but blindsided, subverted, disturbed and fooled.

That's South America in a nutshell. And one day I'd like to go back.

# *Visiting a Rio Favela*

Rio, Brazil 2015

Where I was going there were no maps.

Favelas are essentially slums. There are around a thousand favelas in Rio, many clinging to the vertiginous hillsides and perfectly evident for all to see.

In a strange inversion, these vertical slums have some of the best views on the planet. You'd need to spend millions of dollars for less spectacular vistas in Vancouver or San Francisco.

Yet as far as tourist maps are concerned it's like the favelas are a fiction.

Tourist maps of Rio tend to start at the Copacabana and Ipanema beaches and go as far north as the administrative centre. Above that there's just an arrow pointing towards Sao Paulo a few hundred kilometres to the west.

However, Rio is twenty times larger than the maps suggest. It's as if all of Rio to the north and west just don't exist.

And there's a good reason for that. If tourists had any common sense they wouldn't go there anyway.

Unfortunately, common sense and I had a bitter falling out many decades ago and, though we both occasionally send out hopeful feelers, we've never managed a reconciliation.

So, I decided to visit a favela. I was still travelling with my fearless friend Nick. After several weeks in Sao Paulo investigating spiritual healing, we were ending our trip with a holiday here in Rio.

As far as the whole trip went it had been an adventure, ticking all my boxes, but the whole mythical spiritual quest had been a bit of a bust, although on this aspect Nick's and my perceptions were at variance.

We'd gone for a walk and found an eight-floor-high Spiritist hospital in Sao Paulo. That we'd more or less stumbled (my perception) on the biggest such hospital in the country convinced Nick we had been led there by Spirit. I recall the receptionist at the hotel giving us vague directions to it, but Nick denies such a thing happened. Instead, he believes that after a lot of aimless wandering around we happened to walk into a building where he saw a bust of Allan Kardec (more later) and realised we had struck the motherload.

Then (and now it's my turn to have no recollection of this), a passing woman asked if he needed help. Nick said Spirit had sent him. "Ah," said the woman, "we were told two weeks ago we would have a visitor from Scotland."

I often think of the words of Alexander Pope: *Remembrance and reflection how allied, what thin partitions sense from thought divide.*

Which of us was correct? After a few weeks in South America, neither of us were firing on all cylinders and I wouldn't like to bet either way.

Anyway, we somehow found ourselves at the nexus of Brazilian spiritual healing and this needs some description. You might have to put down your coffee and concentrate a bit here because whether spirit is written with a big or small 's' is important to understanding what happened next.

Spirit (big 'S') is a sort of collective of spirits according to Western Spiritualist thinking. Such a collective Spirit does not, however, exist in the Brazilian Spiritist religion, as far as I can grasp anyway. There, everything is about the smaller 's'—individual spirits.

To separate the two approaches, the Western one is called Spiritualism, the Brazilian Spiritism.

I'm glad we've sorted that out.

Few people outside Brazil even know of places like that big Spiritist hospital in Sao Paulo but there are also 12,000 smaller centres around the country. Forty million people are treated every year by Spiritist institutions in Brazil alone. They treat mental as well as physical illnesses. In one hospital over 1400 mentally retarded children are cared for.

What is Spiritism and does it actually work, you are perhaps asking? Spiritism is a South American off-shoot of Spiritualism. It was started in the nineteenth century by a Frenchman called Allan Kardec. To him the human spirit was immortal but sought to improve itself by going through many reincarnations. According to him, disembodied spirits interact all the time with the living and are responsible for physical and mental illnesses.

Unpaid volunteers are trained for five years to diagnose and treat illness and that single hospital treated 7000 patients a week. As far as I could tell the treatment of physical conditions, from goitre to gangrene, constipation to cancer, infertility to impetigo, consisted of the patient lying on a bed. Four or five of these practitioners sit around this bed staring at the patient and beaming in positive thoughts, while one of them whispers to the spirit within the patient. This lasts for about ten or fifteen minutes.

Err... and that's it.

The treatment of patients with mental illness is entirely different. Four or five of these practitioners sit around the bed staring *away* from the patient. Rather than beaming in good thoughts to the physically ill, they are pulling the bad spirits out of the mentally afflicted.

As to whether any of this works in curing illness, I'll leave it up to you to decide. Everyone was very kind and welcoming to us, even to a sceptic like me, to the point where I felt churlish asking questions.

It didn't stop me, though, and I asked one of the ladies assigned to us whether the efficacy of these treatments, over and above any placebo component, had ever been scientifically tested. For example, in the West efficacy is usually assessed with randomised double blind control trials.

She smiled sadly at my misapprehension and explained that Spiritism wasn't a science, it was a religion. That they believed with all their hearts that it worked so that foibles like randomised control trials were completely irrelevant.

Before you scoff too heartily, bear in mind that half of the Brazilian population, particularly out in the countryside/jungle, have no access to Western healthcare. Spiritism is all they have. Even if Spiritism is only exploiting the placebo effect, that's better than nothing.

I wonder now what happened to all those kind, gentle practitioners when Covid struck Brazil. Their belief was so strong I'm sure they continued their treatments during the pandemic. Nick had kept up some contacts but these ceased at that time and he has had no response to emails since. We fear the worst.

At the hospital, they were so impressed by Nick and his energy that they let him step in as a healer. He came to feel they had given him a model of spiritual healing and it spurred him on to take it up back in the UK with what he regards as favourable results.

Though Nick stuck with the healers while we were in Sao Paulo, I lost interest quickly and spent a few weeks mooching about that dreadful city. I thought Hanoi was pretty awful for reasons that will be revealed later, but Sampa pips it to the post as the worst city I've spent much time in. It's certainly the ugliest.

The city sits on the red earth of a plateau far inland. It's huge, with a population of over twelve million. It manages to be the biggest city in both the western and southern hemispheres, yet many in the developed Western world have never heard of it.

The population, those that aren't subsisting in the 1600 favelas, live in the sort of high-rise apartment buildings that British councils have been demolishing for the last fifty years.

Hot, humid cheek-by-jowl living seems to drive some wild. Graffiti artists risk life and limb hanging off the tops of these buildings to disfigure the corpse-grey facades with ugly black hieroglyphics.

After a few weeks of that I had been more than relieved to fly to the outrageously beautiful Rio.

Before my trip up to the Rio favela I'd been talking to Nick about it. He'd been leaning back against a railing, squinting at the reflected sunlight on the silvered barrels of cannon in the little fort on a headland above the beach. Short, stubby and erect, the cannons pointed out to sea to defend Copacabana Beach from God-knows-what. Here and there little fluffy-eared monkeys with long silver and black striped tails darted amongst the legs of the tourists. Other monkeys lazed in the sun on top of the blue railings of the concrete emplacement.

"Can't be bothered climbing all the way up those mountains," he'd said. "Not in this heat. Besides, who wants to see a slum?"

I was looking down on the long arc of the beach, the placid blue of the southern Atlantic on one side and hundreds of brilliant white apartment buildings and hotels on the other. Only the gentle sea breeze made the heat bearable. To get to the fort we'd climbed from the beach. Two pale, sweating Scotsmen with big floppy hats and slathered-on sun block, we had been almost indistinguishable from the lithe, sun-kissed and barely clothed Latins languorously draped over the sands.

"Then I'll go by myself," I'd said with conviction, full of macho bullshit.

Later, I got talking to a stately silver-haired guy called Vitor who was also staying at our hotel. When I mentioned my proposed trip Vitor had nodded firmly, presaging a rather earnest lecture.

"Let me explain," he said. "There are very many favelas in Rio. These are places where the police do not go. There is no running water and no sanitation. However, eight or nine years ago the government tried to clean up a few of them. It was a process called pacification. Hundreds of police and army attacked... perhaps that is too strong a word." He screwed up one eye, evidently trying to find the right word. "No, 'attacked' is probably correct. They attacked and arrested and sometimes killed several hundred of the more... colourful characters in the favela." He looked round conspiratorially and lowered his voice. "Sometimes the killing followed the arresting, if you understand what I mean."

"And did it work?"

"Yes. BOPE, that is the elite police, cleared out the drug dealers and other criminals, then special pacification units moved in. They consist of specially trained community policemen."

"Community policemen?" I said in surprise. "You mean police who go around checking that old people are okay, giving directions to strangers, issuing the odd parking ticket, that sort of thing."

Vitor looked at me blankly. "Perhaps I am using the wrong word because that does not sound in any way like a favela community policeman. There are no cars to give a ticket to. They are not interested in making sure people are 'okay'. What they are interested in..." and he made the unmistakable gesture of firing an assault rifle, "...is killing any of the drug dealers who try to come back."

That was all a little unnerving but it didn't put me off. I decided to find out how I might go about a visit so I asked the receptionist at our hotel, a mid-scale high-rise a few streets back from the Copacabana.

The receptionist was a tall, thin, solicitous man in his fifties. "Can I ask, sir, why you wish to know?" he had inquired politely.

"I just want to go there."

The man looked crestfallen as if I had rejected a most precious gift. He cast his arms wide. "The beach, the sea, the sun..."

I don't like sand, the sea scares the shit out of me and the sun burns me like a bastard. I gave a dismissive shrug, for once not play-acting.

Alarm spread across his kindly face. "Sir, it is too dangerous. The favela, the *slum*..." he enunciated this last word as clearly as he could, perhaps worried there was some terrible misunderstanding going on here, "...is not for tourists. Bad people. Many bad people. You would be a... target."

I shrugged again, hoping to appear more relaxed than I was beginning to feel.

He became operatic and eventually resorted to begging me not to go. In the end I agreed to take a taxi from a firm he trusted as far into the favela as the road penetrated. There, someone who made a living out of taking adventurous travellers into this recently 'pacified' favela would meet me. The taxi, the getaway vehicle, would wait for me somewhere safe just outside the slum.

"Last things," he said. "Dress poor. Very poor. Don't have your wallet or phone or camera visible. Do exactly what your guide says. Do not stray away from him!"

The word favela comes from the late nineteenth century and Brazil's Canudos civil war, when soldiers hid on the hillsides amongst plants called favelas. Later, freed slaves moved there, which is why favelas are still sometimes referred to as *bairros africanos.*

Around six per cent of Brazil lives in them. As well as no sanitation or electricity, there are no schools or hospitals as favelas have no legal basis. They can hold something like 40,000 people per square kilometre. Compare this with 6000 in London, or 7000 in Hong Kong.

It has to be said that, from an architectural point of view, building tottering stacks of hovels on steep hillsides prone to landslides during tropical storms might be considered a little imprudent. But, then again, if you're poor your choices are limited.

What with landslides and disease and 'stray bullet syndrome', life expectancy there is twenty years shorter than in the rest of Brazil.

The taxi took a circuitous route through the one-way system, almost turning back on itself before zooming into a tunnel cut through the ridge of rock that sandwiched the Copacabana against the ocean. Once through to the other side, the mountains rose high above to the north. Here and there the jumble of favelas rose up on these like scree slopes. On his own peak, Christ the Redeemer was busy absolving them of all their sins. (For what it's worth, the view over Rio from the statue is the most sublime I've seen anywhere in the world.)

Further inland but still almost at sea level, the shops became tattier, not like the plusher ones near the ocean. Occasionally, grand ornate Catholic churches in brown and grey stone nestled between the plain-faced apartment buildings.

We started on a steep climb. The streets were deserted until we found ourselves behind a bin lorry. On the back running board three bin-men in khaki overalls hung swaying as the truck went around the corners. As we got closer, I realised they were all attractive young women, their long black hair whipping out as they flicked their heads or as the truck went round a corner. They did this a lot and seemed to be laughing and joking and having a hell of a time.

Why don't we have bin-men like that back in Glasgow?

Ahead, the road was levelling out and several vans and combi buses were parked to the side. Here the road turned away so that, like a shy lover, it only kissed the favela and never took the relationship further.

On the pavement, such as it was, little blue tarpaulin-covered stalls sold fruit and drinks. A few motorbikes were pulled up and owners leaned against a balustrade above a short drop to a filthy stream.

The sides of the parked vans were open. In the nearest a man sat selling large containers of cooking oil.

As my taxi pulled up, the man I was due to meet stepped forward and introduced himself. He was middle-aged but had the leanness of so many in the ghetto. He was called Matheus and he seemed nervous. He gave me the same instructions as the receptionist but with even more urgency.

I looked up at the impossibly tiered layers of buildings rising steeply above. Tightly packed and profuse, they revealed not a square inch of the mountainside on which they were precariously built. Floor after floor had been added, sometimes growing out over the levels below and held up by bare metal bracers and stanchions and scaffolding.

There appeared to be no spaces between the habitations and the effect was of a sheer walled fortress. "How do we get in?" I asked wonderingly.

"There is a stairway up ahead." Matheus pointed but then he shrugged. "After that, things might become a little... complicated."

I asked what the name of this favela was. He told me in Portuguese, a language in which even a declaration of love sounds like a bitter denunciation. Speaking the name involved a lot of complicated back-of-the-throat action and I forgot it instantly.

I'd have looked the name up on a map but, of course, the place didn't officially exist.

We passed rickety wooden stalls selling fried food and the fumes of old cooking oil made my eyes sting. One stall was a makeshift bar and blank-eyed men in grubby shorts and singlets leaned against it, quaffing vast drafts of luridly coloured and ice-filled concoctions.

Above the street, like the work of a horde of demented spiders, a tracery of cabling hung in loops from high posts. Each little circuit box had the rat's nest of wiring you might expect in a server farm, except every cable was multiply jumped at every lamp post, each individual hack spawning a bowing wire that reached up and into the ghetto.

"So, they have some electricity here at least," I said.

"No, only at the lower levels. The higher you are the further you are from any power. The higher you are the poorer you are because of the more effort to get anything up to your home."

Then he got stern. "No more talking in English. We must be as inconspicuous as possible. You will follow close behind me. The ways up are narrow and we must not get in the way of other people moving around. If we do then there may be trouble, big trouble."

We passed an almost vertical slope of rock and earth, one of the few places where the ground of the mountain was not covered in buildings. It stretched up about thirty metres and seemed to be the favela's garbage chute. People at the top tossed their rubbish over from a platform and it tumbled down into a malodorous pile at the bottom.

"This is what pacification has brought us!" Matheus whispered proudly. "The trash lorries pick it up from here and take it away."

"What happened before that?"

He shrugged.

Later on, and much higher up, I was able to answer that question myself. I looked down on little valleys and crevices in the mountain, all full to the brim with rubbish. The stink was hellish.

However, now still at ground level, I couldn't see any way up. Then, after a few more metres I saw a long run of vertiginous steps hemmed in by sheer sides of brick and cement many storeys high.

We started up the steps but there was a warning shout from behind. I was just able to get out of the way as a wiry man, bent over with the weight of a large armchair on his back, scuttled by and up the steps. I watched in amazement as the man climbed and climbed and climbed without respite until a bend in the steps hid him from view.

Matheus checked around then beckoned me to follow him.

The going was hard and precarious. Made of cement though they were, the steps had crumbled under countless feet. Hidden even from the high sun for all but a few days in the year, the sheer sides of this defile were stained with mould.

A sharp cracking sound made me duck. Deep within surrounding walls as we were, it was impossible to tell where the gunshot had come from. Matheus looked back at me, his eyebrows raised in silent question. I nodded, this time more reluctantly, and he turned and continued his progress upwards.

The steps gave way to a steep incline and the cliffs of rough, unpointed brick and stained cement were broken by dilapidated shop fronts with tatty overhanging polythene. It reminded me of images of refugee camps I'd seen on TV.

Everywhere was the smell of burning wood and paraffin and spoiled fruit and dampness.

More steps. Suddenly all the little figures ahead of us flattened against the wall and a couple of coppers in blue overalls, baseball caps and body armour shoved their way through.

What surprised me was a weapon one was carrying. The other carried an AK-47 assault rifle, so nothing surprising there. If you wanted to 'soften up' these little alleyways then a burst from an AK would be just the ticket. However, the other copper carried a long-barrelled gun which would be an encumbrance in these cramped surrounds. There was so little space in the alley he could only carry it with the muzzle pointing upwards.

The coppers pushed by. Close up they looked worried and their foreheads were plastered with sweat.

Perhaps they were following the sound of the gunshot.

Here and there, dark little alleyways led off either side and I saw barefoot children playing. From higher up, dogs barked in an endless cacophony.

More steep steps and more brief levels, the stalls becoming sparser. Another gunshot sounded, and again I couldn't help going into a reflexive crouch. At least this shot sounded far away.

We came to a level with a single shop and a wooden counter blocking the entrance. Behind the dead-eyed man on the other side of this counter were shelves heavy with everything from tins and flour and cereal to cheap children's toys. This was the last shop we would come across.

Matheus beckoned me into a side alley. After another ten metres we rounded a corner and my eyes slammed shut at the sudden brilliance. When I cracked my eyes back open, I was gripped by a terrible vertigo and had to force my hands flat against the sides of the alley.

Between the heaps of higgledy-piggledy shacks, I could suddenly see all the way down to the Atlantic. I hadn't realised how high we'd climbed and the view was staggering. It was like suddenly breaking through jungle canopy in the Amazon but, instead of tree tops, below us lay several square kilometres of raggedly tiered roofs dotted with blue water tanks. Here and there trees had somehow escaped from the sunless stranglehold of the buildings and erupted into a messy burst of leaves. In the background, framing the V of the Atlantic that cut deep into this vast valley, loomed bullet-shaped mountainous lumps, each a poor man's Sugarloaf.

We kept climbing through the twisty little byways. Occasionally the cramped alleyway opened out into areas too small for even one of these squashed houses. Here at least the sun could penetrate and there were always people lounging around and talking.

In this topsy-turvey world the higher we climbed, the deeper into the ghetto we got. Shacks upon shacks upon shacks rose above us like jagged cliff faces covered with washing draped over wooden rails and corrugated iron. Far above and through gaps I could just make out the sharp brown peak that all this was rising towards. Would the people keep building until they reached the very top or would it finally get too vertical even for the determined poor?

The buildings were becoming even less sturdy; we were just too far up to carry heavy building materials. Everything was shabbier and dirtier and smellier yet, when the buildings allowed, the views became increasingly sublime.

Suddenly, as we moved down one dingy alleyway, Matheus turned left and descended a few steep steps into a gloomy little pit covered by houses. Salsa music on a tinny radio barely concealed the sound of a couple arguing. In a corner, as my sight adjusted to the gloom, what looked at first like the wrinkled finger of a glove resolved itself into a used condom. On the other side of the cement floor was a little ladder leading up to a small wooden landing and a faded red door.

My guide climbed the ladder and opened the door.

This was Matheus' own house and it didn't look too bad. There were chairs and even a cupboard. I noticed in the kitchen a large plastic container containing water. My mind boggled at the idea of carrying this hundreds of metres up through the warren.

Matheus took me out onto a flat roof and I found my vision drawn magnetically to the incredible panorama. Like a snapshot of a raucous river as it flowed down a mountain valley, the jumble of buildings tumbled down towards the azure sea. Above this the clear sky shaded to a lighter blue as it reached down to the horizon. I saw again the several peaks shaped like old coppers' helmets thrusting out of a green peninsula.

And suddenly the copper's long gun made sense. Even from here, and we still weren't at the top, a high-powered rifle could command square kilometres of rooftops. Between them the two coppers could go from close quarters combat in the alleyways to long range sniping on the roofs.

Matheus' wife served me a caipirinha and I drank it, lolling back in my chair with a heavenly view before me and a version of hell just under my feet.

After a few more caipirinhas and the generous hospitality of these poor people, we set off back. By the time we returned to ground level, I'd got used to the gunshots and hardly flinched at all.

Soon afterward the window of opportunity to visit this favela closed. Pacification lasted barely a year, the old drug gangs moving back. Visiting as a tourist went from simply dangerous to actively suicidal.

The next time you complain about the rates, or a new bus lane strangling your road to work, think of the inhabitants of the favelas; think of their noisy, dirty, backbreaking existence played out to the accompaniment of gunfire.

In the developed West we really do need to count our blessings.

## *Leaving your Yurt for a Leak in Mongolia*

Irkutsk, Siberia, 2013

The most decadent experience of my life came on a Japanese Airlines (JAL) flight coming back to the UK from Tokyo at the end of the eighties. A group of us had been on a business trip, buying six MRI scanners for Scotland. In those days, and before a spoilsport government cracked down on 'jollies', such trips were paid for by the companies vying for our business. As a result, I found myself in Plutocrat Class on a Japanese airline intent on making the trip as painless as possible. On being seated I must have hinted at the merest of glancing interests in champagne because I was immediately presented with a whole bottle of chilled Moet to while away the hours.

Time passed easily and at one point I found myself looking down on the wildness and whiteness of Siberia. Idly, I sipped my champagne, checking out the frozen rivers and the endless miles of sparse birch tree forests. It all looked so untamed, so bleak, so absolutely awful.

Slightly jarring amongst the irregularity of nature were some straight lines etched in the snow to form grids. This was clearly the work of man but I couldn't understand why anyone would build anything all the way out here.

Then it dawned on me: here I was drinking champagne in Croesus Class while looking down from a lofty ten kilometres onto the Siberian prison camps.

Like I say: decadence.

Don't worry; the bottle of champagne medicated away any feelings of moral vertigo.

The real take-home message from that flight, however, was that as far as Siberia went, I really never wanted to go there.

So, naturally enough, thirty-five years later I found myself in Siberia. The flight from Moscow to Irkutsk had been a long one (Russia is very big: has anyone ever commented on that before?). As the plane taxied towards the terminal, we passed a line of senescent ex-military cargo helicopters. Some, their wheels and undercarriages scavenged, had tipped over to lean on the shoulders of the ones next to them; just like a row of vodka-swilling drunks in a Russian park.

These ancient aircraft are the only way of getting around Siberia in the winter. After a long and weary life, when the time should come for them to fly away to the big airfield in the sky, instead their ancient parts are ruthlessly cannibalised to keep others working.

Ramshackle and half gone, they stand as a metaphor for all things Siberian.

It was May but we were greeted by driving sleet as we left the airport terminal in Irkutsk, a stolid, blocky Stalinist town ameliorated only a little by the pretty golden onion domes of the Russian Orthodox churches.

Our minibus snaked its way along the road through the forest towards Lake Baikal. We were to partake of its manifold pleasures before catching the Trans-Mongolian express to Beijing.

We were a motley crew. A young guy from Ireland who had never travelled before had quit his job, sold his house and was using the proceeds to journey around the world. He seemed just as surprised as I when he told me about it.

There was also an Australian couple who alternated between friendliness and hostility according to rules I never understood.

Another couple were into their eighties, schoolteachers from the US who had spent all their holidays since they were married travelling around the Arctic Circle. They seemed quietly pleased with this. Everyone else thought they were crazy. The Trans-Mongolian express isn't lauded for luxury and ease and I was pretty sure that one or other of these old teachers would die before we got to Beijing.

Our minibus finally emerged from the endless birch trees onto the shore of Lake Baikal, at Listvyanka. This was supposed to be Siberia's resort town.

Now, I was brought up near Southend-on-Sea, the old resort town for London's East Enders. I know exactly what seaside resort towns look like off-season. Grey, dull, listless, the garish colours of the arcades and fish and chip shops making the place look cheap and gaudy.

Listvyanka in-season made Southend-on-Sea off-season look like Saint Tropez after an injudiciously high dose of cocaine and LSD. The 'Baikal Riviera', as it is known, extends several kilometres along the side of the lake, but everyone hunkers down in several valleys cut deep into the hillside. These are the only places offering some shelter from the scouring Siberian wind, nicely chilled by its passage over the largest freshwater lake in the world.

The lake itself is about six hundred kilometres long and sixty wide and is really, really cold. So cold in fact that I saw lines of ice washed up on the shore.

And this was in May! In winter the temperature can plunge to minus twenty degrees C or lower.

Far across the lake was a long line of snow-covered mountains reflecting in the breathtakingly clear and calm water.

Along the lake front were a few hotels, pink plastered and looking like abandoned birthday cakes. The handful of little shops were boarded up; in the front of one a moth-eaten stuffed bear reared back on its hind legs to menace the few hardy visitors. All the other houses, especially those cowering in the three valleys, were made of wood (as in whole tree-trunks, not wooden planks). Cows wandered freely all over the place.

There seemed little else to do but walk along the front, dressed in as many layers of clothing as you possibly could. Occasionally you could stop to eat the local delicacy, smoked fish called omul from the depths of the lake. Touted throughout Russia as a delicacy it was... okay.

We spent a couple of days there and I can't remember what else I did to pass the time. The only standout memory was when we were heading along the front in the minibus taking us back to Irkutsk and to the rail station. I happened to glance out of the window across the lake and was surprised to see a line of white, all the way across the surface a few kilometres out into the lake. Whatever it was, the damned thing was racing towards us like a shockwave.

I blinked, sure there was something wrong with my vision, but whatever it was kept coming. For a second, I thought the blast wave would scour Listvyanka from the map.

Instead, it got to the shore and stopped dead. It took me a few seconds to realise this had been an ice sheet forming almost instantaneously. I've never seen sea-water ice up but I imagine the salt lowers the temperature of freezing and makes it a more sedate process. However, this was fresh water in Lake Baikal and it seemed that once the process had started it was almost a fast-forward ice-age.

I was left open-mouthed as our minibus turned off the shore road and into the birch forest.

We arrived back at Irkutsk in a charming mixture of rain and sleet. Our guide, who would not be travelling on the train, aimed us at a local grocery store and advised us to stock up on pot noodles. Even though we would be on the train for several days, there would be no restaurant car. All we'd have would be a samovar dispensing hot water.

Hence the pot noodles.

Pot noodles in the middle of Siberia? I'd avoided them like the plague all my life. Now I found myself depending on them for my survival.

Everything of course was in Russian so we had to guess from the picture on the boxes what the noodles might contain. That's how we began selecting, studiously and earnestly but then the guide shouted the train was leaving so we grabbed what we could and dashed for it.

The train was very long and, like so much in Russia, rundown and dog-eared. The join between each carriage was as airtight as a tennis racket. When you stepped gingerly across you could see the Siberian dirt whizzing by beneath.

The carriages were sectioned off, with foreigners quarantined in two adjacent carriages. Not until we crossed into China was it possible for us to walk from one end of the train to the other, an odyssey on such a long beast.

Each compartment slept four in bunk beds either side of a narrow aisle with a little table at the window. There seemed no easy way of climbing up to the top bunks other than stepping up on the table, which was usually covered in water bottles and mugs.

There were no staff to make the beds so the bedding was there pretty much all of the day, either neatly refolded or scrunched up and spilling over the sides of the bunks. I don't have the patience to make beds so mine was messy. Luckily, I had a top bunk so it didn't matter much. It did matter if it was a bottom bunk because that's where everyone sat during the day.

The train slowly pulled away from the station and we headed south-east towards the Mongolian border.

A lot of the villages in Siberia look like conglomerations of garden sheds, often surrounded by raggedy tree-trunk fences, like the stockades you might have found at the Alamo.

This begged the question as to what these rather Germanically over-specified fences were there to protect against. What were the equivalent of rampaging Mexicans or Sioux?

My guess is wolves.

Wherever there are houses in Siberia there are piles of garbage. They lie festering under glowering gunmetal grey skies.

I had to keep reminding myself that this was the summer and we were seeing the place at its best.

Despite the weather, station platforms on the line were uncovered. I'm guessing it would take substantially strengthened roofs to cover the platform area to withstand the huge weight of snow in the winter.

Then again, perhaps hardy Siberians full of antifreeze (or at least vodka) regard roofs in railway stations as fripperies.

Long lengths of welded rails may be the norm in Europe but on the Trans-Mongolian there were no such things. Crossing from one section of rail to another produced a *chuggeda* sound. As we rarely, if ever, on the 1600-kilometre journey went over forty-five kilometres an hour, the *chuggeda-chuggeda* was a never-ending background beat to our lives. I dreaded the thought of long nights of this. Would I ever be able to get to sleep?

As night drew in and we drank vodka for anaesthetic purposes, the time came for me to climb up to my bunk. Three sheets to the wind, scrabbling for handholds like a frightened monkey, I eventually hauled myself up and tried to make the bed while I was on it.

Sharing a bedroom with other people has always been rather tricky for me. Firstly, if they snore and pass wind, it wakes me up. Infinitely worse, however, was my effect on them. As I've said, I'm a dreadful snorer and physical violence is a real possibility.

So, with the snores and rumblings of others, and the dangers of an assault on my person, and the rattling of the carriage and the monotonous *chuggeda-chuggeda*, I resigned myself to long and sleepless nights.

But the instant my head hit the pillow I fell deeply asleep.

Eight hours later I struggled back to consciousness. The sleep had been delicious.

And that was the pattern throughout the journey. Indeed, even during the day, all I had to do was sit back on the seat and close my eyes for Morpheus to sandbag me. Getting to sleep for long periods of time had never been easier.

I reckon it's all to do with the *chuggeda-chuggeda*. Perhaps it resonates with the foetal memory of my mother's heartbeat. Maybe the little compartment, crowded though it was, was like her womb.

Whatever, those were some of the finest sleeps I've ever had in my life.

And so we made our way across the endless steppe. The land was almost flat, with the train taking long sinuous turns around the few little rises. Sometimes, on the curves, I could see the engine, a quarter of a mile ahead.

Riding shotgun on the foreigners in our carriage was a heavy woman in a stern-looking uniform. It was soon clear she neither liked us nor spoke English or any other foreign language. I couldn't even work out why she was there, except to replenish the samovar and look down her nose at us.

However, when we got to the border with Mongolia her role as guard came into sharp focus and was frankly alarming. The border wasn't far from Irkutsk. The train had taken a route around the south end of Lake Baikal and we'd gotten there by nightfall.

Just as we stopped at the border, the guard suddenly leapt up from her bunk in her cubbyhole and strode down the corridor like she was taking point in a military parade in Red Square. She got to the toilet, fished out a large key, and locked it from the outside. Then before anyone could think to say anything, she got off the train and locked the carriage door behind her.

Border checks have to be done by both nations and so it can take up to half a day to make the crossings. Up to that point we'd dismissed this possibility as just irksome. But suddenly this was a much more frightening prospect, especially for the women who couldn't easily or discretely piddle into an empty bottle.

Not only were we locked up, but railwaymen de-coupled our two carriages from the rest of train and we were shunted to the periphery of the rail yard. We lay there becalmed like a plague ship; the surrounding area cleared to minimise our foreign contagion.

As eight hours ticked by the only sounds were the whimpering of women and the creaking of bladders.

Why does it take so long to frank a few passports? I don't know. Why did they lock us in? Again, I can't say. I'm told it doesn't always happen which, of course, begs the question: why does it happen at all?

Finally, we were shunted back into the rest of the train which then pulled up to the station platform. As the doughty train guard unlocked the carriage door, she was mown down by a rampaging band of Western women carving a savage path to the station's toilets.

The women left with clouded brows but returned with beatific smiles.

The guard was disapproving, the small size of Western bladders redolent of decadence and weakness.

Siberia had been empty but Mongolia took it to the max. Mongolia is a strange place in that almost everyone lives in the city of Ulaanbaatar. Those that don't are nomadic, moving their herds of yaks and horses and sheep across the sparse grasslands of the steppe.

After the never-ending emptiness of the steppe, the sprawling twenty-five kilometres of Ulaanbaatar is quite a shock. It's not a nice city to look at as Mongolia has had rather a torrid relationship with its Russian and Chinese neighbours, often being invaded by both. Blocky Soviet buildings still litter the centre and these are surrounded by endless suburbs of yurts.

Except they're not called yurts. That seems to be a general Central Asian word for these little circular tents, but the Mongolians call them gers. Once upon a time the gers moved with the herds of yak but over time the herders have been sucked into the vast eddy that is Ulaanbaatar. With 1.3 million inhabitants, the city contains over half the country's population.

That's like New York having a population of 150 million, or London 30 million.

Then again, if the choice was between the not conspicuously bright lights of Ulaanbaatar and the frightening emptiness of the rest of Mongolia, then I'd gladly become a city boy myself.

Ulaanbaatar, by some measures the coldest capital city in the world (in January the average temperature is –22.5 degrees C but usually gets down to –30 at some point and can get down to –40), means 'Red Hero' and was renamed to glorify the latest Russian invasion. The Russians destroyed the beautiful old temples and monasteries and in return put up their usual soul-crushing apartment blocks.

We took a minibus that would drive us out to the steppe but we had to run the gauntlet first. As we drove through the vast suburbs of dingy gers that surround the centre, the problems with the roads became evident.

In the West we complain about potholes but we really haven't got a clue. Potholes are called that because you can usually fit a smallish cooking pot into one.

In Mongolia, even on the main roads, you could fit a minibus into some of them. As a result, there is no lane discipline, everyone weaves from one carriageway to the other to avoid the deeper pits.

Even the smaller potholes are bigger than any I've ever seen in the West.

Vehicle suspensions in Mongolia must have the lifetimes of mayflies. Chiropractors must make a fortune in this country. Several times, on a drive of only about eighty kilometres, my spinal column was driven right up through the base of my skull, or at least that's what it felt like.

Sometimes we'd drop into a big pothole, leaving us in free-fall for an instant, before the van's roof came smacking down on our heads.

Somewhere in that brutal automotive assault, we left the bedraggled gers behind and entered nothingness. Mongolia is the most sparsely populated country on earth (two people per square kilometre, compared to 93 in the US, 279 in the UK). The nomadic tribes must sometimes think they are the only people in the world.

We travelled through a gently rolling country, here and there broken by craggy rock formations that took odd shapes. One looked exactly like a turtle but was the size of a large pub.

The potholes, if anything, got worse and with the van performing a frenzied dance to avoid the worst of these as well as dodging the oncoming cars slaloming into our lane, the going was slow. For hours we chugged through an empty landscape, sparse blades of grass the only living things to be seen.

Amongst this primal emptiness one felt like an intruder. I could well understand why so many of the descendants of the once-mighty Mongols huddled together in Ulaan-B.

This wilderness has always been populated by ghosts, although latterly they have taken an unusual form. Long-bearded old Chinese men in flowing silks, supposedly the ghosts of Chinese merchants who even in death parasitically exploit the wealth of Mongolia.

A more prosaic interpretation is this simply represents the perfectly valid insecurities of a small nation living cheek-by-jowl with a muscular neighbour who has four hundred times the population, one hundred and fifty times the military and three hundred nuclear warheads compared to none.

Perhaps in the West we should take comfort from the fact that Mongolia hasn't been either subsumed or consumed by China recently. It suggests modern China may not have the kind of colonialist ambitions we in Europe pretty much made our own.

After an hour or so of jolting up and down I was as tenderised as the minibus's suspension.

The endless sky was mesmerising and that's why what happened next came as such a surprise. Suddenly, rising out of the emptiness rose a gigantic silver statue glinting in the sun.

It was like stumbling across the Statue of Liberty poking up out of a Scottish glen but much, much shinier.

Massive though it appeared, I was still underestimating its size. It wasn't until we pulled into its empty car park that I finally grasped its magnitude.

I'm interested in travel, and I read about it a lot, but I had no idea this thing existed. Christ the Redeemer in Rio, the Easter Island heads, the Sphinx. This damned statue is in the same ballpark but as yet so few people know about it.

The statue is of the mighty Genghis Khan sitting triumphant on a horse. The statue stands on and dwarfs a two-storey circular building that's ten metres tall. The Khan himself is forty metres tall, made from stainless steel and weighs 250 tons.

It's incredible and imposing yet something isn't right. Genghis is magnificent but the horse he's on looks short and fat. There is something almost Sancho Panza-like about the whole thing—Don Quixote's fat servant following the great man while sitting on a mule.

The overall effect, and I'll whisper it in case some Mongolians are reading this, sort of makes the Great Khan look rather bloated and not a little ludicrous.

I'm actually okay with this. The guy was a dreadful thug who launched the Mongol invasions at the end of the thirteenth century. Whole populations of peaceful cities were massacred. He manufactured, by force of his mighty will, the largest contiguous empire the world has ever seen, conquering Central Asia, much of China, and the Levant. In doing so he, or his successors, wiped out many millions, amounting to several per cent of the entire world's population at that time.

Maybe making him look like a rotund Sancho Panza is appropriate revenge; ridicule rather than awe being what he most deserves.

This is a very poor country yet this expensive statue, out in the vast nowhere with nobody around to admire it, shows how much the present-day Mongolians adore this bloodthirsty old tyrant. Perhaps they feel so beaten down and forgotten, menaced by the Russians at their northern border and the Chinese at the south, with only the ghosts of the otherwise empty steppe to keep them company, that harking back to the past is a comfort.

When the minibus came to a halt we struggled out, massaging our limbs and relocating our bones in their appropriate sockets, then climbed the stairs to the edifice.

The Genghis Khan Equestrian Statue, to give it the official title, is actually hollow with a stairway leading up through his body and then out of the great Khan's chest and up the neck of the horse. From the top the views are fabulous, if many square kilometres of lightly grassed nothing is your thing.

Inside the building and under the horse's feet is a ten-metre-tall Mongol boot and a wardrobe full of Mongol clothing you can dress up in. We were the only people there so it wasn't a struggle to get the clothes we wanted.

However, as marauding Mongols we were less than convincing.

And why is this magnificent building in the middle of nowhere, where the only way to see it is to fracture your spine and liquidise your guts over scores of kilometres of potholes?

Apparently, this is where Genghis found a golden whip.

One mystery explained!

Now, more perplexed and culture-shocked than ever, we left Genghis behind and made our way even further out into the wild. On the way we stopped at a building high up in a rocky valley. A long staircase led up to this garishly painted temple full of Buddhist figurines.

The place looked exactly like something out of *Conan the Barbarian*. At any second, I expected James Earl Jones as the snake demon Thulsa Doom to appear at the temple entrance right at the top of a long flight of stairs, only for a loin-clothed figure to sneak up behind him, lop off his head and send it bouncing down.

Robert E. Howard wrote *Conan the Barbarian* back in the 1930s. The books take Conan through many exotic locales, from jungle-shrouded temples, to minareted and pavilioned forts.

In my travels I've sometimes felt I've been following in Conan's footsteps and indeed from reading his books it's like I've been to these places before (Ankhor Wat in Cambodia, and the forts of Rajasthan, correspond to the two examples above). I've begun to call these instants of recognition Robert E. Howard moments. This is a testimony to Howard's imagination as the man hardly ever travelled further than the limits of his small town of Cross Plains in Texas, before he killed himself when he was only thirty. He did this because his mother was on her deathbed, and indeed the next day she would follow him into the dark.

So, this journey out of UB had already been quite a day. I'd seen a magnificent but demeaning statue of one of the worst people there'd ever been. I'd also had a Robert E. Howard moment, seen a rock formation shaped like a turtle and had my bones transformed into jelly.

It was inevitable I would top this all off by ending the remarkable day in a ger and that's where we were headed next. Soon, the gently rolling grassland was being broken up by small mountains emerging like wolf's fangs. On a gentle rise leading up to one set of these emerging dentures, twenty gers had been set up.

As with all gers, they were fabric-wrapped, circular, white and with conical roofs from which emerged a chimney. The structures were held together by three blue bands that were secured to the door frame. The doors were orange and ornately painted.

Inside, the roof was held up by two pillars and between them lay a stove. Twenty or so ornate struts supported the roof and around the walls were three single beds and a couple of little cupboards.

The ger certainly looked the part. Mongolians have spent countless generations living in gers so how bad could it be?

As it turns out, pretty damned bad. For a start, even though the stove had a chimney we were advised not to burn anything at night as carbon monoxide poisoning was a distinct possibility. The last person to go to sleep had to put the fire out otherwise everyone might wake up dead.

That shouldn't have been too much of a problem as it was May so there was no snow. Trouble is, the wind off the steppe takes no prisoners. The waving grass doesn't seem to attenuate it one little bit. The wind bites its way through the paper-thin walls and chills you to the bone. Perhaps lying hunched up in the foetal position and covered with an avalanche of yak pelts might have kept the cold out, but modern blankets just didn't do the trick.

And the evening meal hadn't helped much. The yak cheese, sour milk and yoghurt hadn't really cut it and I'd hardly eaten a thing. Same with the Irish guy who was sharing the tent with me. He had to resort to beer to numb himself into unconsciousness.

Me too.

The downside of this was that in the dead of night (and when there isn't an artificial light for twenty miles there's nothing deader than a night on the steppe) I needed to pee.

And that's when I heard the wolves. They were howling away and didn't sound at all happy. Then again, there was so little to eat out here that maybe they'd had to resort to yak cheese as well. That's never going to make anyone chirpy.

So, I lay there, trying to ignore my filling bladder, while the wolves held a spirited and feral conversation.

There was a toilet hut but it was about fifty metres away and I doubted I could find it in the dark. I did have a torch but I thought that might be a bit of a giveaway as far as hungry wolves were concerned.

In the end, and in desperation, I decided to go outside, feel my way around the back of the ger, let the waters flow, then scramble back to safety as quickly as I could.

There was the sliver of moon presenting a lop-sided smiley face as I lugged my swollen bladder out onto the steppe. Freezing in my jammies, and accompanied by the howling of a pack of wolves, I voided copiously, a sound no doubt appreciated by my other travelling companions on the other side of their own wafer-thin walls.

Relieved, I turned to retrace my steps but froze in terror. Dark though it was, I made out a dozen even darker shapes creeping silently towards me. Already the nearest was between me and the door to the ger.

It was a good job I'd just emptied my bladder.

Turning and running wasn't an option as they'd be on me in an instant. I could try to get to another ger but finding the door quickly in the dark would be a problem.

So, like countless small, frightened creatures since the dawn of time, I stood as still as I could and hoped the bad things would go away.

This didn't work and almost immediately they were upon me. Fur brushed across the back of my hand. I pressed my back against the ger and braced myself for the first bite.

These were damned big wolves, almost up to my chest, with a pace that was slow and deliberate.

And they just kept coming out of the dark. There must have been forty or more, moving in a wave across the campsite. Were they here to eat us all?

Belatedly, I realised they weren't coming at me but rather across me, their furry backs jostling me and filling my nose with a musty, sweaty animal smell.

Then one of them snorted and I realised these weren't wolves at all. It was a herd of black yaks, on some nocturnal migration too compelling to make them deviate from their course. This had taken them right through an inconveniently placed campsite.

Suddenly I realised I hadn't breathed for a minute or more, and I blew out a lungful of carbon dioxide noisily. This startled the beasts. The nearest ones snorted and stepped away to avoid me.

I took my growling, empty stomach back to my bed, to the cold and to the sound of the wind off the steppe and reflected that Mongolia would not rank high on the list of countries I might ever return to.

~~~

We got back on the train after another pothole gauntlet, our vertebrae like castanets.

Again, the thirty or so carriages made their sinuous way around low hills as the sparsely grassed steppe began to lose its fight with the sands of the Gobi Desert, all eight hundred thousand square kilometres of it.

Beside the track was hundreds of kilometres of fence, its wire catching the tattered litter blown across the desert from far distant cities and towns. It looked like scrappy bunting for a procession that had never turned up.

The desert was, if anything, even emptier than the Mongolian steppe but occasionally we could see mining lorries, their position given away by clouds of dust. Wild Bactrian camels, with their large, distinctive double humps began to make an appearance.

That evening another traumatic urinary experience befell the ladies of the tour. Though Russia and Mongolia at least share a common railway gauge, China has a different one.

To an ingenue like me, the obvious solution would be to change trains at the border but for some reason this is not the case. Instead, the far noisier, time consuming and
~~~

presumably hugely expensive process of changing the bogies on the trains is resorted to.

Our long train pulled into a huge shed. The lifting apparatus could only handle raising a couple of carriages at a time, so for eight hours we were shunted back and forth, carriages undocked then raised to slide out the Russian bogies and slide in the Chinese ones. The two carriages were then lowered and pulled forward to form a new train, while the back of the train was shunted forward for the next two to be uncoupled and lifted.

The shaking and banging went on all night and, of course, the Gestapo train attendant had locked down the toilets yet again lest they discharge over the lifting gear.

When you're awake you generate more urine than when you're asleep. And, as we couldn't sleep because of the pandemonium, an awful lot of urine was being generated. Again, men were refilling empty water bottles while the women moaned and twisted in their bunks. When the changeover had finished and the doors were unlocked, they rampaged across the platform to the nearest toilet.

Finally, as we pulled out of the station, long after we'd arrived at the border, the toilet door on the carriage was unlocked. Too little too late.

Travelling through China was a revelation. This was in 2013 so things may be very different now. China started out as the empty Gobi Desert but as we moved south-east down through what was then the most populous country on earth, the first little habitations began to appear by the tracks. They seemed to be made of adobe, some perfectly hemispheric in shape, others more like beehives. The few inhabitants we saw as we rattled by had broad Mongolian features with skin browned by the sun.

Over the six hundred kilometres to Beijing, things slowly changed. Mud-brick houses gave way to more solid looking brick structures that nevertheless looked just as filthy. Litter was everywhere, not just crucified against the railway fence but now covering the muddy unmade ground between buildings, eddied into piles at which stray dogs rooted.

Brick then turned to grey concrete, the buildings rising up out of the earth, from single storeys up to thirty. From little villages you might miss if you blinked, to vast dispiriting conurbations it took half an hour for us to roll through.

Everything looked grubby and dingy. Each little shop with its cracked signs and dust-caked windows seemed transitory, as though designed for a brief, sordid existence.

Camels had soon had their day and now we saw donkeys dragging heavily laden carts behind them.

It took a while to notice another unusual feature. At first, I put them all down as land markers, but soon I realised these were graves and they were everywhere. Some looked like dolls' houses, some had the usual tombstones, some looked like the little cupped seats you'd ride on in a Wurlitzer or dodgem car with a raised section at the back and rounded sides.

These were usually on little rises, perhaps only a metre above the flat farmland. And they were so plentiful; the second most populous country on earth is bound to produce an awful lot of dead.

The Chinese are into ancestor worship and like to keep them close.

The further south we penetrated the rockier and more uneven the ground became and soon rail bridges were needed to span steep valleys and chasms. The railway began to follow the longer valleys, the tracks high up on the mountainsides to give wonderful views as we paralleled the snaking rivers below.

Cute little pagodas could be seen on hilltops as we slalomed our way for the last hundred kilometres into Beijing.

Each visit to China is like a snapshot giving a restricted view of a maelstrom of change. Come back in a couple of years and it won't look the same at all.

I wasn't surprised by the poverty and filth of China. I'd seen something similar in the Northern Territories when I'd been in Hong Kong in the early 1990s. The British were still running the place then, though corruptly and still denying the HK people democracy as they had been for the previous hundred years.

Then, just before yielding HK back to China, they beneficently bestowed it. The British were more than happy to let democracy tangle the feet of Chinese authoritarianism, though they hadn't tolerated it for their own subjects in the far-flung and dying British Empire.

However, even in 2013, as the train rolled into Beijing, I realised that other changes were afoot, although it would take another visit years later to show me just how monumental these would be.

In 2013, Beijing still had a run-down sort of quaintness. Many people still lived in the old-style hutongs, acres of tiled roof single-storey buildings.

Communal latrines every fifty metres serviced the needs of their inhabitants. There were no sewers so, once a week, a truck would arrive along with a biblical cloud of flies to empty the holes under the latrines. On sweltering hot summers days, the smell was poisonous.

Bicycle rickshaws took us through narrow streets where we could peer through open doors showing developing world interiors of cracked flagstones, peeling plaster and cats' cradles of electrical wiring.

The streets were lined with piles of old furniture, broken TVs and bird cages. Small flat-bed trucks navigated these narrow streets, the backs piled high with junk, though whether taking it out or bringing more in wasn't clear.

Outside the hutongs, life in Beijing wasn't as I'd expected. I'd seen endless items on TV showing rivers of bicycles cascading through intersections with hardly a car in sight. There were still bicycles but now they were challenged for supremacy by cars and buses.

We only had a few days in Beijing and it went by in a blur. The Great Wall, Tiananmen Square, the Forbidden Palace—whatever.

I figured one day I'd come back and do it properly.

And, a few years later I did.

I was in for one hell of a shock.

# *Visiting China with a Sniffy First World Attitude*

## Beijing, China, 2017

Culture shock may be a psychological rather than a physical danger but it can still be rough. At the very least it changes your view of the world forever.

If you're wanting to mainline culture shock then China is your man. In this chapter we'll explore just some of the ways the country messes with your head.

## The Fuck-you Airport

When I returned to China in 2017 for a tour around the country, I arrived with lazy First World assumptions. I was coming from the UK, which is part of the so-called developed world while China was a developing world nation. The Chinese were struggling out of crippling poverty, the result of the dead hand of socialism strangling the economic life out of the country for seventy years. Only now were those poor damned Chinese emerging blinking into the light.

At least that's what I thought.

I first began to sense something was amiss when the plane reached the outskirts of Beijing. Below were featureless grey high-rise blocks and they just kept on coming, kilometre after kilometre. Nowadays they surround the city like an endless thicket of tombstones.

The hutongs in which ninety-five per cent of the inhabitants had lived, and for which Beijing had been so famous, were disappearing fast.

In the vast burgeoning prosperity since Deng Xiaoping finally took that dead hand of socialism off the free market in the 1980s, the hutongs had been one of the first targets.

Anyone flying into Beijing can work out where all the old hutong inhabitants had gone, namely those hundreds of square kilometres of tower blocks.

As for the old sewerless hutongs, so many have been bulldozed to make roads and shops and office blocks that a preservation movement has sprung up to keep a few for old times' sake.

The next undercutting of my faulty world view came when we landed at Terminal 3 of the Capital airport. At a million square metres it was the biggest I'd ever seen, though Dubai's Terminal 3 has since surpassed it.

That's recently changed yet again as the biggest single structure airport in the world is the new Daxing airport in Beijing (the old Capital airport is still operational).

The Daxing terminal is like a giant starfish splattered down onto the flat Hebei plain. Inside it is disturbingly organic, as though colossal white mushrooms have sprouted, their broad caps spreading out and melding to form a roof. It's white and bright and looks like something heaven would aspire to.

By 2025 it was expected (pre-covid) that it would be handling 100 million passengers a year and be the busiest airport in the world.

Even the older Capital airport seems designed to make foreigners feel unworthy. In 2017 it was like arriving at Nuremberg when Hitler was master, or Rome at its height of empire. The whole thing is set up to intimidate foreigners, to drive home their inferior status in this new world.

It is, in other words, a fuck-you airport.

The next hint that I had things all wrong was the trains. On this trip we zoomed for thousands of miles through the countryside on high-speed rail lines. HSR is becoming ubiquitous in China. At one point we pulled into a station at a regional capital that only served HSR trains (another couple of stations served conventional rail). The number of different HSR lines leading into the station was mind-blowing and the station itself was the biggest rail station I've ever seen.

China opened its first high-speed rail line in 2008 yet by 2020 it had over 30,000 kilometres of line, accounting for two-thirds of the entire world's HSR. This is expected to double in the next fifteen years.

Meanwhile in the UK we have yet to open our first purely internal HSR. It's not due until 2026. We do have a hundred-kilometre stretch from London to the Channel Tunnel to link in with the international Eurostar service. This was opened at about the same time as China's first HSR link. We haven't built another centimetre since while they've built 30,000 kilometres.

The usual HSR trains in China do a mere 350 kph (compared with 210 kph on main lines in the UK). There is one exception, however. Coming in by bus from Shanghai airport at night I was startled by what looked like a line of tracer bullets that zipped by the window. These were the lights of the fastest train on earth and it runs by magnetic levitation. Rather than metal rails the 'track' just looks like a wood and concrete plinth. The Maglev can reach a maximum speed of 431 kph. We were lucky enough to catch it back to the airport and it was a real thrill to blast through a crowded city at ground level almost at airplane speeds.

And that Maglev is already old hat. The next version will do 600 kph.

The HSR gap between China and the 'developed' world is bad enough but it's mirrored by air travel.

With a fifty-fold increase in air travel since 1985, the Chinese have built around one hundred new airports in that time. In the UK the only significant new airport development is the third runway at Heathrow and even that hadn't been completed at the time of writing.

The counter-argument is that China was desperately under-served by rail and air and road for a population that size. That's true, but the point is that in barely a human generation it hasn't simply gone from a dearth but has leap-frogged right over the West.

China changes more in a week than the West does in a year. China is looking back at us in the rear-view mirror as it accelerates away just like its Maglev train.

It's not just in existing technology and infrastructure that we in the West are dead men walking. China is pouring vast resources into robotics and AI, space travel and genetic research. One example is 5G where they are already two years ahead of us.

These advancements are evident in everyday life in Chinese cities. Even in 2017, cash was becoming a rarity in the big cities in China, with even vending machines taking payment from customers' phones. The West has caught up now but mainly because of the covid pandemic which made handling cash much less attractive (it had never been very attractive but we somehow ignored the health issues of touching stuff that had been in the pocket of scores of other people along with their bacteria and snotty handkerchiefs).

None of these massive advances by China is surprising, at least with the benefit of hindsight. Add the population of the European Union and the USA together, then double the result and you get, more or less, the population of China.

That means they have nearly five times as many really smart people than in the US alone. Where before they had to steal or buy technology developed elsewhere, now they're the ones doing the developing.

And nowadays Chinese are far better educated and far healthier and far richer than they were before. Indeed their per capita income has quadrupled in the past thirty-five years. Meanwhile their GDP increased thirty-fold (compared with around five-fold in the UK).

In less than a single human generation over 750 million Chinese have been lifted out of absolute poverty, and not just by a small margin. Never in the history of mankind has such an improvement been made to so many people in such a short time.

China is unstoppable, a rampaging bulldozer. This is why we in the West are roadkill but we just haven't realised it yet.

Perhaps to stop ourselves wilting at just how disturbing the rise of the totalitarian Chinese state is, in the West we cling to the notion that increasing wealth will bring a desire for liberal democracy in China.

We're in denial.

Rather naively I brought up this very point to a Chinese woman called Ling I met in Beijing. She pointed out that fifty years before, during a famine caused by the incompetence of Mao and his government, her mother could only survive by eating grass and the bark from trees. Ling contrasted this with the biggest worry her own daughter had nowadays: which model of iPhone to buy.

The hard truth is that the Chinese system, totalitarianism in conjunction with a more or less free market, is a winning combination. What they lose in terms of human rights, they gain in terms of wealth and extremely effective government.

After all, resisting a compulsory purchase order in the UK to stop a runway or HSR track being laid down is easy.

You can fight it in law, appeal if you lose, then take it to a higher court if you lose again, then to even higher courts. You can mobilise public opinion, find a previously unheard-of animal whose habitat may be damaged by the development, get politicians on board who are trying to make a name for themselves, and so on.

In China if the government want to compulsorily purchase your land, then they purchase your land. End of story.

The overwhelming size of China and the sheer effectiveness of its political system are going to make China the centre of the world. Some would say it actually has been for several years already.

Those of us in free-thinking Western democracies may not like any of this but that isn't going to amount to a hill of beans.

Many in the West do not understand just how far behind the Chinese we have fallen in terms of development. In the last couple of years our newspapers and TV news are starting to wise up, but they still have a long way to go. The penny will only finally drop when we understand just how relatively poor we have become. Rather than liberalism triumphing in a prosperous China, how long will our liberal values last in the face of us being demoted to developing world status?

I was as oblivious as anyone else to this and so, after my previous trips to China, I went there in 2017 with the patronising attitude that someone from the First World can't help having when they visit a developing country.

However, this time when I returned home, I did so as a Second World citizen returning to a Second World country.

## Death

Eating grass and bark leads us nicely into another zap of Chinese culture shock.

Why was it necessary to resort to such extreme measures to survive?

The reason is, of course, to avoid death. And death is something the Chinese know a great deal about. So much so that it's profoundly disturbing to Western eyes. Writing about it like this is my way of trying to process the horror.

My family and I went on a number of trips within China and we often found local guides who spoke English. I began to notice that these guides couldn't be bothered to mention anything if the death toll involved less than half a million people.

For example, the guides might casually mention how a million people had died building the Great Wall, or how 750,000 were executed after building the First Emperor's crypt, or how 850,000 died in an earthquake.

These historical figures are grotesque but they pale into insignificance compared to what has happened in China over the last eighty years. Some estimates put the number of Chinese killed during the Japanese occupation at fifteen million.

The disastrous agricultural policies of Mao led to the deaths of something like twenty million in the ensuing famine. Our tour guides seemed proud to point out that the present-day Communist party is magnanimous enough to admit this had been a 'bit of a mistake'.

The Cultural Revolution saw the often-gruesome murders of ten million or so middle-class people (or at least slightly better off peasants) and intellectuals. The Communist Party now has the good grace to admit this was 'unfortunate'.

You'd imagine such an eye-watering death toll within living memory would crush the spirit of a country but the

Chinese are nothing if not resilient and they've come bouncing back with a vengeance.

Coupled with the extreme durability of its people, the Chinese government has the power, the will and the money to effect rapid change.

China is the greatest threat to our liberal world view there has ever been. Developing countries around the world used to aspire to become like Western democracies. Nowadays they aspire to be anywhere near as effective as China.

China is like a black hole, warping the space around it and funnelling everything down into its gaping maw.

You're probably thinking I've gone over the top and I hope you're right.

Just don't say I didn't warn you!

### An unhealthy predilection (mine, not China's)

As well as dishing out so much death themselves, some communist leaders have tried to beat it, in a way.

My commie leader death fetish began over fifty years ago in Moscow when I saw Lenin's pickled corpse.

Early evening in Red Square, the psychedelic patterned onion domes of St. Basil's cathedral, the strains of the balalaika wafting through the balmy air, my first girlfriend on my arm, we stood queuing to see a corpse.

Can I show a girl a good time or what?

This was back in the late sixties and I was on a rather unusual school trip which had somehow been organised while the Cold War was at its most vicious.

I'd been brought up in the West where we were constantly being told how awful things were in Russia. Crude and blatant Western propaganda this may have seemed but, in the event, it turned out to be the unvarnished truth.

Moscow around the Kremlin was a place of wide-open streets but no cars. The food was dreadful. Even worse, the grey and down-beaten people had to queue for hours to buy it. Shortages of even the most basic foods were a daily fact of life.

Russians may not have liked us but they really liked our money and whatever we owned. People would sidle up to us in the street trying to sell us anything provided we bought it in foreign currency. They'd also offer vast amounts of worthless roubles to buy the tee-shirts off our backs.

The national need for foreign currency was so all-consuming that our party of wild school kids was allowed to jump the queue to see Lenin's remains.

And what a queue it was. Poor peasants had made the pilgrimage from many thousands of miles away in this most massive of countries. What must they have thought, in this queue-culture society where you had to stand in line for hours to get a loaf of bread, to see a bunch of mouthy Essex kids being ushered in ahead of them?

So much for the egalitarianism of communism. Lenin should have been turning in his grave, except he didn't have one.

Instead, he lies in a mausoleum. This is a squat red granite, marble and porphyry pyramid just outside the imposing and similarly red walls of the sprawling Kremlin.

For many years Stalin's body lay next to Lenin's. When Stalin fell out of favour in 1961 his corpse was smuggled away and entombed elsewhere.

Seeing Lenin's corpse is pure militaristic theatre and it worked its magic on me. I'd never seen a body before (although, bearing in mind that Lenin has had a hundred times as much restorative work done on him as all the Kardashians combined, one wonders if there's anything of the old Lenin left). The thought of seeing my first corpse was giving me the wobbles. The statue-still soldiers with guns lining every corridor weren't helping.

The Russians shuffling in were silent and one sensed the weight of their awe.

I was pretty stressed out by the time we were ushered into his/its presence. Lenin lies in a glass box like Sleeping Beauty. And he looks like a waxwork (all pickled commie leaders do). He looked as buffed up and as perfect as sixties make-up and lighting would allow.

I may have been a little frightened but I couldn't deny the morbid thrill.

'Mmmm,' I thought at the time, 'I've got to get me more of this.' Thus began the hobby of a lifetime.

Sadly, travel in those days was very expensive so many years passed before I managed to bag Ho Chi Minh's vinegared cadaver in Hanoi.

Same sort of scene, same pack-drill, except the corpse and the surrounding soldiers were more obviously Asiatic. The queuing Vietnamese were also quite a bit noisier than the Russians.

So, I'd bagged two out of three, but the Big One had still escaped me. When it comes to mass killers, nobody can beat Mao Tse Tung who is thought to have seen off as many as fifty million people either directly via state-sponsored murder, or indirectly through his incompetence.

Now that's what I call a communist leader!

My first chance presented itself when I came whistling into Beijing on the Trans Mongolian Express. My itinerary was so condensed I had either the chance to see the Forbidden City or to queue for a few hours to see Mao. I may have a predilection for these corpses, but it's not an obsession, so I went to see the Forbidden City, which was gob-smacking in its extent. It also showed how China was once the greatest country in the world, just as it is becoming again.

Not for nothing do the Chinese call China *Chung Kuo*, which means Middle Kingdom, as it is midway between Earth and Heaven.

So, in 2017 here I was back again in Beijing and now I had more time available. Mao lies in a building on Tiananmen Square and I headed there early to try to beat the long queue.

Except there wasn't one. Mao's mausoleum was closed as Mao was being renovated (perhaps something had dropped off).

I was bitterly disappointed, of course, but I took some comfort because there was a chance it was all a sham anyway. The Mao that people see is not the real Mao, according to Li Zhi Shui, Mao's personal physician.

After being purged for supposed neglect in Mao's death, although he claimed the charges were fabricated, Li eventually escaped to Australia and wrote the book *Private Life of Mao Zedong*. The real Mao is supposedly in bits in the basement. All these bits are in jars, preserved to prove to potential investigators that his death involved no foul play. According to Li, the Mao that people see today is a wax dummy bought from London's Madame Tussaud's.

Dr Li later admitted he had had no idea how to embalm someone and had asked Hanoi for help because of their experience pickling Ho Chi Minh. Despite this advice, Li reckoned he put in way too much formaldehyde and Mao's ear and cheek fell off after his head swelled up 'like a football'.

Hence the need for a trip to Britain to get the wax version.

Still, I would have liked to see him/it. That's the thing about travel. It provides so many wonderful experiences but it also produces equally big disappointments. You pays your money, you takes your chances.

A bit like life, really.

So, strike one for something I'd wanted to do on this trip to China, but I had another lifelong itch I wanted to scratch.

## In Search of JG Ballard's Shanghai

JG Ballard was a dystopian science fiction author known for conjuring surreal but detailed apocalyptic visions. His writings were full of crashed planes and drowned worlds. Even so, there is a coldness to Ballard's prose, a sense of detachment from these nightmare worlds into which his protagonists are hurled.

I've found his writing both weird and clinical to the point where I sensed a lurking pathology. It wasn't until I read his semi-autobiographical novel *Empire of the Sun* that I realised where this all came from.

Ballard's view of the world, but also of Shanghai in particular, was coloured by his being imprisoned there by the Japanese when he was a boy in the Second World War.

He had been brought up in the Concessions, international enclaves full of the mansions where the British and French lived. These mansions were commandeered by the Japanese and turned into brothels and gambling dens.

The displaced foreigners were interned in concentration camps and Ballard spent two years in one of these. The atrocities he saw in these camps, and his unexpected discovery of a crashed Japanese Zero fighter half submerged in a paddy field, finds expression in the images of his adult writing.

The seminal life lesson he learned from his experience, reflected so often in his work, is that civilisation is but a patina. He had led an affluent life and yet this had been ripped away almost in an instant. In his own words: "I don't think you can go through the experience of war without one's perceptions of the world being forever changed. The reassuring stage set that everyday reality in the suburban west presents to us is torn down; you see the ragged scaffolding, and then you see the truth beyond that, and it can be a frightening experience."

Shanghai is a malign presence throughout *Empire of the Sun* and indeed the last three words of the book are '...this terrible city'.

Even before Ballard's time there, Shanghai had an awful reputation. In the 1900s it was said to have more prostitutes than any other city on earth. They serviced sailors bringing opium from India, usually on British merchant ships with British government approval.

Back in the 1850s when the Chinese rebelled against this trade and the resulting drug enslavement of their fellow countrymen, the British had sent in gunboats to teach them a jolly good lesson.

We Brits were such charmers in those days. Yet sometimes nowadays when we go abroad, we can't understand why not everyone likes us.

Shanghai was drowning in vice. For a hundred years it had been the centre of the Chinese opium trade and for the smuggling of women from provinces all over China to service its voracious needs.

What made it all worse were the colonial powers who ran the place. The British and the French had entered into a pact with the Devil himself. The colonials were at a loss to deal with a culture they barely understood so they acted through a ready-made army, the hundred thousand or so members of secret societies such as the Green Gang. These gangsters ensured the Chinese didn't rebel and in exchange the colonial powers let them get on with their brothels, gambling, drug and women trafficking.

The Green Gang ran nearly a thousand opium dens in the city. The Gang had started out as a Buddhist sect about five hundred years before. At that time, Shanghai was a modest sea port but it blossomed to become a way point for grain as well as an entry for foreign opium.

Such was the need for crewmen in a thriving port whose business was expanding like the most malicious of cancers, the word *Shanghaied* came to mean drugging and kidnapping men to crew the ships.

This historical background and Ballard's chilling work had always intrigued me and so I was keen to visit this dark city that made him the writer he was.

But, of course, things had changed. Shanghai is now the biggest city in China (twenty-five million, compared to Beijing's twenty-three million).

The second disappointment was that I never saw a single body drift by on the Yangtze, though in Ballard's time this had been a commonplace.

There wasn't even a hint of malnutrition or even abject poverty. In fact, it looked exactly the opposite.

The view of the financial district of Lujiazui across the Huangpu River from the Bund, is a staple in news items of China, with towering skyscrapers painted in shimmering electronic motifs. On the sides of these futuristic buildings waterfalls cascade, strings of Chinese characters sinuously climb the towers and undulate across the spheres. It's all breathtaking, though already this digital choreography is becoming almost standard across skyscrapers in the bigger Chinese cities.

So that's all good, right: no more poverty, no more corpses on the Yangtze, no Green Gang, no Japanese massacres?

Yes, except that the city is transforming itself into the sort of shallow, bling-heavy consumer paradise that Ballard spent the rest of his career satirising and condemning.

I reckon Ballard would be turning in his grave, if only he could work out which way to revolve.

## A Cruise up the Yangtze 'with Chinese characteristics'

We joined the cruise ship in Chongquing, a town hemmed in by tree-covered hills. The town itself crowds in on the river with densely packed black and yellow office and apartment blocks. These shimmer into electronic life at night.

They were matched by little party boats blooming with psychedelic light shows and tinny music as they drifted along the river, the Chinese on board drinking heavily and having a hell of a time.

Our large river-going cruise ship certainly looked the part. Just like a sea-going cruise ship but scaled down, though still much larger than any you'd see on the Rhine or the Nile.

However, it was run by the Chinese and therefore suffered from a surfeit of Chinese characteristics.

The phrase 'socialism with Chinese characteristics' is an interesting one and is used to describe Deng Xiaoping's political changes to China in the 1980s. Essentially, Deng freed the markets, allowing outright capitalism (and as a result lifting the aforementioned 750 million people out of absolute poverty) while still committing itself to communism and, of course, maintaining the communist party's absolute grip on power.

In other words, 'socialism with Chinese characteristics' means a totalitarian state with unchained capitalism, which in my untutored view means not socialism at all. So, the phrase 'with Chinese characteristics' is like a negation of whatever went before. Similar to the use of the word 'not' as in: 'I believe in every word he says, not.'

Let's look at some cruise-related Chinese characteristics. For example, every morning at 7 a.m. the loudspeaker in the cabin blared that breakfast was being served and we'd better hurry as the restaurant closed at 8 a.m.

Try doing that on a Western cruise ship and the captain would become the first seamen in centuries to be keel-hauled.

There were only a handful of Westerners amongst the four hundred or so passengers. The first day we heard this announcement, we sauntered down for a leisurely breakfast only to find the restaurant picked clean.

The Chinese by comparison had been queuing long before seven for the restaurant to open. When it did, they swept in like locusts, stripping the place, then sweeping back out.

After breakfast more Chinese characteristics manifested. Getting out on deck is an important part of cruising (if it wasn't then why not just take a bus or a plane from one destination to another?). And so, the Westerners would stroll around the deck, admiring the fabulous views and breathing in the fresh river air.

The Chinese in general took a different view and, once they had eaten, they retreated to their cabins not to be seen again until the next meal or the next shore visit.

The contrariness didn't end there. The floors in the boat were beautifully and lushly carpeted. Nevertheless, the authorities felt it necessary to put up warning signs telling the Chinese not to spit on this carpet.

These didn't always work.

I tried to put all of this out of my mind as the cruise through the Three Gorges revealed the most magnificent scenery I've ever seen from a ship. In the spring, snow melt from the Himalayas swells the river and scours the lower mountainside, so that in summer the waters retreat, leaving a ten-metre belt of white rock between the river and the tree-line.

Pagodas and little forts top the steep hillsides and it all looks so picturesque.

The Three Gorges dam isn't quite as spectacular to look at as the Aswan dam—which is essentially just a very long, smooth and imposing barrier—while the Three Gorges is broken up by locks for letting big ships through.

That said, in some ways it is much more impressive. It has the largest capacity of any power station in the world and it reduces the risk of catastrophic flooding, which has always bedevilled the Yangtze. It has also made the river navigable, previously possible only in some places and at some times.

However, this improvement in navigation came at the price of raising the water level by over ninety metres. Over a thousand archaeological sites were flooded and there were huge changes to the river's eco-system. Some 1.3 million people were displaced.

Again, this testifies to the power and effectiveness of the Chinese state. Compare this with the tens of thousands who might be far less affected by a third runway at Heathrow. Relatively small in number they have held up the project for over thirty years.

Those 1.3 million river dwellers could object all they wanted; the dam was still going ahead.

This is why China is accelerating but the UK is languishing. I'm certainly not saying it's good displacing 1.3 million people. I'm just pointing out how effective the Chinese system is in achieving its ends.

One downside is that the Three Gorges Dam is a huge security liability. Blowing up the dam would not only drown millions as the wall of water surged down the many hundreds of miles of river valley, but it would slash the country's electricity generating capacity.

This is something the Taiwanese military have considered as retaliation if China ever used force to reclaim what it considers to be its recalcitrant child.

Real trouble is brewing there, as we'll see later.

Meanwhile our trip next took us to some of the most famous artefacts in the world.

## The First Emperor and Indescribable Horror

The Terracotta Army is an amazing sight but it's built upon terrible barbarity and so, of course, we had to see it.

Some 8000 life-size, individually crafted warriors stand ready and marshalled in three vast pits. These pits were dug over two thousand years ago in Mount Li, itself a source of gold and jade. It can be found outside the large city of Xi'an in Shaanxi.

The First Emperor of China had a vast mausoleum built there and this included the Terracotta Army. The complex was built by 750,000 people and, when it was finished, the emperor had them all put to death and buried with him.

Not for him the hassle of returning all those P45s.

As well as the statues of soldiers there are also more than a hundred chariots and six hundred horses.

The tomb of the emperor has not itself been breached. Inside the mausoleum legend has it there is a huge model of China with a hundred channels of flowing mercury to represent its rivers.

There may even be some truth in this: high levels of mercury have been found from probes inserted into the tomb.

So perhaps the tomb does contain a model of China with cities and towers and palaces for the emperor to rule after death. There are supposed to be jewels in the ceiling of the tomb to represent stars.

Why haven't the Chinese authorities opened the tomb to find out if this is all true? The official story is that when they'd opened other 3000-years-old tombs, everything crumbled to dust. They say they're waiting for the technology to do it safely.

Some caution may indeed be necessary. Crossbows are said to have been rigged to shoot anyone trying to break in. Who knows what other fiendish tricks the emperor may have up his sleeve to protect his place of rest.

His name was Qin and he was the first unifier of China. As well as his tomb he is famous for constructing the precursor of the Great Wall of China. Hundreds of thousands, perhaps even a million men died in its construction.

His people originally disdained him as his mother, a dancing girl of one rich man, had become instead a prince's. It was rumoured that she had been made pregnant by the previous owner, a merchant, rather than the prince. In other words, he was considered both illegitimate and devoid of royal blood.

He was brought up in a bizarre and brutal royal world. Musicians would sometimes use lead-weighted lutes as weapons in attempted assassinations. Wiping out your enemy's families to the third degree (first cousins, great grandparents and great grandchildren) was commonplace.

Assassination attempts against Qin himself included a strongman hurling a 100 kg metal cone down onto his procession while he was travelling through mountains. The wrong carriage was destroyed and the king survived.

No academic, Qin burned many books and buried alive the scholars who kept them.

As he grew older, Qin began to fear death and sent hundreds of men and women out into the world to find the elixir of life. None ever returned, though probably from fear of being executed for their failure.

He had tunnels and passageways carved between his palaces so he could travel without being seen by evil spirits who might kill him.

One terrible portent literally fell from the sky in the form of a meteor, landing near the Yellow River. Some wag had inscribed on it *The First Emperor will die and his land will be divided.* Qin had the meteor smashed to pieces and everyone in the vicinity executed.

This didn't help, though, and within a year he was dead from poisoning, perhaps self-administered as mercury was used in some elixirs.

Qin took horror with him even in death. Fearful that news of Qin's death would cause the collapse of the empire, his prime minister kept it secret as he and the king's entourage made the two-month journey back to the then capital city of Xianyang. It was summertime and soon the emperor was stinking badly so the prime minister had carts containing rotting fish placed ahead of and behind the King's carriage.

Perhaps an appropriate way to go for the man.

Before we leave China, we've got to talk about one more bit of unsettling culture shock.

## HP Lovecraft Food

Food is often a reliable way of inducing culture shock, though usually you have to get into the backwoods to experience the truly bizarre. In China, you can find it in the major cities, although now it is hidden away in crowded little markets on side streets. These lead off the main trading streets rammed with high-end Prada-selling stores and Western fast-food joints.

Street food in Beijing includes boiled snakes (head and skin intact) and deep-fried tarantula. The Chinese also have a predilection for taking little birds, smashing them flat, then barbecuing them

You can also find racks of tiny scorpions impaled on skewers and eaten like kebabs. Before they're eaten, they wiggle for ages in the dance of death.

Dogs are also eaten in China, typically in specialist restaurants. They're usually roasted whole so when they're served, they still look exactly like dogs except without hair.

For Westerners, roast dog makes an unforgettable sight, no matter how hard they try.

~~~

So, all in all, China is challenging to the Western eye. If you're oblivious to its history you can have an interesting time as a tourist. However, scratch the surface just a little bit, and its horror all the way down.

Next, we'll visit a country which is just as weird but an order of magnitude less scary.
~~~

## *Seeking out Snakes, Bears and Intelligent Toilets*

Japan 2019

I was due to hike an old Shinto pilgrimage trail but, as with any Westerner arriving in Japan, there was first the problem of culture shock. We'll go through a few of the more surprising aspects before boots actually hit trail.

Again, this is what you shouldn't do if you want to avoid trouble.

### Pick a fight with an intelligent toilet

Japan is a dual personality country and it can flash from one to the other in an instant.

You get off the plane and even the immigration officials welcome you with smiles and bows. Your cab driver wears a peaked cap and a dinky pair of spotless white gloves. The receptionist at your hotel is immaculately dressed and earnestly helpful. Your room will be small but surgically clean.

And thus, you are charmed. You feel safe in a country where everyone takes pains to be scrupulously polite and efficient.

Then you try to use the toilet and the sheer otherness of Japan is thrust right in your face or, if you're unlucky, up your bottom.

Every time I come to Japan, I struggle with that most implacable of foes: the intelligent toilet. Dulled by jet lag and in need of release, I find yourself staring at a device that has more controls than an upmarket hi-fi. The last one I used had eighteen knobs and buttons.

There are instructions but these are usually on the underside of the seat lid and, of course, they're in Japanese. Some are augmented by little drawings but these alarm more than help because several definitely show things going *up* the bottom.

The first time I came across one of these I was very keen to find the control that commanded one of the more basic functions like... oh, I don't know... like flushing away the ordure accumulated by international travel across ten time zones. So, I began pressing buttons at random, though being careful to avoid the ones with 'up the bottom' drawings.

Tragically, my fumblings awoke the toilet's malevolent slumbering intelligence and it took against me from that point on. For the rest of my time in Japan it would spitefully raise the temperature of the seat to scalding hot whenever I sat down. The babbling brook sound it produced (both to promote and disguise micturition) was poor compensation.

I had considered the Intelligent Toilet a purely Japanese artefact so I was blindsided when I found one in my hotel room on a recent trip to the Lake District.

The intelligent toilet is taking over the world and it's coming for you next.

And don't get me started on the subject of toilet slippers

The Japanese have a fetish for slippers. When you enter a Japanese house, inn or temple, or even some restaurants and museums, you've got to take your shoes off first.

And make sure you do because this is something that the otherwise relentlessly polite Japanese get very annoyed about if you don't.

Once you've taken off your shoes you have to put on yellow or white house slippers. That's all manageable, so far. However, before you've gone more than a few feet you come across a tatami mat and you have to take these slippers off.

It doesn't seem to matter that your socks or bare feet may be dripping with sweat after eight hours of walking. It's perfectly fine to walk on their expensive and carefully woven tatami mats with your smelly feet, but it's absolutely forbidden to do so in their perfectly clean house slippers.

Also, judging by Japanese porn, perspiration-slicked bodies toiling away on these mats is pretty much *de rigeur.* So, pressing a sweaty bottom against them is okay, but the clean sole of a slipper is beyond the pale.

Go figure.

You have to wonder why the Japanese need slippers at all as the streets are spotlessly clean so you're never going to drag in dog shit on the soles of your trainers anyway.

Okay, so it's all a bit of a foible but one you're willing to forgive as the Japanese are so nice.

Unfortunately, it doesn't stop there because when you come to a bathroom, you have to step out of your house slippers and into special blue toilet slippers.

*What the hell is it with these damned slippers*, you're thinking but soon, being in a bog, your mind strays to other topics.

And that's why it's oh-so easy, once you've finished your business, to step out of the bathroom and forget you've still wearing the toilet slippers.

Better to step uncaring into a minefield.

That you've entered a world of pain becomes evident when your Japanese hosts react like you've raped their chihuahua. As soon as they've thrown you out into the street, they'll phone the authorities who will immediately shut down all their ports and airports. Then, at their leisure, they will hunt you down like the wild animal that you are.

The whole slipper bestiary is part of their culture and it sounds churlish not to put up with it. However, if you're touring around and you have to lace and unlace your hiking boots a dozen times a day, the whole thing gets old pretty fast.

Also, when you've stumbled to the bog in the dark and tripped over their silly toilet slippers for the umpteenth time, you find your patience beginning to wear thin.

There's another problem. I believe things are beginning to change, but the Japanese have long made a virtue out of not having slippers that will fit your foot size. Something to do with everyone being equal. So, whether you're a bull-throwing sumo wrestler, or a fawn-like ballerina, you have to make do with the same size slipper.

Thus, the sumo is reduced to mincing around while the ballerina has to wallop about in clown shoes. Nobody looks comfortable, every brow is furrowed. Everyone moves in short flat-footed strides. Everyone has to clench their toes, like a monkey clinging to a branch.

Walking like this is the antithesis of elegance.

And God help you going up the stairs. If you don't slip and break your neck, you'll inevitably leave at least one slipper a few steps behind. On the other hand, if you're going down the stairs, a slipper will inevitably fly off and take someone's eye out.

There are times when you're travelling through Japan that you just want to tear out your hair and shout *Why*?

But...

Just when alienation threatens to overwhelm you, you'll suddenly be won over by the charm of the culture.

For example, I once came across a shrine in a village out towards Mount Fuji. Japanese postal workers had donated money to build this shrine and dedicated it to relieving the spirits of the 1.8 million pieces of mail which, because of poor handwriting or incorrect addresses, are undeliverable every year in Japan. The shrine itself is framed by the snow-capped peak of Mount Fuji, in a tiny graveyard full of trees heavy with white and pink and red cherry blossom.

One's heart can't help but melt a little.

Back in the UK I mentioned this to Jim, a friend who works in the Post Office in Glasgow, and asked if he and his colleagues would consider doing something similar here.

"Fuck off!" he said and went back to his pint.

Then again...

This dichotomy between the disturbingly weird, and the charmingly weird, form the two-headed Janus-like aspect of Japanese society. This always keeps you off balance.

Akihabara is a district of Tokyo dedicated to geek culture. My wife needed a replacement charger for a phone which had originally been brought out to celebrate the rise of the dinosaurs. I held out little hope that such a charger would be found anywhere except in some fossil layer.

We found a shop selling around a million bits of technology in rack after bulging rack. This left so little room you had to shimmy around in the narrow little aisles. Our quest seemed hopeless but we showed the assistant the old charger and he walked without hesitation through the jungle of racks and boxes and displays. He came to one box, reached in unhesitatingly and brought out exactly what we wanted. Words like assiduous and dedicated and even wholesome came to mind.

Smiling and bowing our thanks we turned the wrong way and instead of leaving the store we found ourselves in another section where the racks were full of magazines of girls of sixteen (if that). All were either naked or stripped to the waist, any pubic hair airbrushed out to make them look even younger. The aisles were full of men, young and old, poring over these magazines greedily.

Leaving quickly, we decided to have a drink and found a bar that overlooked the main drag of Akihabara. It took us a moment to realise the bar was full of young women dressed as pre-pubescent girls. They served the beer and food and posed for selfies with the geeks. Nobody seemed the least bit flustered or ashamed.

The two-sided nature of the Japanese is also to be found in their focus on detail. Their food looks fabulous, though its usually bland to Western tastes. Bento boxes, made of lacquered wood and having a myriad of tiny compartments full of tantalising morsels, are exquisitely beautiful. The tea ceremony is elegant and serene. Kimonos are works of art. Flower arranging reaches giddy new peaks of artistic perfection. Everything small is as perfect as possible.

It is all so fabulous that you might think the rest of Japan would be beautiful too. And it is, around April time at least, when the cherry trees blossom. Trees have been planted in parks, along roads and rivers for just this effect. Whole families come to parks to picnic under their favourite trees and drink a lot, though never enough to become antisocial.

Unfortunately, for the rest of the year urban Japan looks just a little bit crap. Japan's population is getting towards double that of the UK's but is constrained within a long thin island, much of which is impossible to build on because of the jagged hills born from vulcanism. As a result, most Japanese live in urban conditions, in tiny houses shoehorned into vast conurbations stretching for hundreds of miles, the cities and towns only demarcated by the dividing lines of the jagged hills through which the high-speed trains dart like startled snakes.

High density, higgledy-piggledy housing, separated by tiny roads through which vehicles have to crawl, makes the place look a mess. The roads and houses are also rather dingy.

Such houses in such drab little streets coupled with the terrible crowding in cities like Tokyo must put real strain on the people. Perhaps this is why the Japanese focus on the beauty of the small. If you prepare an exquisitely presented meal or floral arrangement, then at least that is something over which you have control.

And perhaps control lies at the heart of much of their sexuality. They surrender so much to maintain social order in this pressure cooker that perhaps they find their missing control in sex and why there is so much S&M in their manga and their world-famous pornography.

Perhaps the not uncommon but deeply disturbing sight of middle-aged men snapping away with their cameras at bands of pre-pubescent girls belting out pop songs, is again about control. Worried, powerless men may feel the only partner they could control would be a very young girl, even if it is only in their imagination.

## So, let's talk about sex, baby

Strangeness just bubbles away below the surface. Walk the back streets of Osaka and you're surrounded by multi-storey buildings all sandwiched together. These seem to consist of floor after floor of tiny bars each with their own bright signs, ascending the sides of the buildings like garish neon bunting.

There's no evidence of people streaming in and out of these places, so what exactly is going on there?

One night my wife and I decided to try one. A tiny lift served the building and as we entered it two drunk office workers in their fifties or sixties (it's difficult to tell in Japan) followed us in.

By the time we got to the sixth floor we were just about asphyxiated by the booze fumes from the men so it was a relief when the doors opened. We stepped out quickly, the guys following.

Almost immediately a worried looking proprietor, presumably alerted by a camera in the lift, came rushing out and thrust a drinks menu in English into my hand. I did a double-take at the astronomical prices.

I hesitated, though more from shock than uncertainty, but this was enough to get him really worried. He started to wave his hands, palms towards us, clearly not wanting us as customers at all.

Meanwhile the salarymen had staggered by us and opened the door. Inside I could see an empty bar except for a table at which sat two teenaged girls. As soon as they saw the old guys their faces lit up like it was Christmas.

I was intrigued, my wife less so. We made our way back into the elevator to the proprietor's gushing relief.

I'd heard much about this aspect of Japanese culture. What we had glimpsed was the first gentle incline on the slippery slope to all-out prostitution.

These hostess bars are claimed only to provide the company of pretty young women for tired and stressed businessmen. Young women to laugh at their jokes, pour them drinks, be impressed by their stories. All the things their wives, who hardly ever see them because of their long working hours, have long since given up on.

The men and girls have a nice flirtatious evening, the men paying for overpriced drinks (although not as overpriced as they would have charged us. The grossly inflated gaijin's menu I had been given was just to deter us).

It sounds innocuous but I'm just not buying it. The women can string these men along for a while but sooner or later, not in the bar, but perhaps at one of the many love hotels around the big cities, a more physical transaction will be inevitable. Perhaps the hostess manages to keep these older men on the hook but one day she's not so appalled by one of them, and he offers her an eye-popping sum, and it's just too much to resist.

And there's the slippery slope.

Prostitution is illegal in Japan and this has forced them to develop all sorts of ingenious ways to not actually have penetrative sex. Sex workers will manipulate, suck, blow, wet, oil, and adapt all sorts of positions like an obscene game of Twister. They'll dress up as nurses, office workers, dancers and, especially, schoolgirls. They'll play dominance and submission games, will whip, beat and scratch. You can eat sushi off their naked bodies, they can pee on you or even worse.

But at no point can penis enter vagina for that is against the law and the Japanese are pretty strict about these things.

The one exception to this law is bathhouses. There are plenty of lawful bathhouses in Japan but there are also ones, called 'soaps', which provide a range of tariffed services. Everyone, even the police, seem comfortable living with the fiction that, as pretty young girls working there are soaping your flabby salaryman body down with their own naked bodies, they suddenly, being merely human, are sometimes overcome with lust and need to have sex with you no matter how old and ugly you are. That you have previously paid the highest tariff to the manageress is pure coincidence.

And that's how the circle is squared. Paying for sex can never be eliminated from any society so in Japan it is sublimated as far as it can be. Where it can't be then everyone pretends it's something else.

This tariff is so high that only the well-off can pay and that may partly explain why virginity amongst adult males is high in Japan, with nearly half of the population not having lost theirs by their mid-twenties. This rate has been increasing over the last thirty years. Money is certainly a major factor with higher income males up to twenty times less likely to have had no heterosexual experience.

Despite all this screwed-down sexuality bubbling away, a lot of which is violent and sado-masochistic in tone, there's nowhere safer than walking the city streets of Japan.

Nevertheless, still waters run deep.

## A walk in the wild

The idea of spending ten days walking an old Shinto pilgrimage trail appealed to me. The thousand-year-old trail is called the Kumano Kodo. It's about 100 km long and winds over and through the mountains of the Kii peninsula. Because these are jagged, tectonically produced hillsides, there would be an awful lot of ups and downs requiring climbing and descending about 20,000 feet in total.

When my friends heard I was going to walk this pilgrimage trail they said things like, 'But Bazza, you're already way spiritual so why do you need to go on a pilgrimage as well?'

Patiently I had to explain to my acolytes that even the most enlightened souls occasionally need their spiritual gas tanks topping up. What better way to do so than this? Shinto believes that all things, such as rocks and trees, are imbued with spirit. I figured that if I could get to the holy shrine at the end of the trail and bring myself to believe that even a babbling brook can have a soul, then perhaps I could come to believe I had one myself.

Blackened and shrivelled though it might be.

So, I met up with the crack team of pilgrims in Osaka. They were all from the West, mainly North America. This turned out to be emblematic of the trail. Although the trail is very beautiful and not that difficult to get to from Tokyo, Osaka or Kyoto, it's never busy and foreigners easily outnumber the few Japanese who hike it.

The ever-efficient Japanese rail system got us to the start where a large train/cable car hybrid, passengers sitting in raised rows like in a lecture theatre, were pulled backwards up the steep mountain to the trail.

Right from the beginning on the top, it became clear that the going would be more difficult than I'd expected. A huge typhoon the previous autumn had wreaked havoc on the densely packed hillsides of cedar and cypress, toppling many trees. Their fall down the steep hillsides had been arrested by others. This made the hillsides look like they were covered in a grid of trees, the vertical ones still standing, the horizontal ones fallen and dead.

Some trees had crashed down onto the path, others had come down on shrines and temples. All this was in addition to an ever-present problem on the trail. The extensive surface roots of all these trees were treacherously slippery when wet. This made life interesting as there was usually a vertiginous drop on at least one side, and on both sides when we were walking along ridges.

Gravity was therefore always a big issue but, even if you fell, the densely packed trees would arrest your tumbling fall soon enough. Falls were likely to be sore rather than fatal.

When you got to the mountain tops and weren't surrounded by trees, the views were spectacular. Even when you were deep within the green there were many charming shrines and statues along the way. Sometimes the path led us through beautiful green tea growing mountain villages.

When I told a writer friend about how I would be spending ten days walking through the wilderness in Japan with ten complete strangers, he said that sounded like the cliched plot of a murder mystery. Inevitably a serial killer in our midst would slowly bump off the pilgrims one by one.

He was sort of right because the person who nearly did us all in was the one you would least expect, namely... (drumroll)... our guide. She managed to get us lost in a country full of bears (I had no idea Japan had bears!).

It's kind of funny now but not quite so much at the time. We were high in the cold mountains, it was late in the afternoon so we'd eaten all our food, and the light was fading fast. It slowly dawned on everyone that the guide's map no longer corresponded to the route. Crouched over it, as we all stood around her in a circle, she eventually gave up trying to decipher where we were and started calling people on her phone. The conversations became rather animated.

It had got to the point where I was mentally rehearsing a cogent and compelling case along the lines of: 'I'm old and stringy and, if we have to eat anyone, then let's start with that plump young couple from North Carolina.'

Just as we were getting out our cutlery, the guide got through to someone in the mountain rescue services who was able to direct us safely down off the mountain. Taxis were waiting for us and we were rushed to our hostelry for emergency infusions of beer.

The problem was that the very severe typhoon had entirely destroyed part of the trail. Not realising this, we'd taken a side trail thinking it was still the main one. The local authorities had re-located the trail to an alternative, less-used track but had not altered the signposts to reflect this. This was uncharacteristically sloppy for the Japanese and I'm sure heads rolled somewhere.

Also, full disclosure about bears: although there were warning signs about them I never actually saw one.

Japan, it turned out when I consulted the internet from the safety of my hotel room, has both brown and black bears. Some have even been seen prowling the streets of Kyoto, for God's sake. One bear succeeded in cutting off electricity to 850 houses by climbing an electricity pole and getting electrocuted.

The Japanese regard bears as pests and shoot around 3000 a year. Their gall bladders fetch a hundred dollars a gram as they're used in Asian medicine to treat liver diseases such as cirrhosis.

Black bears are found mainly on the Kii peninsula. In all of Japan there may be 12,000. They can grow to over two hundred kilograms and have a crescent of white fur on their chest; hence the name Moon Bear, which might not sound quite so adorable when they're outrunning you, as they can.

Even worse, they build feeding platforms high in the trees so I guess they can even drop down on you unexpectedly. They usually eat acorns but oaks have been declining due to competition from the introduced cedars and cypresses, so the bears have to look for other sources of protein like, for instance, brightly clothed Western hikers.

A few times a year bears also have knock-down drag-out fights with people seeking wild bamboo shoots, something the bears also prize. Unless the bamboo shoot hunters are armed, they lose.

In 2009 a black bear took on nine people at a bus terminal in Takayama and won.

Even though there can be as many as 150 bear attacks a year, bears kill only a few people in Japan every year—though they badly maul many times that number. That said, one brown bear killed seven in a single night in Hokkaido, including biting the head off a baby. The bear buried one of the victims, as bears sometimes do, for more leisurely consumption later.

So, all in all, I was happy never to have seen one of the damned things. I did however see another wild animal. I came across it on the trail, almost stepping on it.

The conversation went as follows:

"SNAKE, SNAKE!" I squealed like a little girl.

"Yes," mused the guide. "Funny, but they don't usually come out at this time of year."

"BUT IT'S A SNAKE!"

"Don't worry, it's probably not poisonous."

"GIMME A REFUND AND A CHARTER FLIGHT TO THE NEAREST PSYCHOTHERAPIST!"

"Look, it's got its head stuck in its burrow. It thinks that if it can't see you then you can't see it. It's far more afraid of you than you are of it."

"OH NO IT FRIGGING ISN'T," I said but by then the pitch of my voice had risen beyond human hearing.

Did you know Japan was big in venomous snakes? Nope, me neither. There are a dozen of them, though most live in the sea. Of the land-based ones, the highly venomous Mamushi pit viper is a real charmer, although not up there with the Habu pit viper which doesn't necessarily kill you (it only kills around ten a year) but the venom turns your tissues to mush.

Other land-based killers you can find in the Japanese woods include the Asian hornet, the wild boar which can stab you to death with its tusks, redback spiders accidentally imported from Australia but now flourishing, and the mountain leech.

For some reason the tour brochures never mentioned any of these.

## The unvarnished truth about Japanese accommodation

On the walk along the Kumano Trail we stayed in a startling variety of accommodation, although most came under the heading of ryokans (inns).

You'll have seen images of the bedrooms in these inns, featuring rice straw tatami mats instead of carpets and with a white mattress on the floor rather than a bed. The walls are sliding panels, some with opaque screens for windows. Meanwhile, everyone is wearing those thin black and white patterned dressing gowns tied with a blue belt.

It all looks impossibly stylish and so pretty and elegant. But here's the dirty secret: it's a perfect example of style triumphing over substance.

The tatami-matted floor is hard and that thin mattress they put down doesn't help. It's like you're sleeping on a board.

The walls and sliding panels look paper thin because that's what they are—paper. You hear everything happening anywhere in the inn; someone breaks wind three bedrooms away and your walls rattle.

Not only that but the paper lets in a lot of light and, to top it all, it makes the room absolutely freezing. In old Japanese paintings not for nothing do people inside inns and houses seem to be wearing padded clothing.

This was in the Kii peninsula, almost in the middle of the 1000-kilometre-long island of Japan. Five hundred kilometres north is Hokkaido where the *average* January temperature is minus eight degrees C. The Japanese are a hardier people than they look.

So, if you go to Japan and have the choice between a modern hotel room and one in a ryokan—well, I think you get the drift.

The buildings that had been made into ryokans were surprising. The first night we stayed in a monastery that hired out rooms to travellers. With its little Japanese gardens and shrines, lichen-covered boulders and enveloping mist, the whole thing was straight out of an Edo period scroll. The monastery was big but with the sound proofing being so poor, whenever a monk chanted or snored somewhere, everyone else heard it.

Another ryokan was a converted schoolhouse, complete with communal toilets featuring banks of the cleanest urinals I have ever seen. In the West the receiving bowls of urinals are usually at the height of the male member, so the long drop doesn't make the urine splash over your feet. For some reason in Japan the bowl is only about a few centimetres above the floor. Do the Japanese men have metre-long penises? Having bathed with a few hundred of them in volcanic spring bathhouses I can attest that the answer to that is 'no'.

I guess they just have to put up with the splash-back and maybe that's why they have toilet slippers.

At least here the dangerous intelligent toilets had not penetrated, though the alternative was the much stupider but equally unsettling squat down versions.

In another ryokan in a valley deep within the mountains, I spent the coldest night of my life despite wearing everything I had with me, bulking me out like an overstuffed Pooh bear. So much so I could no longer reach my arms down to pull up my third layer of trousers. Even after all this, I was still too cold to sleep.

It wasn't all bad, however. A couple of ryokans, perched high on ridges giving exquisite views over valleys and mountains, were more like Western guest houses with proper beds and warm rooms and a good night's sleep.

Other ryokans were on hot springs, and even if they weren't they all supplied full body hot water baths, with or without the sulphurous smell of the genuine article. The word 'hot' in hot springs is no hyperbole. Villagers in a town with a hot spring often can be seen boiling their eggs there in little nets.

I have to say that after a hard day's hiking, the scalding waters really washed away the aches and pains and I was never stiff when I woke up the next day.

The most startling place we stayed in was like one of those Bond villain's headquarters, a hot springs complex built like an encrustation of gigantic barnacles onto a long line of rocky islands with subterranean tunnels linking them all together.

Inside were marble-covered floors, giving an initially classy impression. On closer inspection it became evident this was a garish resort, like Butlins, but brightly lit and teeming with Japanese in bathrobes. The place was full of families, even though the schools were in session. Family entertainments such as little theatres and games arcades as well as endless shops selling cheap foods, soft toys and blingy crap could all be found in its underground reaches.

After strenuous days of hiking in the wilds it was jarring to arrive in such a bright and gaudy place, so much so that I wondered if my travelling companions had slipped hallucinatory drugs into my water bottle.

Inside these chained islands, sulphurous springs bubbled up in large caverns and this was where everyone bathed.

Japanese are fussy about their bathing routines, as indeed they are about so much else. There is a strict decontamination procedure before you can even get into the bath. Like with the toilet slippers, this is something you don't mess with.

You're not allowed to take in towels, except for a small one more like a facecloth. You have to crouch on a dinky little plastic stool, so your knees are almost on a level with your chin. If you're well-built your bottom will flow over the top of the stool and make it like the head of a mushroom.

Behind the line of little stools are a row of shower heads. You use these to wash yourself down and get clean. In the West that would be enough washing for most people and you could cut out the whole middle-man smelly egg bathing routine.

Most hot springs are open to the air so it's nice to lounge in really hot water and look at the view. The bath itself is artfully strewn with big rocks and the bubbling hot streams flow down over these in a comely manner. It's pleasant to do once or twice but it's difficult to see its attraction as the main activity for a whole holiday.

After your bath you have to go through the decontamination procedure again, though presumably this time to stop you reeking of rotten egg for the rest of the day.

~~~

There were so many things on the trail that were amazing. Shrines and Tori gates, some over twenty metres tall, as well as beautifully ornate temples. Even the packed lunches were works of art.

Near the end of the trail was the incredible Nachii waterfall, at 133 metres the tallest in Japan. In the foreground was the three tiered red and black Seiganto-ji pagoda. Set amongst the cherry blossom and with the backdrop of the waterfall this was something from an oriental fairy-tale.

A fitting end to the whole trek.
~~~

Did I achieve spiritual enlightenment? If you've got this far into the book then I reckon you can guess the answer to that.

Japanese barbers: don't, just don't

After the long walk, my beard and hair had grown and I looked like an unsuccessful drug dealer who'd sampled too many of his own wares. When I got back to Osaka, I noticed a shop called John Wayne Barbers on a side-street and thought, 'Nah, that's gotta be a cowboy outfit' so I kept on walking.

Big mistake. I should have taken my chances there but instead I tried one that had pretty receptionists and stylish young barbers in a brightly lit emporium at a big cross-section in the centre of town.

I've long believed that the less hair you have the shorter you should keep it. Growing a long strip of hair on one side so you can plaster it over your otherwise bald pate hides nothing. So, I trim my beard and head hair fairly closely.

But how was I to communicate my instructions in a language I couldn't speak?

Luckily there is a lingua franca for trimming which barbers all over the world understand.

Except, it turns out, in Japan.

Professional trimmers come with guards fitted over the blades and these govern the length of hair remaining after the cut. The *One* guard cuts the hair as close to the skin as possible and leaves about three millimetres of hair. *Three* leaves nearer ten millimetres.

So, I held up one finger and pointed to my chin, then three and pointed at my head. The barber nodded sagely.

I lay back in the barber's chair, relaxed and confident. The barber took the clippers and ran it back along the mid-line of my head. Trouble was, he hadn't used a guard at all. Now I had a bald strip five centimetres wide in a sort of inverse Mohican.

The staff, alerted to my disappointment (perhaps it was the tears) gave me a full refund. This didn't make up for my luxuriant (a man can dream) tresses lying strewn all over the floor like the cypresses on the Kii hillsides.

And, of course, once you've started down that road you've got to go all the way. I waved for him to continue and he took the whole lot off.

The John Wayne barbers were sounding pretty good by now.

I'd wanted to tidy up as my wife was flying out to join me from the UK that same day. I made my way out to the airport hoping for some sympathy. When she caught sight of me, even after twenty hours of emotionally numbing air travel, she laughed her head off.

Food

My wife is not an adventurous eater, and indeed she would go on to lose half a stone in her two weeks in Japan.

So, my dining options were going to be more limited after she arrived. The night before she got there, I decided to treat myself for surviving the Kumano trial by indulging in a Michelin starred Japanese meal.

Michelin star meals are, aside from travel, my most expensive indulgence. The thing that really characterises them is the insane amount of work that goes into each course. More cynical observers might suggest that what actually characterises Michelin restaurants is the insane amount you pay.

The best Michelin meal (and indeed any meal) I ever had was on the Isle of Eriska near Oban in Scotland. There were seven courses, and each had taken more work than you'd put into a Sunday roast with all the trimmings.

Once, in a Michelin restaurant in Edinburgh, where a glass screen separated the kitchen from the diners, I watched seven chefs clustered around and bending over a table. They were assembling a single portion of dessert with the care and attention you'd associate with defusing a bomb.

In Eriska, one course was a single scallop, without even a shell. Underwhelming, until I took a bite and realised it was the best tasting scallop I'd ever had.

Another course was some fish in a foam which was good, but what rocketed it into the stratosphere were five smoked mussels arranged around the side. Shell-less, almost just a garnish, they looked like an afterthought. But, again, these were the best mussels I've ever tasted.

So, with the Japanese already putting so much work into their everyday dishes to make them look like works of art, what on earth would a Japanese Michelin star restaurant be like?

It's worth noting that the three cities in the world with the most Michelin restaurants are in Japan (Tokyo, Kyoto and Osaka). The restaurant I went to was the Osakana-ryori Asai amongst the myriad tiny back streets of Osaka.

The restaurant wasn't even really on the back street, but tucked away down a corridor off one.

Not speaking Japanese I'd had my guide on the walk phone through a booking. Just as well as nobody at the restaurant spoke English. Even so, when I rocked up, they all knew my name. Being the only gaijin customer that evening may have been a giveaway.

I also was the first customer there and was seated at what looked like the bar but was actually a counter. On the opposite side was the kitchen where seven chefs dressed in white uniforms with little white hats working quietly with obsessive attention to detail.

Dish after dish was brought, each looking ethereally beautiful. If I'd seen them displayed at a modern art museum, I wouldn't have felt cheated even if I'd paid good money to get in.

The thing was that I didn't have a clue what I was eating as there was no English menu.

Each of the ten or so courses had around six different components. These might, or might not, have containing anything. Smoked butt cheek of bear for all I knew.

There were morsels of fish that seemed to have been chosen more for colour than taste, artfully arranged on a half shell that itself looked like the profile of a fish. Tiny little dabs of condiment formed a crescent on the marbled plate. I recognised green horseradish and a wedge of lime but the rest weren't anything I'd seen or tasted before. Sprigs of cherry blossom added to the aesthetics of some dishes.

Tiny bowls of soup held leaf-wrapped fish or fried octopus with the finest of batters exploding out like the plume of water from a grenade tossed into a pond. Delicate and with just the right texture, the batter managed to be both crispy and moist at the same time.

Plate after plate came, as did the wine, so in the end I forgot to take pictures and the rest is lost in a kaleidoscopic blur.

After all that, the desert was a comedown as is every dessert in Japan. However, the Western propensity for sugar and fat (when I bake a cake, I basically take everything in my kitchen that is bad for me and chuck it into a mixing bowl) is beginning to corrupt the Japanese. Even so they haven't got it quite right. Dessert bars are starting to appear in the many malls and they proudly display sundaes of every description. Foamily cream-topped, with layers of mouth-watering chocolate, and a crunchy biscuit base, they look just the ticket.

Enough at least to make you buy one, only to find that it is as satisfying as a wet weekend in Bridlington. The 'cream' has about as much fat as a Kenyan marathon runner, the 'chocolate' is in fact coffee flavoured jelly, and the biscuit crumbs at the bottom are basically crunched up cornflakes. *Sad* is the most precise word to describe it.

Japanese entrepreneurs are missing a trick. I first grasped this when I sat down at a cafe while my wife went to stare mesmerised at the displays of clothes in a department store. I was drinking a coffee and minding my own business when I saw a beautiful young Japanese woman passing by who turned her head towards me, slowed down and gave me a look of burning desire.

I froze, my coffee mid-way to my mouth.

After a few seconds she reluctantly continued on her way. I was left blinking and bemused. I may have been okay-looking when I was a young man but now I'm in my sixties and white haired where I'm not balding.

Answer to a maiden's prayer? Not so much.

Had the woman escaped from the local asylum? She'd seemed rather well dressed for that.

Just then another young woman passed and did exactly the same thing.

This just wasn't making any sense so I looked around for an alternative explanation. I found I was sitting right next to a cold cabinet. Inside was an unusual thing in Japan, a patisserie display with real cakes and with real cream.

This had been the focus of the women's lust.

So, it's not that as a race the Japanese don't like sinful Western deserts, it's just that they haven't had much exposure to them, but they're beginning to succumb.

The Japanese are by and large a slender people but I'm going to go all Nostradamus here and predict that that is going to change.

So back to the Michelin restaurant in Osaka. Unfortunately, the dessert was again of the tasteless jelly variety. It didn't matter though as I was buzzing from the rest of the meal. The care and the love the chefs had put into it had been extraordinary.

As I was leaving, a waiter rushed up and stopped me because he had found a translation for one of the courses. Somewhere in there I'd eaten 'Soup made from the entrails of sea cucumbers'. Not something I would have chosen, and I couldn't remember what it had tasted like, but by then I didn't care.

And so, it was back out into the usual glittering-to-buggery Osaka and restaurant dishes where the translations on the helpful English menus were uncompelling: like 'oily scum udon' and 'guts hot pot'.

Sugar is very much a feature of Japanese cooking, if not in the dessert courses. It's used for the sour-sweet taste which is the basis of much of the tastiest Japanese food. Sushi is raw fish on rice yet, let's be honest, raw fish is generally pretty tasteless if it's fresh. What gives it the taste is the rice which isn't just rice. It's prepared in a vinegar and sugar mixture.

Even so, and to generalise terribly, Japanese dishes can be works of art but they actually don't have a lot of taste. It may well be that my taste has been so dulled by curries that I can't appreciate the subtlety of Japanese food. However, it's interesting that teriyaki dishes, loaded in sugar, are almost ubiquitous on menus in Japan. It's also interesting that Indian restaurants are taking off there and you'll find them even in high-end places like the Ginza.

There's no avoiding it—Japanese food really is beautiful but rather bland.

## Physics red in tooth and claw

I'm a physicist myself. After the TV show The Big Bang Theory, and even before, physicists were dismissed as ineffectual nerds, but we aren't. The forces we deal with can shatter worlds.

I'm not saying that's something to be proud of, nor are the abuses that politicians have put our work to.

Hiroshima was a place where the power of physics had been made manifest and I had always felt drawn to visit it.

The first time I visited the city was when I was at a week-long conference in Kyoto. One day I bunked of and caught the high-speed rail. This ate up nearly two hundred miles like it was a pack of Doritos. I was able to get to the city, wander around stunned, then return to Kyoto before anyone noticed I'd gone.

You can't get the old newsreels of a flattened Hiroshima out of your mind, so when you arrive it's a surprise to see everything so built up and modern. In fact, Hiroshima is nicer than other Japanese cities because it has much wider tree-lined boulevards. Why can't all Japanese cities be like this, you wonder? Then you realise why.

The reason is, of course, that the atom bombing allowed the civic planners to build again from scratch. You can't do that in Tokyo where railways, roads and canals twist around each other like mating snakes. Bridges over bridges—is there any civil planning in Tokyo at all?

In Hiroshima there are many rivers and, unusually for Japanese cities, they're not buried under concrete or bridges. Ironically it was the confluence of two of these that was the target for the crew of the *Enola Gay*. In Hiroshima the rivers at least remain and the Japanese have planted blossom trees all along them. They look sublime when the sakura come out.

In the epicentre stands the Atom Bomb Dome, a building made of reinforced concrete that was able to withstand the terrible force that stamped directly down. Weaker buildings, or ones struck from the side, fell like cards.

The Hiroshima Museum is built on the opposite side of the river to the Dome. It has to be visited even though it's full of disturbing sights such as photos of keloid disfigurations: scar tissue formed due to superficial radiation effects. There's also examples of the twisted black fingernails of the Hiroshima Maidens. Radiation affects cells with the most rapid turnovers, such as the cuticles from which black twisted nails sprout.

That's all bad enough but right at the end of the exhibition hall, just near the exit (this has changed in the new museum) was one exhibit that reduced me to tears. It's a glass case in which stands a tricycle, paint bubbled and stripped away by the heat wave, its seat and pedals missing.

It belonged to a little boy called Shin. He had been pedalling his bike one and a half kilometres from the blast. He was burned so badly he died that night. Because he had loved his tricycle so much, his father had buried it with him. Forty years later his grave was opened so he could be reburied in the family cemetery and the tricycle was donated to the museum.

Few buildings survived, although one is a Bank of Japan building four hundred metres from the blast. People entering the building were vaporised but their shadows were etched onto the concrete steps by the flash.

However, over time, the rain has washed even those terrible reminders away.

~~~

It's worth re-iterating that the joy in travel comes from the differences. If you want to go somewhere which is the most different, but also is about as safe as you can get, then Japan is the winner. Nevertheless, the culture shock it can produce should not be minimised. After my first trip to Japan, my brain felt like I'd gone three rounds with Mike Tyson.

If you want a gentler introduction to the Far East then the next country on our itinerary may be just the ticket.
~~~

## *If You Can't Stand the Heat, Try Far East Light*

Taiwan, 2019

When it comes to the Far East, Japan is hardcore just because it's so weird and disturbing though not actually scary.

China's implacable totalitarianism makes it genuinely scary, as does its increasing dominance in technology and development.

If you've never been to the Far East and all that sounds rather discouraging, can I suggest you start with an easier introduction to the Orient?

Taiwan is my favourite country in the Far East because it has the safety and convenience of a modern democratic state yet still retains its Eastern exoticism. It's not as harsh as China, nor as regimented and buttoned-down as Japan.

I've never understood why it hardly features on the tourist map as it is also very beautiful. Indeed, the island was originally called Formosa, which means 'beautiful isle' in Portuguese. Its lush green hillsides rise almost vertically out of the Pacific and reminds me very much of Hawaii.

True enough, it does suffer from earthquakes and typhoons but then again, nowhere's perfect. It also has a very large neighbour who thinks it owns Taiwan even though the people there beg to differ (less than 6% favour reunification). One day China will reclaim what it believes to be its own and there will be hell to pay.

That there is undoubtedly an intertwining is evident from the names. China calls itself the Peoples Republic of China.

Taiwan calls itself the Republic of China. Both claim to speak on behalf of the other.

China demands that other countries recognise their version of reality, namely that Taiwan is part of China. To a very high degree the rest of the world complies. If a country recognises the ROC as an independent state, then China will cut off all diplomatic relations. China is so powerful that pretty much all of the world pays lip service, to the point that although Taiwan was a founding member of the United Nations, it is not officially a member state.

Taipei, the capital city of Taiwan, with its modern architecture reminds me of Judge Dredd's Megacity One, except that rather than a high wall surrounding it all, the city's edges are defined by steep mountainsides shrouded in mist and jungle. Where the concrete ends the jungle begins. Little temples dot the hillsides with well-maintained steps and paths to make a series of fabulous walks.

Tea plantations and universities sit at the top of the hills, some reached by cable cars on four-kilometre-long lines. Meanwhile, down in the city itself, some of the cleanest subway trains in the world sashay around the tower blocks.

Lovely and civilised, Taiwan is full of wonders exotic to the Western eye.

## Food

Taipei has tremendous restaurants but it also has food that is far more challenging. Its Chinese influences can be seen in its predilections for swallows' nests and deer antlers, squished birds and squids and lots and lots of offal.

One popular delicacy has the size and appearance of a respectable-sized human penis but that's not what it is at all. When pigs are young, their tails are lopped off because otherwise they grow curly and can get caught in things. This lopping off leaves a stub which grows as the animal matures and that is what these penis-like objects are.

And, no, I never tried one and, no, I never will.

In Japan the food may look like a work of art but doesn't taste nearly as good. In Taiwan the food looks like a mess but tastes great. Taiwan cuisine has strong Chinese influences but the country has also been ruled by Japan and that too is reflected in the food. It has also sucked up all the other cuisines from south-east Asia. The food stalls in the night markets contain so much that is unrecognisable, much of it smelling great.

It has to be said, though, that Taiwanese eating has a distinctly bizarre and deeply morbid aspect. Toilet-themed restaurants can be recognised by a neon toilet hanging suspended over the front door. At the table you'll be seated on an actual toilet, although it's not plumbed in. Food is served in bowls shaped like miniature toilets. Sometimes, the lights are shaped like faeces but that's not the worst bit. That honour is reserved for the food that is also shaped and coloured like turds.

Some (not me) might argue that the two functions of eating and defecating so assiduously decoupled in the minds of Westerners demonstrates an unhealthy attitude. They say that the Taiwanese are simply taking a more holistic and healthier point of view.

Some (including me) think that being fascinated by the latter function is simply infantilism.

However, the liberal Westerners' attempts to rationalise away such Taiwanese behaviour founders on another sort of restaurant there: the concentration camp restaurant.

Shackles, straw on the floor and murals of emaciated inmates look down at you as you eat. Large photographs show actual Nazi victims starving to death.

My Taiwanese friends claim that this is done out of innocence, that people there just haven't a clue what happened in Nazi Germany (though they have a lot to say about Japanese atrocities during the war).

A similar naivety, they say, led a Taiwanese company to advertise the German domestic heaters they sold with a picture of Adolf Hitler.

So, in some ways the country is highly insular but at the same time it grasps new ideas and runs with them. That's why 'Made in Taiwan' was so common on poor quality toys made of the new-fangled plastic back when I was a kid, though they've moved onto much higher technology exports since.

Like China, Taiwan too can change fast. When I first visited the country in 2014, Taipai was a wasteland when it came to pubs. In that huge city you could just about count them on the fingers of one hand and they were all full of foreigners.

On my visit in 2019 pubs were everywhere. They weren't just serving stuff like gassy bottled Asahi; instead, they were serving twenty or thirty different types of draft ale all produced by microbreweries that had sprung up almost overnight.

### Trains (again)

For several years I've been boring people with my assertion that Britain is no longer a First World country, using arguments along the lines of those in a previous chapter. I've cited as evidence that China has built a hundred airports over the past ten years while we have spent thirty years pissing around about a third runway at Heathrow. I've pointed out that in ten years China built many thousands of kilometres of high-speed rail (HSR) line while in the UK we still don't have a single domestic operating line..

Some of the people I've ranted at respond by saying that it's all a question of scale and population size and that's why we don't yet have HSR. China is physically much bigger and also has over twenty times the population. Obviously HSR makes more sense there.

The Taiwan HSR gives the lie to this view as Taiwan is much smaller in terms of both physical size and population than Britain yet its HSR works fabulously well. Their massive trains can travel at 350 kph and pull into stations every six or seven minutes, arriving within a second of schedule and at exactly the same point on the platform every time. Vast numbers of people are carried over long distances quickly, easily, reliably and cheaply. It makes our rail system look like it's run by Neanderthals on barbiturates.

The only trouble I have with HSR trains is that they scare me a little bit. When I saw my first bullet train back in Kyoto in 2004, it had an unfortunate effect. I hate snakes and when this huge serpent-headed beast slid noiselessly into the station towards me, I may have wet my pants a little.

What also unnerves me is when you're standing at a station and a HSR through-train passes. I defy anyone to see that happen for the first time and not have their breath taken away. It's like five Jumbo jets shooting by within a few feet of your nose. The train is travelling so fast you don't see it coming and by the time you've worked out what it was, it's already gone.

I was taking the Taiwan High Speed Rail to visit a writer pal of mine who lives in a city called Taichung. I wasn't expecting much from Taichung itself. The guidebooks are not kind because most of that cheap plasticky stuff we bought labelled 'Made in Taiwan' came from there. In other words, it's a city of light industry and is to Taipei what Birmingham is to London.

However, when my friend showed me around, I was pleasantly surprised. The centre seemed full of large interconnected parks and, being Sunday, people were there picnicking with their families. Youngsters danced under the shadows of the skyscrapers and it seemed that everyone was showing off their pets, not just cats and dogs and rabbits, but also more exotic species like meerkats and iguanas.

Though the dressing up of some of the dogs as samurai, and cats as 1920s air aces replete with scarf and goggles, was a trifle weird, Taichung itself seemed safe and wholesome and full of well-behaved people. Those are words you don't often associate with Birmingham.

It has to be said that in my travels around Taiwan I found the people far less jaded and cynical than in the West. For someone so jaded and cynical myself, it was all rather touching.

## Marvels

Taroko Gorge is a wonder of the world but hardly anyone outside Taiwan has ever heard of it. Nearly twenty kilometres long its marble-sided cliffs form a gorge 3000-3700 metres deep, double that of the Grand Canyon (average depth 1600 metres). It also looks far more spectacular. The problem with the Grand Canyon is that when you're on the top peering down into it, it just doesn't look a mile deep. If there was a little house or a car down there it might give some sense of scale.

The thing about Taroko Gorge is that, first of all, you're right at the bottom of the thing and, secondly, the walls are so close together. Looking up, it's like you're deep within the earth. Sometimes the walls are so close people at the top can throw things to one another. Compare and contrast with the Grand Canyon which even at its narrowest is 200 metres across but can be up to nearly 30 km wide.

Geologically, Taroko Gorge was once all coral at the bottom of the sea before the tectonics of the region compressed it into marble and limestone then thrust it up out of the water.

Its volcanic origins have twisted the multi-coloured layers of rock into strange and beautiful shapes.

The Gorge is also very dangerous with a number of tourists getting killed by falling rocks every year. At the most hazardous bits you're given helmets although, judging by the rocks that litter the road, they may not do a whole lot of good.

We were only there for a couple of hours but at one point an ambulance sped by carrying a tourist with a split open head.

My Taoching friend related what had happened when he had last visited. The roads in and out are very narrow and someone had tethered a goat to a tree. The goat had wandered into the road and was leaning forward trying to get at something just out of its reach. A woman tourist on a scooter was coming down the road and struck the stretched-out rope, sending her flying off her scooter and into a tree, knocking her brains out.

If health and safety were anywhere near as big a deal in Taiwan as in the UK, then nobody would ever be allowed into Taroko Gorge at all because of the falling rocks, never mind the goats.

Another wonderful place to visit is the fabulously quaint village of Jui Fen. This was an old Japanese gold mining village with mountains on one side and a steep drop to the ocean on the other. The village is a single long street, although in fact it's so narrow it's really a path. Either side for most of the way are little stalls selling trinkets and food such as the egregiously smelling but reasonably palatable stinky tofu.

The street leads up then turns back downhill and this is where it takes your breath away. Leading down are some of the oldest and most beautiful Japanese-style teahouses and restaurants, their red lanterns leading down in curving chains. You can sit on one of the balconies with a cool beer in the hot night and watch the people passing below. It's a bit like heaven.

Taiwan is indeed the beautiful isle.

If I had to summarise the Far East: Japan is startling, China is bracing, while Taiwan is just plain nice.

Let's hope China keeps its paws off it.

## *Don't bother your pretty little head about the political instability*

Egypt, 2018

Below me, the flow of the Nile had been so reduced it was almost a pond, its motive force more a caress than a current. For millennia the fierce brute of the Nile would carry away tens of thousands when in flood but now it lies tamed, a milk nurse for Egypt.

Watching the river from the dock, I was distracted by a couple of coppers sidling up to our tour group.

Then a few more appeared, then a whole bunch of them.

I began to count.

By the time our tour group was ready to head off for the buses, the coppers were arrayed before us like a shield. Sixty tourists were being accompanied by twenty police: ten in uniforms and with assault rifles, ten in plainclothes with pistols.

This would turn out to be our minimum security detail in this troubled region.

We climbed aboard our little buses and set off in convoy. Behind us the comforting bulk of the heavily defended boat slipped from view and we were out onto the dusty roads and picking up speed. The theory seemed to be that the faster we travelled, the less chance of trouble.

We roared through little mud-brick villages. At the head of the convoy was a couple of blues-and-twos motorcycle outriders. These were followed by three cars full of coppers, then the tourists in our bright pink minbuses, then another couple of police cars bringing up the rear.

We were one of the first tourist groups to come here in years. Maybe that's why the villagers looked up at us open-mouthed as we barrelled through their little villages.

Then again, perhaps our little pink buses and armed escort looked like a state visit from the Queen of the Fairies.

Back in Egypt in 2018, political stability was still an aspiration so any trip there was risky. This was reflected by the passengers we sailed with. Generally, they were all so old they didn't give much of a damn what happened to them. Anyway, it gave them a perfect excuse to leave their kids and grandkids behind.

My wife and I figured that with all the recent problems, this might be our last chance to see the country before it all went completely to hell.

In just the previous seven years Egypt had seen a revolution and successful coups against both a dictator (Mubarak) and a democratically elected leader (Morsi). The country also had a long history of Islamist attacks against tourists, the worst being the murder and mutilation of sixty-two of them in Luxor in 1997.

And that's over and above the occasional pot-shot and rocket propelled grenade aimed at the river boats.

Because of all this, several hundred kilometres of the Nile had been closed to tourists, devastating an already very poor local economy. However, this section had recently re-opened and we were one of the first ships to sail right back into it.

On our armed excursions things could go sideways very quickly. Once, our little Queen of the Fairies motorcade came to a checkpoint at a T-junction and I was watching idly through the window of the minibus as some of our coppers got out and strolled towards the intersection.

Just as they got there an oil tanker came turning in from the right. The coppers waved for it to stop. For some reason the driver didn't understand and kept on coming towards us.

Was this a terrorist intending to detonate the oil tanker and kill us all? The coppers seemed to think so. One leapt on the running board of the truck, wrenched open the cab door and leaned in, shoving his pistol into the driver's face.

The driver jammed on the brakes, the truck juddering to a stop with all sorts of screeches and bangs.

Just for a second, I thought we'd all had it.

By the time the truck had stopped, the coppers were all over it like white on rice. Our buses started and we drove slowly by. The driver was looking down in surprise at his lap.

I'm guessing he'd piddled himself.

Tension then relief. That seemed to be what it was all about. The upside was that we saw the tombs and temples undisturbed because, for some strange reason, we were the only tourists there.

I like travel with an edge, where there is a sense of adventure. You can still find it, even if you're paying top dollar as in this trip. It's just a matter of determinedly going to the wrong place at the wrong time.

But in this particular case, I begin to wonder if I'd bitten off more than I could chew.

Welcome to Egypt!

~~~

Imagine a massive all-powerful beast sustained by the tiniest thread of life.

That's exactly what you see when you look down on Egypt and its people from the air. Their fragility is nakedly revealed because all that keeps them alive is the slender, meandering capillary of the Nile.

Egypt is the Nile and the Nile is Egypt.

Some 96% of the country is desert and not the sort of pussy half-desert you find in places like the US. There, scrub and cactus can just about survive. In contrast, Egyp-
~~~

tian desert is sand and rock and nothing else and that's why almost all of the country's 104 million people live within a few kilometres of the river.

That's what makes it so terribly vulnerable. In bygone ages millions starved because the yearly Nile flood never came or did so only feebly. Other years, it roared down the Nile valley like a rampaging lion drowning people and animals and crops.

And where does the Nile come from? This was a question that intrigued many Victorian explorers, not to mention countless generations of Egyptians. For thousands of years, it was believed the waters came from the Mountains of the Moon.

Would that they did as it sounds straight out of a Rider Haggard romance. Unfortunately, the Mountains of the Moon are a legend. The prosaic truth is that the Nile waters come from the drainage basins of eleven north-east African countries. On its 6500-kilometre journey the river hoovers up enriched sediment and deposits it as a bountiful gift on the flooded riversides of Egypt.

So fertile is this muddy sediment that ancient Egyptian farmers claimed that the first shoots would pop up from the soil even before they'd got to the end of the seeding trench.

These alternating periods of drowning and starvation went on for thousands of years until the Nile was spectacularly tamed. Dammed far upriver, its flow became so carefully regulated that two miraculous harvests a year were engineered.

Egyptians could also now build their mud-brick houses right down to the water, until then an extremely hazardous undertaking.

The river is held back by two Aswan dams 900 kilometres upriver from Cairo. The first, the Low Dam, was the largest masonry dam of its day, at 2000 metres long and nearly 36 metres high. It was built by the British in 1902, or so the history books would have you believe.

I'm going to go out on a limb here and suggest that, in fact, possibly one or two Egyptians might have had to toil under the blazing sun to make it happen. The British designed, the Egyptians built.

The dam was raised on the sight of the First Cataract. This had marked the limits of navigation for the ancient Egyptians even when the Nile was at its mildest. Today you can see the dry riverbed and where the current must have exploded against the huge boulders scattered across it.

You pass over this first dam when you come in from the airport to the city of Aswan. That's also when you first notice the intense military presence. Egypt is riven with internal dissent but that's not the main reason there's so many soldiers around this first dam.

There's even more around the High Aswan Dam, further upriver. As you approach this, the desert bristles with air defence systems, making the dam the most heavily defended structure on the planet.

The High Dam makes the Low Dam look like a sandcastle on the beach constructed by an indifferent toddler. It's the largest embankment dam in the world and was completed in 1970. Designed, financed and built by the Soviets, although again it's conceivable Egyptians may have scooped out the odd shovelful of sand. This dam is four kilometres long, 111 metres tall and nearly a kilometre wide at the base. It holds back 132 million cubic kilometres of water in the form of Lake Nasser, the biggest man-made lake in the world. The lake is 500 kilometres long and up to 35 kilometres wide.

And now we really are talking about vulnerability.

Breach this dam and all that water would race for 900 kilometres down the Nile valley before emptying into the Great Green, as the ancient Egyptians used to call the Mediterranean. Remember those 104 million people living within a kilometre or so of the river? Should the dam be breached then the wall of water would literally wash populated Egypt into the sea.

This is why Egypt plays nice with its neighbour Israel: they have nuclear bombs. Indeed, Egypt tries to play nice with all its neighbours as it is insanely vulnerable to anyone with a half-decent air force.

Not only is the dam a terrible hostage to fortune but building it came at a great cost. Filling the artificial Lake Nasser displaced 120,000 people both in Egypt and neighbouring Sudan. Ancient temples and monuments, including the astonishing Abu Simbel, and its four twenty-metre-tall statues of Ramesses the Great, had to be moved.

Abu Simbel was built over 3000 years ago. It stood on a bend in the Nile near the southernmost border of Egypt. It served two purposes and was not unlike Beijing's new Fuck-You airport.

Firstly, it would provide marauders out of darkest Africa, who had left their dung and straw huts to sail down the Nile to pillage and plunder, with a truly cataclysmic WTF moment. The marauders would have seen nothing like it where they came from. Indeed, thousands of years later, neither had I.

Secondly, it made the subliminal suggestion that coming in peace would be a sagacious move. If not, then turning around and buggering off back where they came from would definitely be in their best interests.

Abu Simbel and the dams were something to marvel at but they weren't why we were in Aswan. Rather, we were to join a boat there and cruise all the way downstream to Cairo.

Nile cruisers are large by riverboat standards, with fifty or so cabins. They're around seventy metres long and fifteen wide. Their draft is shallow and it has to be because there are so many sandbanks in the Nile. The captain must know the river like the back of his hand so he can shimmy his boat around these obstacles. Boats also have to dock or anchor at night as there are few lights along the river and hardly any buoys to indicate shallows.

Cruising on the Nile used to be extremely popular. Before Thomas Cook introduced steamboats, it was all by sail-driven houseboats called Dahabiyas which might take fifty days to get from Cairo to Luxor. It took even longer if you wanted to sail all the way down to Aswan. So popular did this industry become that at one time it made up over a tenth of Egypt's GDP.

Hundreds of ships cruised the Nile and you can still see them, though now they lie rotting along the riverbank. It makes the Nile look like a graveyard for whales.

The boats fell into decrepitude when the tourists stopped coming following the unrest during and after the 2011 revolution. Nowadays only a handful of boats navigate some stretches of the river.

And thus, we sailed north, stopping at various points to visit temples and tombs. On either side of the river were green strips sometimes kilometres wide, sometimes just a hundred metres where the valley was narrowest. At these tighter points the desert loomed high above, waiting to pounce.

Each day we saw something breathtaking. Even sunrise and sunset along the Nile is so magical I don't think I missed a single one. And, of course, the far away cry of the muezzin only made it even more exotic. This really was Rider Haggard.

I'd expected to be impressed but wasn't prepared for the magnificence.

For a start I hadn't fully realised that it doesn't rain in Egypt; indeed the Nile is the only source of fresh water. This means buildings don't weather. Some still look brand new even though they were built as long as 4500 years ago.

That's not to say there isn't some deterioration. The temperature changes between night and day stresses the rocks. Cracks form and sometimes big chunks fall off.

Otherwise, the ancient buildings look more freshly minted than anything put up in Scotland more than a couple of years ago.

Many of the carvings in the tombs and temples seem as fresh as if they were carved yesterday. Those on the outsides have lost their surface layer of paint but that's made them all the more refined. The paint, before being chipped off by desert winds, would have looked garish, with strong golds and blues and reds. Bordello-like, really.

Stripped of paint, the carvings' elegance and ethereal, almost alien nature are revealed.

Humans have done far more damage than the desert wind. Antiquities were plundered wholesale by European archaeologists and adventurers. Their carelessness and lack of respect seem incredible to modern sensibilities.

For example: the Egyptians mummified animals on an industrial scale and their underground catacombs held millions of cat and baboon and ibis mummies. These were looted and sold as kindling to the European market, as indeed were countless historically priceless papyri. Mummies were sold as fertiliser.

As the cruise progressed the security situation became more and more pressing. I've mentioned the twenty coppers who accompanied us ashore who were our minimum security detail. Sometimes we needed considerably more than that.

When tourism returns to troubled regions it doesn't just start where it left off. Instead, each new tour takes a small incremental step back towards normality. With our tour it was more like a giant leap of faith.

We were due to call in at a town called Minya, a Muslim Brotherhood stronghold, to see some tombs. The locals call Minya the Bride of Upper Egypt as it's dead centre between Upper and Lower Egypt. Only four years before the government had sent in tanks to restore order to the town. The 'small incremental step' was that we would do a walkabout through the town centre.

The night before and further upriver all the senior coppers in the region had come on board to work out what they were going to do. They must have been under terrible conflicting pressures. On the one hand they were desperate for tourist money to come back to this impoverished region, but on the other hand if a single tourist was killed by insurgents, then it would cost the Egyptian economy hundreds of millions of dollars in lost income.

The coppers argued long into the night before coming up with a cunning plan.

This consisted of not only our minimum protection detail but also at least another twenty plainclothes. In addition, they positioned rooftop marksmen.

The real clincher was that we were also given two dedicated SWAT teams. Even I could work out what they were because on the sides of their black SUVS was helpfully emblazoned in big white letters the word *SWAT*. Who knew that Special Weapons and Tactics was the same in Egyptian as English?

So, right from the start we tourists were outnumbered by our protection detail. This disparity became even more obvious when half the tourists decided they weren't willing to risk their lives for the sake of the Egyptian Tourist Board and so stayed on the boat. Pussies!

After assembling in the boat's lounge, the braver of the tourists crossed the gangway and headed up through the dock gate. This was guarded by the first SWAT team, all dressed in black from feet to helmeted head, masks obscuring their features (and this was before Covid made masks fashionable). They climbed out of their truck to join us.

One was left guarding the boat. He stood behind a slab of bullet proof metal, his AK-47 resting on the top and pointing out into the square. People walking by found the sides of their heads passing within centimetres of the gun barrel. Some flinched, some stooped to get out of the line of fire. Nobody looked very relaxed.

Accompanied by the rest of the two SWAT teams and a horde of coppers, we set out for our leisurely stroll.

The square we found ourselves in was tree-lined and contained a few little stalls selling fruit. The line of tourists snaked across it, flanked on either side by the SWAT guys. At the head of the line, and also bringing up the rear, was the usual security contingent, ordinary cops dressed in their green uniforms and all with assault rifles. Embedded within the line with the tourists were the plainclothes guys, giveaway pistol butts sticking out of pockets or tucked in waistbands at the back of their trousers. I could see how anxious they all were and that's what scared me most.

We crossed the square and turned into a road overshadowed on either side by five and six-floor buildings. On the faces of these, and also hanging from lines between poles, were the images of Abdel Fattah el-Sisi. At ground level were little shops and bazaars selling flat disks of bread, as well as vegetables, fruit and shoes.

Normally in Egypt, little stallholders rush forward to sell you stuff but here they edged back. Normally, we would have had to dodge the incredibly aggressive Egyptian traffic but the sight of a SWAT guy standing guard in the middle of each intersection calmed all the drivers right down. One of the most eerie sights of the trip was those crazy Egyptian drivers waiting patiently and silently while thirty elderly Westerners took an eternity to hobble by in front of them.

Passers-by stood stock still, mouths open, staring unblinking at our well-armed procession. Some clutched little children to their chests. The kids laughed and pointed. One or two of the parents also began to smile and they started to wave. The old white folk smiled and waved back enthusiastically.

The plainclothes men's eyes were searching everywhere for threat but the townspeople, although surprised, seem glad to see us. The elderly white people were rich and a sign money might be returning.

Suddenly a man stepped forward from the crowd of onlookers, hand outstretched. The plainclothes guys leapt forward, reaching for their pistols, but an old tourist guy beat them to it. He was very tall with hair almost as pale as his skin. He grabbed the outstretched hand and shook it firmly. The police froze, conflicting emotions skirmishing across their features. By the time the handshake had finished, the Egyptian was surrounded by police, all leaning in close.

A growing crowd of little kids had been following us and the braver ones started to dash into the group of tourists, grabbing the nearest withered hand. The tourists looked delighted, the policemen less so. A few of the local cops peeled off to shoo away other kids before they could do the same.

Our walk was turning out to be a circuit and we soon found ourselves back on the little square by the river. Ahead I could see the lights of the boat. With safety so close yet still so far, I could feel the policemen's tension.

Ahead of me an old white woman was stepping up a kerb, but I could tell she wasn't going to make it. Her toe caught, she staggered and would have fallen but three plainclothes officers, thrummingly alert with the stress, instantly leapt forward and caught her, breaking her fall so she landed like a feather. They helped her up but then backed off quickly, too inhibited to dust her down.

When we returned to the boat, the sense of relief amongst the policemen was palpable. They started clapping each other on the shoulders and laughing.

And thus ended the most uncomfortable leisurely stroll of my life.

~~~

We'd seen marvels day after day but the best was yet to come.

The pyramids at Giza are the last remaining Wonder of the ancient world. The Great Pyramid, even after at least 4500 years, is a startling sight. At 150 metres high, it was the tallest man-made structure in the world for nearly 4000 years. It weighs six million tonnes and is made of over two million blocks of granite and limestone. It rises out of the clutter of Cairo streets like a glimpse of another world.

Remarkable though they are, they're only a shadow of what they once were. Originally encased in limestone they would have gleamed white in the Egyptian sun. The pyramids must have been the most sublime structures man has ever built.

Unfortunately, over time, Egyptians have cannibalised the limestone to ornament buildings in Cairo in what is possibly the greatest act of architectural vandalism the world has ever seen.

That one man, King Khufu, had the power and authority to build such an incredible artefact as the Great Pyramid so long ago is amazing. Less surprising is how little we know about him, consisting mainly of a few words from the not always reliable historian Herodotus writing two thousand years after Khufu's death.

According to Herodotus, Khufu prostituted his own daughter to pay for her tomb. This hardly seems likely. Khufu
~~~

had constructed the most magnificent building ever, so he probably wasn't short of a bob or two.

These magnificent tombs were like launch pads to take the Egyptian kings (the word pharaoh would not be coined until a couple of thousand years after Khufu) to meet the gods. There the kings could intercede on behalf of their mortal subjects for a plentiful but gently rising Nile flood. They would also accompany the sun god Ra in his path across the sky and help him fight the chaos god and enemy of light: the serpent Apophis.

If this was the cunning plan then it didn't turn out so well, for all three main pyramids on the Giza plateau—Khufu's, his son Khafre's, and the smallest that of Khafre's son, Menkaure—were all looted. The mummies were taken, no doubt so they could be unwrapped at the thieves' leisure and the golden amulets and talismans filched. What became of the mummies is unknown.

That's all pretty terrible because the ancient Egyptians believed that without an intact body the dead person could not function in the afterlife. Hence, they went to such lengths to preserve them as mummies, storing their viscera in separate canopic jars so they wouldn't rot the bodies from within.

Interestingly, in the time of these Fourth Dynasty kings, the brain was simply considered stuffing to fill out the head and was thrown away. The heart was supposed to be the seat of the soul and was preserved.

Naturally we jumped at the chance to get into Khufu's tomb. The original entrance is high up and still sealed. Down from this and barely six layers up from its base, there's a dark space which was how the tomb robbers had burrowed their way in. Nowadays this rat hole is the entrance everyone uses.

To get there, you wind your way back and forth up across the lower face of the pyramid, climbing up steps carved in the blocks. Once you get inside, the first thing you notice is the smell. A multitude of people have come this way, their sweat condensing out onto the cool of the walls.

The passage is roughly hewn and twisting and the floor is uneven. You emerge into the Grand Gallery which rises steeply up into the heart of the pyramid. A sloping wooden floor with little ridges for steps helps you climb. The gallery is high and tapered and everyone has to stoop as the ceiling gets too low. You find yourself shuffling subserviently upwards, your back bent like a farmer carrying a sack of grain.

I'm guessing Khufu would have liked that.

The smell gets worse. Countless thousands have been this way to disturb Khufu's sleep.

The Grand Gallery leads unerringly up into the King's Chamber. Huge dark red granite blocks, weighing up to eighty tonnes and transported all the way from Aswan, crowd around you.

The tomb has been emptied of grave goods and all that remains is Khufu's sarcophagus, tucked away at the back like an afterthought. The lid is gone and a corner has been hacked off. There are lights in the tomb but there's still a sense of profound darkness.

The terrible emptiness at the core of this mighty pyramid seems all kinds of wrong.

Once back outside, with the desert sands and busy old Cairo throbbing away, you're back in the real world but the plateau hasn't finished with its weirdness.

The Sphinx is unforgettable. Its features, moth-eaten by millennia of wind-driven sand, are supposed to be those of Khafre, a bullish-looking man judging by his other statues.

The Sphinx is half man and half lion and nobody really knows why.

Next to the Sphinx is a funerary temple for Khafre, and just below that is where a canal had allowed boats to bring the quarried blocks to the plateau. This canal has long since vanished and been built over with Cairo suburbs.

The dry desert sand may destroy rock but it also preserves wood, of which there was very little in ancient Egypt. At Giza, several solar boats have been discovered and these are an incredible 4500 years old.

The one on show in a special building behind Khufu's pyramid is fifty metres long. Its one long elegant curve makes it the most beautiful craft I have ever seen. It was designed to carry Khufu as he crossed the sky with the sun god Ra. Whether it might actually have been able to float on the Nile is another matter, but it is without doubt a boat made for a god.

After the grandeur of the pyramids, the chaos of Cairo can never be anything but a come-down. In the streets stall-holders sell everything from loofas to fly-swarming meat, while tuc-tucs whizz by with tatty cardboard boxes stacked high on their roofs. Posters for politicians are stuck everywhere, making the building facades looks like sheets of postage stamps.

However, even Cairo couldn't diminish the memories of what we had seen. There really is nowhere else like Egypt on the planet.

As for whether the political situation will settle down, I don't think anyone can say for certain. So, I guess the take-away message from all this is: high risk but high reward.

## *Go Looking for Dead Bodies in Cuba*

Cuba, 2010

Havana is like a beautiful woman whose face has been ravaged by age. Once smooth and elegant, now it's all sadly crumbling away. Plaster is cracked, paint is peeling.

Like any old woman who has lost her looks, Havana prefers the dark. Perhaps that is why the streets and alleyways have no lighting.

That or the piss-poor economic management of the Cuban government.

Piles of rubble and barred windows make the city look broken and guarded despite the life and warmth of the people.

Drinking mojitos in the rooftop pool of our opulent hotel, my family gazed out over rooftops that looked like they had only recently survived the apocalypse. Mildewed plaster and bird droppings, lines of drying clothes, corrugated iron, men and women in shorts and singlets lying around slumped in the recovery position.

Havana is the sort of place you look at and go 'Uh oh!', though the guidebooks assure you it's safe. If so, it's presumably because any thief who steals from foreigners risks a whole lot more than a fine and a severe telling off.

Maybe this is why I was less cautious than usual, despite travelling with my wife and daughters. That first night, after a swim on the roof, we emerged from the hotel onto a fine old square and glanced around looking for somewhere to eat.

We were immediately accosted by a tout who charmed us into following him to a local restaurant.

As soon as we left the square, we noticed the lack of streetlights. The empty crumbling arcades smelled of urine. Grubbily dressed man smoked in the dark recesses.

I rapidly got cold feet and was just about to turn and usher the family back the way we had come when the tout dived into one of the tenement blocks. Cautiously, I had a look inside and found it completely hollow with a set of wooden stairs spiralling all the way up to the top floor. Far up there we could see a building within a building. Supported by beams, it hung there like a foetus within a womb.

It certainly had the awnings of a restaurant. Through its windows we could see chairs and tables and lots of people.

I couldn't believe it would be any good but, as we'd come this far, we trudged up the stairs and were shown inside. Later, belated inspection of the guidebook revealed this to be one of the finest restaurants in Havana, though it looked more like a downscale American diner.

What was different from a diner, and what made me stay, were the huge bubbling tanks full of lobsters lining one wall.

I love lobster though the rest of the family hates it. The lobster wall made them nervous and they all wanted to go back to the hotel and its extremely expensive food.

But, then again, they weren't the ones who were paying so the hell with them!

So, while I was demolishing several lobsters for the princely cost of a fish and chip supper back home, my family had ordered chicken and were poking away at the small, stringy looking things that arrived.

"This isn't chicken!" said my daughter Juanita, the accusation so loud and final my hand froze, a delicious chunk of lobster almost to my mouth.

"It's rat!" said my daughter Aurora.

Struggling to maintain the calm and paternal authority for which I'm famed (at least within the confines of my own skull) I took a closer look at the meat on their plates. I had to admit the scrawny legs and breasts didn't look much like chicken, though they were too big for a rat. Or did they run to really big rats in Cuba?

"*You* taste it," ordered Ann, my wife.

So, I did taste it and, sure enough, it didn't taste at all like the chicken back home. Even so, I knew immediately what it was, for I remembered tasting it forty years before.

It was *chicken*. Real chicken. Not some poor fowl genetically manipulated so its muscles puffed out like balloons, who'd spent its life pecking away nervously in a tiny enclosure surrounded by thousands of its fellows.

The creature on this plate had fought and fucked and foraged its way around a farmyard, dodging trucks and feet while ferociously seeing off cats and rats. This bird had *lived* and its flesh revealed every moment of it. It was gamey and a little tough, not like the pillow-soft meat of the birds we got back home.

Somehow chicken in the UK, even that labelled 'organic', has lost its flavour but very gradually over so many years we just haven't noticed.

My family didn't believe me when I swore this was chicken.

Thankfully, they ate the rice and black beans and the cabbage which accompanied this and, it turned out, pretty much every other meal we had in Cuba. If you don't like them, no matter how dedicated a socialist firebrand you might be, you'd better strike Cuba off your bucket list.

Rice and beans are all that many Cubans have to eat and this is despite the cheap-as-chips lobster, and even though they pay only a twentieth of what foreigners have to. This is because Cuba uses two parallel currencies, the one for tourists worth twenty times that for the locals.

This disparity was bad enough, but it became even more brutally clear when we left Havana and travelled fifty kilometres down the coast to the resort of Varadero. This is on a wafer-thin peninsula sticking a dozen kilometres out into the water (I have to be a little unspecific as I've looked at the map and the water there could be called the Gulf of Mexico, the Atlantic Ocean or the Caribbean Sea. I've heard all three used). Strung along this peninsula are some of the plushest resort hotels I've ever seen.

We went there because part of the deal when I'm travelling with my family is that at some point, we have to spend time by a beach. As it happens, I loathe beaches. I don't like the salty crust that forms on my skin. I hate the sand getting between my toes and into sundry other crevices. On top of all that the sun ravishes my skin. Like most Scots, my ancestors hadn't had their skins kissed by the Mediterranean sun for ten thousand years or more. In the words of Woody Allen: *I don't tan, I stroke*.

Our skin is white because it has adapted to our paltry high latitude sun so that it can suck up the diminished goodness. When exposed to the tropical sun our skins drown in the sudden surfeit of radiation.

However, my biggest problem with lounging about on the beach is that I can't lie around doing nothing. You're going to spend a long time doing nothing when you're dead, so why aspire to it when you're still alive?

So, the beach is torture for me but my family loves it.

Hence, we were staying at Varadero, which doesn't seem to inhabit the same universe as Cuba, and the Cuban authorities are very keen to make sure that continues.

We set out from Havana, travelling along empty motorways, passing shacks and villages. Along the coast were little nodding-donkey oil rigs, just a few of which were still working. They dipped their beaks half-heartedly into the ground, their seals long since worn away, the smell of oil overwhelming.

When we got to Varadero, guards with assault rifles manned the little gate blocking the road where the peninsula met the land. At first, I figured it was to keep all the foreigners locked up there. Later excursions showed this wasn't true at all.

No, the armed guards were there to keep the Cubans out.

Wise move, because if the Cubans saw how the Westerners were living and the incredible food they were eating, then there would be another revolution pretty damned quick.

The hotel was a low, wooden open affair with large pools full of fish under the walkways. There were profuse displays of orchids, marble-floored rooms, free bars and a huge restaurant with scores of little stalls all laden with a kaleidoscope of delicacies from around the world. I'd never seen such variety.

Meanwhile, at the landward end of the peninsula, Cubans were spending a lifetime eating rice and beans.

Hence the guards with assault rifles guarding the entrance.

What it comes down to is that the free market, ugly and soul-less that it is, actually works. It raises everyone's standard of living but institutes a huge disparity in wealth. Pure socialism, and its relentless suppression of the free market, makes everyone equal but poor.

Yet here in socialist Cuba there was dazzling inequality. Such a step change difference between rich and poor I had seen only once before, on the Mexican border between Tijuana and San Diego. There you moved from developing world to advanced Western in the thickness of a barbed wire fence.

Our Varadero hotel was, of course, right on a sandy beach gently massaged by azure waters. That's where the family went, leaving me to fend for myself.

So, I spent days travelling around Cuba on its vast motorways, almost empty except for a few donkey-drawn carts. Cubans would stand around in little unsheltered groups waiting patiently for the rare lorry to slow and let them leap up onto the back for a free ride.

Cuba's a tropical paradise and the people are beautiful and lively but dirt poor. The only new constructions I saw were of monuments and statues to revolutionary heroes. Many of the older buildings are elegant and spectacular though they're rapidly fading away. There was a lot of money here once but it has slipped away.

Travelling around a new country is always interesting but I'd heard about one destination right on the hotel's doorstep that intrigued me. It was a tropical jungle nature reserve in just a few acres of fenced-off ground. According to a brochure I found, somewhere in this were the gruesome remains of someone who had died. How long ago seemed open to conjecture.

Gruesome, tropical and jungle are all words that work their magic on me. String them all together and they're irresistible.

So, I set off, looking quite the tropical dandy in my sandals, straw fedora and newly laundered white shirt and shorts. I walked unchallenged through the hotel's gate, also guarded by armed men, and within a few hundred metres came to the entrance to the reserve.

This took the form of a sign attached to a post and pointing to a gap in the fence. Beyond lay jungle.

There was not a soul about. There were roads within a few hundred metres but the traffic was almost non-existent so all I could hear were insects gnawing, dying, mating and beating their wings.

And that was pretty much the only sign of industry I'd seen since I'd come to this island.

I wandered in and found many little paths snaking away through the ferns and palm trees. There were so many holes in the pumice-like rock of the path that it looked like a solid sponge. Sometimes I could hardly see the path amongst the encroaching vegetation reaching in from the sides and hanging from above.

The deeper I got, the denser the jungle became. Amongst the insect cacophony I began to notice an almost continual rustling sound. There was no breeze to move the leaves and I was trying to work out where the noise was coming from when I saw something that almost stopped my heart.

On the path, and just ahead of me, I saw a reptilian tail disappearing into one of the myriad holes in the rock.

Suddenly alerted and looking round more carefully amongst the fronds and shadows, I realised I was surrounded by countless lizards, all flicking their tongues at me.

Lizards I'm okay with, snakes not so much. Where you get one, you usually get the other.

I stepped forward and all the lizards scuttled into the underbrush or dived down into the pumice. It wasn't until they moved that I understood just how many there were.

The reptilian presence squeezed out all the fun from the day. I decided to call the whole thing off and turned back the way I had come.

Within seconds I was lost. Intersecting little trails led all over the place. I hadn't bothered to memorise my route as the reserve hadn't sounded that big.

With the jungle pressing in, I had no idea where to find the fence, never mind the entrance. By now I had definitely wandered off the main path, such as it was. I found myself crashing through vegetation accompanied by the swishing of numberless reptilian tails.

Suddenly I blundered through a curtain of fronds just as the path ended and my nose came within centimetres of a rock face. I stumbled to a halt, face-to-face with a huge nest of hornets embedded in the rotten rock. Centimetres long with big heads, they looked like wasps on steroids,

I inched backwards very carefully. Was the buzzing sound from the hornets rising in pitch or was it just my imagination?

The curtain of fronds closed back over and hid the nest as I retreated backwards into the jungle. Suddenly I didn't know where to look. Back to see if the hornets were coming for me, or below to see if a snake was about to sink its fangs into my bare ankle.

Could this day get any worse?

Why, yes, yes it could.

Taking a little path to the left I came across another outcrop, this one with a cave. This must be what I'd been looking for.

Since I was here, I bent down and I shuffled into the cave. After a few metres the cave opened out into a central domed cavity a few metres high. Across the cavity the cave continued for a short way before it opened out again into jungle. With light coming in from both ends I could see well enough.

Certainly well enough to see the corpse.

What separates human remains from a corpse? Maybe nothing in law but, in my mind, human remains suggest some decorously laid out bones in a glass case in a quiet museum.

A corpse, on the other hand, is something still recognisably human and that's what I was looking at now. It had dried out a bit so the skin over its back had contracted enough to show all the knots of the vertebrae. He'd died on his side, curled up in the foetus position. His head was buried so deep within his shoulders that I couldn't see his face unless I looked more closely, something I was strongly disposed not to do.

The corpse looked so fresh the cave should have been a crime scene rather than an archaeological site. Assuming the body had lain here for decades then why hadn't it been eaten? I could see how this thin, heavily fenced off and guarded peninsula would stop larger predators from getting in but what about rats? Surely there had to be rats!

Then I thought again about the rustling. Lizards don't eat rats but snakes do. Was this place so heavily populated with big snakes that even rats didn't stand a chance?

What on earth was I doing here? Lost amongst hornets, snakes and with only a corpse for company, I suddenly realised this wasn't so much a holiday as a standard-order nightmare.

Somehow, I had to get out without getting stung or bitten by venomous fangs or asphyxiated by muscular coils tightening around my neck.

Feeling very sorry for myself, I turned back towards the cave entrance, bending down to so I didn't bump my head.

And indeed I didn't, so that was good. Unfortunately, the bending down made my back 'go', a spasm of excruciating pain sending me to my knees. My bare flesh was now pressed against the holes in the pumice in which God-knows-what was lurking.

I started to shuffle forwards, my suddenly unhinged mind full of images of the corpse reanimating and reaching for me, the desiccated skin over its fingers ripping open to reveal the bones beneath.

The next few minutes were a blur. Somehow, I crawled out of the cave but getting back upright was agonising, the slipped disc in my spine sticking so far out it must have looked like a prehensile tail. I blundered through the leaves and fronds, sure to be struck down by snake bite or the hands of a long-dead man around my throat.

After an eternity of horror, I found the gate and staggered out onto the quiet road.

Dirty, sweaty and hunched over in agony, I lurched up to the security gate but the guard held out a hand sternly, palm towards me. He didn't seem to be able to equate the dirty, bedraggled, sweating wretch grimacing in pain with the cocky European who'd swaggered by just an hour before.

Even showing him my room key didn't help; he clearly thought I'd pinched it. Neither of us spoke the other's language so in the end he phoned through to reception. The English-speaking receptionist, only able to hear me and not see my wretched condition, was easier to convince and soon I was hobbling back to my room.

I was wise enough not to expect sympathy from my family and it's just as well. They listened to my sorry tale, trying to keep their faces straight and suppressing fits of giggles. They hadn't had so much fun since I stumbled into a nesting ground in the Orkneys and was attacked by a flock of skuas. Damned things nearly took my eyes out!

When it comes to travel, it's funny how little things can colour your perception. Two weeks of luxury and good food in a beautiful tropical paradise were swept aside by one hour of communist hornets and reptiles and corpses. Even ten years later I just have to hear Cuba mentioned on a TV news item and my lips purse in disapproval.

Don't let me put you off, though.

## *Sharing a garden swing with a monkey*

Agra, India, 2017

It was idyllic. The hotel—white marble, towering atrium, staff in impeccably pressed uniforms, brightly coloured paintings of Mughal emperors filling the walls—had been an oasis of calm after the chaos of Agra. Shut firmly outside were roads full of combative motor bikes, tuc-tucs, camels, donkey-drawn carts and suicidal pedestrians. The hotel even managed to block out the smell of two stroke engines, ubiquitous in most Indian cities.

India is always colourful but also hot, noisy, smelly and poking its sharp fingertips in your chest for attention. If you're an effete Westerner like me, used to a quieter lifestyle, then it's worth splashing out on a good quality hotel when you go to India. India is wonderful but after a day out in the maelstrom of city life, you just want to retreat into an upmarket air-conditioned hotel and shut it the hell out.

However, it was now approaching sundown and I'd had the chance to shower away the dust from our long journey across India's endless plains. I made my way to the top of the hotel and its little roof garden from where I could see the Taj Mahal across the low roof tops of the city.

India may be bracing but at dawn and dusk the atmosphere is magical. The heat for once is not oppressive and there is a quality of the light that transports you and makes you love the place, whatever disturbing sights you've seen during the day.

So, there I was, rocking on a swing seat, and appreciating the dusk and looking across at the marvel that is the Taj Mahal. I'd been expecting to be underwhelmed but when I first caught sight of it my heart had risen like a bird from a cage. It has an otherworldly beauty, the ineffable stuff of heaven.

I watched the Taj as the red orb of the sun disappeared, the wear and tear of the day dissipating in the sublime light.

Then the monkey rocked up.

Monkeys in an Indian city aren't a surprise; they perch on roofs and telephone poles like crows in the West. They can move very fast and very suddenly. Put your snack down beside you on the bench and it'll be gone in a flash.

But now here was one climbing up to the fifth floor to join me. The beast came over the parapet smoothly, lithely, menacingly. Close up it was much bigger than I'd expected and I found myself marvelling at thick muscle sliding easily under furry skin. The eyes, cartoonishly close together, regarded me with disdain. 'What the hell are you doing here?' they seemed to ask.

It advanced slowly but unhesitatingly. Smaller than an Alsatian but much more thickly built around the arms and torso, it must have weighed about as much. It showed me a full set of wickedly pointed teeth.

It had that strange lope you see when long arms are doing a lot of the walking. As it climbed onto the swing seat and sat beside me, the swing creaked under its substantial weight.

The monkey turned and looked out at the Taj. The seat had been gently swinging and, though I immediately stopped pushing, it continued moving lazily back and forth.

Neither the monkey nor I seemed inclined towards conversation. Me from fear because the monkey was all muscle and fangs while I was all fat and fear. If things kicked off then I didn't fancy my chances.

For long minutes we sat there. I wasn't enjoying this but I was afraid what would happen if I tried to make a move. I was hoping someone would appear on the roof and send the monkey into retreat but nobody came to my rescue.

Would I be there all night? Would a whole bunch of monkeys climb up to this roof? Would they carry me off back to some lofty minaret or to some underground temple dedicated to the Monkey God? Once there, would they tear open my chest, rip out my heart and lift it high for inspection by their malevolent deity?

No, as it turned out. Instead, after what seemed like an eternity, the monkey scratched its armpit and gave a yawn showing more teeth than a year of toothpaste commercials, then made its way to the parapet and disappeared over the side.

The monkey, it appears, had been enjoying the sunset and the Taj Mahal just like me.

Hazards in India come at you like this, straight out of left field. You just don't see them coming, and that can be fatal.

For example, on the motorways. India does have motorways although they are more like the dual carriageways back in the UK. They're way better than other roads in India because at least there's a consensus about direction of travel. Oncoming traffic doesn't veer into your lane because there's a divider preventing it. On other roads it's a more free-for-all affair with oncoming lorries aiming right at you just to ginger you up a bit.

On the bigger highways lane discipline still doesn't really exist but at least on one side of the divider you're travelling in the same direction.

Except for cows and other animals. They don't seem to have heard of lane discipline at all. We travelled for many hundreds of miles across the plains and I became quite an expert on the subject of Indian roadkill.

In Britain the most prominent forms of roadkill are foxes and hedgehogs. In India it's cows. Cows are venerated here, are never eaten (at least by the Hindu majority) and are free to roam wherever they wish. Unfortunately, they seem to prefer the fast lanes of motorways.

Often the only notice you get of approaching calamity is when the truck ahead of you swerves to the left without warning because its driver has seen the dead cow that you can't. If you're quick, you can swerve to the left too but otherwise the roadkill can kill you.

Also, unlike dead hedgehogs, cows can't easily be flattened and forgotten. What happens instead is that the bodies are eventually battered off the side of the road where they wait, bloated and blackening, for the carrion birds. The birds' modus operandi is to peck away at the cow's bottom until the hole is big enough for them to get their heads all the way inside to reach the tasty bits.

As motorway sights go, I'd take a Roadchef any day. So would my daughters, although it's difficult to be certain as they haven't spoken a word since.

I use the expression *carrion birds* rather than vultures advisedly. This is because there are hardly any of the latter left and that has resulted in a rather startling change to Zoroastrian burial ceremonies. These used to take place on the Towers of Silence.

I've had a morbid interest in the Towers since reading of them in the works of Paul Scott (and they're also the basis of the Towers of Set in good old Robert E. Howard's Conan books). Vultures wheeling over Indian cities in the past might have been an indication that a Tower of Silence was nearby. Zoroastrians and also Parsees placed their dead in the open on top of these so the vultures could eat them. This was called a Sky Burial. The Parsees do it as an act of charity to the birds, the Zoroastrians to prevent the Corpse Demon Avestan from getting at the bodies.

Unfortunately, in recent years the population of vultures in India has fallen catastrophically by 99.9% (perhaps they ate something that disagreed even with them) and as a result the practice has had to be discontinued. Instead, the Towers are now lined with large lenses and mirrors and the process is called a Sky Cremation. However, even under the intense Indian sunlight, this process can still take four or five days.

And, if you get close to one, it will put you off barbecue for life.

So, cows can and do kill in India but there are plenty of other hazardous animals (snakes and tigers, I'm looking at you!). However, the real problem is dogs, as I found to my cost.

We were in Goa and I was having an idyllic experience while walking along a beach. The cobalt blue waters of the Arabian Sea and a broad swathe of sand stretched before me to eternity. This magical moment suddenly turned pear-shaped when a group of wild dogs comes snapping at my ankles.

Wild dogs in India are nothing if not a problem. If you're lucky they won't be big but a single nip from rabid teeth and your brain will swell up like a balloon. Which is a shame as it is firmly constrained within the unyielding bone of your skull.

Not right away of course; it can take several months for the rabies virus to crawl its way up your peripheral nervous system before it reaches your brain. Once it gets there your chances of surviving are theoretical rather than actually achievable.

In fact, if you'll allow me go all quantitative, as of 2016, only fourteen people are known to have survived rabies after the first symptoms appear, even though rabies kills more than 15,000 people a year, and four times that annual number before the vaccine was invented. It's worth bearing in mind, however, that if you can get the vaccine within ten days of being bitten, then you will almost certainly live to tell the tale.

One of the symptoms of rabies is hydrophobia. No matter how parched the patient, they can't bring themselves to drink water. Even just the thought of drinking sends the muscles of their throats into an agonising spasm.

If rabies has got into the dog population in any country, then they will be responsible for 99% of the cases in humans. The number of stray dogs is why more humans die of rabies in India than any other country in the world.

Other factors contribute to this high death rate. The killing of dogs was outlawed in 2001. One reason for this is that dogs feed on the mounds of garbage all over Indian streets, thus performing a rubbish disposal function, and they also keep the rats down.

The second reason is that as a predominantly Hindu based culture, animals are not supposed to be killed, even dogs.

This is crazy because you won't just be attacked by dogs on deserted Goan beaches, but also in the heart of big cities where dogs routinely attack the urban poor, especially children. Stray dogs number in the tens of millions and, even if they don't have rabies, their dental hygiene is less than impressive and their teeth harbour a bestiary of viruses and bacteria.

Dog bites also form the kernel of an unusual form of mass hysteria. Many Indians believe that people bitten by dogs will develop puppies in their stomachs, men as well as women. As medical professionals don't share their belief in this condition (they have a name for it: puppy pregnancy syndrome), the patients spurn them in favour of charlatans and their ludicrous and totally ineffective treatments.

So, if you go for a walk in a city or for a run on an idyllic Goan beach, take a stick or carry stones you can chuck at the brutes.

I didn't have any such things on my lonely Goan beach so had to escape by running fully clothed into the ocean. The little bastards milled around barking for half an hour at which point I was able to make my escape.

So again, hazard and horror can spring out at you from nowhere. The first day we arrived in India also revealed another challenge for pedestrians.

We set out from our hotel in New Delhi to look at some Mughal tombs that were well within walking distance. It was early afternoon and we strode off confidently, waving away the tuc-tuc drivers who stopped to offer us a lift. Our refusal seemed to baffle them, and indeed one of them, named Mr. Patel as we were to find out later, was so concerned he followed us for the rest of the day.

The tombs were amazing, as were so many of the other places we visited in Delhi, but it eventually came time for us to return to our hotel. It was nearing rush hour and traffic that had been already quite fierce was now a ravening river of moving metal following no rules that we could discern. There were pedestrian crossing lights but the drivers ignored them.

Crossing the road had become a charter flight to Dignitas.

Suddenly we found ourselves stranded. I was getting pretty worried when Mr. Patel came weaving to our rescue. Somehow the four of us, and Mr. Patel, were crammed into his tuc-tuc and we went careering off through the torrent. It was the worst ride of my life, especially as I had my family with me.

Somehow, perhaps it was the magical green and yellow paint of his tuc-tuc, but there seemed to be a kind of force bubble around us, so he got us back safely.

Big tip for Mr. Patel!

~~~

Bollywood films aren't India's only source of drama. There's also a rich tradition of hotel security theatre.

During the 2008 Mumbai Massacre, a famous hotel was attacked and many guests killed. In response, the larger hotels in India seem to have gone overboard on security. Even just to get into the hotels, we first had to pass through heavily guarded gates with thick metal poles, buffers against car bombs, which could be retracted back into the road. Guards would check under the bonnet of our car, in the boot and would slide a mirror under the chassis.

When we got to the hotel itself, we had to put our bags and cases through an X-ray machine, its aperture built into the outer wall. Then, once inside, we had to go through a metal detector.

In one hotel in Southern India a guard patrolled the restaurant with the longest and thickest barrelled rifle I have ever seen. It looked like some sort of elephant gun.

This all sounds impressive but it was a complete charade. At the gates the guards either looked under the car, or they looked under the bonnet, or they looked in the boot. None of them did it all. On top of that none of them ever looked in the passenger compartment. The back seat could have been up to the rafters in heavily armed Mujahideen and they'd never have noticed.

As for all those metal detectors: I set off every single one. I don't know why this was as I don't have any metal implants. Dutifully, the guards would bring out their hand-held metal detectors and run them over me. I always set these off as well.

At that point they would just give up and usher me through. Expensive hotels in India go out of their way not
~~~

to piss off their guests so the truth is they weren't going to search me.

Ever.

As for the elephant gun: one day I got a close look and noticed the piddly little bore in the thick barrel and realised it was actually just a massively over-engineered air rifle. How useful would this be as the terrorists came storming off the beach, their AK-47s chattering?

In summary: all these security measures were simply cosmetic and designed to reassure the guests but in the event were utterly useless.

Is this a quintessentially Indian phenomenon or is such ineffectiveness also true of security in the rest of the world but just a bit better disguised?

Answers on a postcard.

~~~

Despite all the above, India is a truly fabulous place to visit. In Rajasthan in particular you can find abandoned cities, vast citadels, exotic temples: sometimes India seems straight out of Robert E. Howard's tales of Conan the Barbarian.

Actually, come to think of it, I guess it's the other way round.

It's well worth visiting despite the hazards, even those from the monkeys.
~~~

## *Taking to the roads in Vietnam*

Hanoi, Vietnam, 2013

Figures show that the biggest risk you run in visiting non-Western countries is death by road traffic.

India, described in the last chapter, is very bad with 16.6 road deaths per year per 100,000 inhabitants. If that's just not high enough for you then might I suggest Vietnam as your destination at 24.5? Both, however, yield precedence to some African countries where the rate is over 30.

In comparison the rate in the UK is 2.8. The US, incidentally, is surprisingly high at 12.4.

So, when you're in-country, is it obvious why Vietnam's death rate is almost an order of magnitude higher than in the UK?

Duh!

There is a dual carriageway that takes you east from Hanoi out to the beautiful Halong Bay. It is one of the best quality roads in the country, although there is no central reservation to keep the two directions of traffic apart. As in India, the side of the road you are supposed to drive on is more guidance than instruction. Oncoming vehicles may well veer into your lane but the real hazards of travelling along these roads in Vietnam are as small as a grain of rice.

Because that's what they are.

The rice harvest is around September and October and the mounds of grain have to be dried by spreading them out on a large dry surface. And what better surface than a lane of a highway even if it is one of the busiest in the country?

So, your coach is travelling at top speed (any other speed is forbidden on pain of death in Vietnam) in lock step with a long line of other vehicles, when, and this is the only warning you get, the vehicles ahead of you all veer like a serpent into the fast lane. If you are already in the fast lane, then the slow lane cars veering into your fast lane makes you veer into the fast lane of the oncoming traffic.

It all gets very febrile.

Imagine barrelling down the M6 in England and having to take sudden and dramatic avoiding action because of a pile of mangelwurzels that a farmer has dumped on the motorway.

One wonders about the mindset of these rice farmers. Every day they are risking hundreds of lives just because the highway is the most convenient place to dry their rice. Is it a kind of *idee fixe* where they focus on this one thing to the exclusion of everything else? In this case rice rather than people's lives.

There's another even more dangerous and fatal problem with traffic in Vietnam.

As in so much of the Far East, the weapons of choice to kill Westerners are small motorbikes. It seems that everyone has one and the *idee fixe* the Vietnamese have is that it is going to get them to wherever they are heading and to hell with any collateral damage.

There are pedestrian crossing points but these have little significance. It doesn't matter whether the lights are red or green or fluorescent purple. The Vietnamese motorcyclists act as though they are colour blind, without a single exception.

Traffic is extremely dense but has a sort of flow, like a ballet performed by a football crowd. Whatever the colour of the light the dense wall of motorbikes never stops. If the light is green there is at least the notion, though vestigial and exposed on a hillside at birth, that if you cross then they may, if there is an 'x' in the month, try to avoid you.

Some Westerners resort to hiring orphans to walk with them around Hanoi. While running down a Westerner, or anyone young and fit, may be regarded as something of a prize, mowing down a cute little Vietnamese child would be the equivalent of a yellow card. When they cross the road, the Westerners literally keep the hired kid between them and the traffic, using them like a shield.

If you don't happen to have an orphan handy, when you arrive at a crossing for the first time you stand there bemused at the endless stream of metal flowing by. Sooner or later, you have no choice but to commit and you just have to start walking. Once you do, there is no going back.

The absolute cardinal rule is that you cannot start to cross then hesitate. If you do then you're going to have bikes on you like a bad rash.

When the pedestrian light is green the hordes will usually try to avoid you, and the tidal wave of bikes will part to flow around you. You become submerged, front and back in moving metal.

As long as you don't hesitate and, God forbid, alter your stride, then the riders can compensate and steer round you. However, if you hesitate or speed up or slow down then the game is a bogie and all hell breaks loose.

I was once crossing the road on the green pedestrian light. I had sort of got used to it by then and had learned to set off with a regular stride, not meeting the bikers' eyes (that might be seen as a challenge and they won't even try to avoid you). The never-ending stream of bikes was flowing around me but I was keeping my nerve. I felt like Moses parting the Red Sea.

Suddenly, out of the corner of my eye, I saw a girl on a bike coming right at me. There was no way she wouldn't strike me.

The fright made my steps falter. I'd already had more than a gut-full of this nonsense and my nerve snapped at the absurdity of this utterly ridiculous situation. I pointed my finger at the traffic light and screamed, "Green light!"

The woman, and a whole bunch of the nearer bikers, all stopped dead, brakes screeching. Bikes coming behind had to swerve, which in turn made others turn aside too.

Chaos ravished order and the whole cavalcade came to a halt.

In the sudden stillness I shimmied around the stalled bikes to the safety of the other side.

The most disturbing thing was that the becalmed bikers didn't shout or scream or peep their shitty little horns at me.

No, they all just looked at me sadly, pityingly. Here was a representative of the white race unashamedly losing face in front of a crowd of Vietnamese. I had let myself down, I had let my country down, I had let my whole race down.

For once I began to feel some sympathy for Nixon and Kissinger and their carpet bombing of Hanoi.

I didn't like Hanoi and in fact it's the city I like least behind Sao Paulo in Brazil. Aside from the horrors of the traffic, I didn't like the cramped streets or the muggy air. I didn't like the hawkers with their large woks full of boiling oil on the sidewalks that people had to carefully step around. Sometimes Health and Safety can go too far but definitely not in Vietnam.

Vietnam did, however, furnish me with a couple of those experiences that stay with you for the rest of your life. The sort that makes travel so worthwhile.

I had gone on a hot and humid night to an upmarket restaurant in the heart of the city. It was a several-storey building with a courtyard surrounded by a high wall. As I had arrived early, I was given a table outside in the open and that suited me fine.

I'd ordered my meal and was passing my time people watching as I do when I travel alone. The restaurant was beginning to fill up but was not too busy, allowing the head waiter to lean against the high wall by the gate and smoke a fag.

He was having a relaxing time when something made him do a double take. He quickly put a finger to his head then pulled it away and inspected it.

He screamed like a banshee.

Everything changed. Almost like it was choreographed, and perhaps it had been practised like a fire drill, all the waitresses in their beautiful cheongsams came streaming out of the building. One grabbed my plate and crockery, while another grabbed me and pulled me to my feet. I found myself being dragged out of the courtyard and into the restaurant. Just as I reached its shelter, a wall of water fell from the sky, crashing down like an avalanche on the corrugated iron roofs all around.

I've never seen a downpour quite so bad. I suppose they're common in Vietnam and the locals know exactly what to do. The head waiter had felt a single drop of rain on his head and that had been enough.

However, I'd seen something a bit like it in Taiwan. I was with my friends Gary and Emma. Emma is Taiwanese and we were going out for a meal. It was night and the sky was overcast but it seemed a perfectly nice evening otherwise.

Suddenly Emma said, "We need to buy umbrellas."

I laughed. It didn't look or feel like it was going to rain and, anyway, what was a few raindrops in this hot climate? It would all evaporate in seconds anyway.

"Now!" she said.

That's when I realised that, as though by magic, hawkers had appeared all around us selling cheap plastic umbrellas.

Unnerved, I brought an umbrella with only seconds to spare. Again, there was a sudden deluge.

Back in Vietnam, I ate my meal and watched from the window as the rain thundered down. When the time came to leave, the headwaiter summoned a cab and sheltered me under his umbrella as I climbed in.

I got back to my hotel, a tall, thin mid-range affair, and got a beer and sat on my little balcony to watch the rainstorm. By now the lightning had started but it wasn't like any lightning I'd seen before. The flashes were so frequent, almost one a second, but diffused by the clouds so that the whole sky looked like a flickering TV screen.

Across from me was a sepulchral Catholic church. So much in the Orient is baroque, fever dream ornate, especially when it comes to religion, but this church was very different. It was completely plain with a tall, heavy square-sectioned tower. Years of heat and rain had left dark stains down the long lengths of the sides. It appeared like it was in shadow even when it wasn't. It was spooky even in daylight.

I watched this old church, limned by the flickering lightening and through sheets of falling water. The tower was like some old missionary, alone and dying and far from home in a country he would never understand. A person so long away he was neither European nor oriental.

I sat and watched it for hours as the lightning played, lost in a world so unlike my own.

## *Journeying into the lands of ice and darkness*

### The far north, various times

Norway is a very long thin country, almost 2400 kilometres in length. None of it is balmy, but in the northernmost bits you're left in no doubt that you're within the Arctic Circle.

The Arctic Circle encompasses the parts of the northern hemisphere where the sun never rises above the horizon on at least one day of the year (if you're a glass half full person it also represents the places where the sun is always above the horizon for at least one day). This region corresponds to around the top 24 degrees of latitude.

To live in places where on some days it never gets dark and on other days it never gets light, must produce a strange mindset. I was only there for a couple of weeks but I began to feel like I was in another world.

As well as the psychological hazards, in these high latitudes polar bears can be a bit of a pest. Weighing up to 700 kg, perhaps three metres in length and with more teeth than you ever thought possible, they can leave a very nasty bite. They are known by many names in the circumpolar world: nanook, umka, ice bear, white bear. These charmers can smell prey up to a mile away.

I was told on good authority that this makes Norwegian Arctic policemen behave in a very strange manner. One extremely long road runs the length of Norway. If you take it very far north then the police will pull you over and check if you're carrying firearms.

And, if you aren't, they'll give you one.

In Svalbard, previously called Spitzbergen, an archipelago off the north coast of Norway (human population 3000, polar bear population 300) you aren't allowed to leave the few settlements without a gun.

Not that anything less than a high-powered rifle fired at a very long distance will help you much if you get into dispute with a polar bear. Closer, and it would take an exceptionally icy-minded shooter to stand their ground and score a critical hit on a polar bear sprinting towards them at 40 kph.

Really, firearms in these circumstances are to make a loud noise in the hope, and let's not get any more aspirational, that it will frighten the creature away.

The hungrier the animal, the less likely that will work.

Risk averse as ever, I decided not to take that chance. That's why I made sure I was safely encased within the metal bulwarks of a cargo ferry that sails up the Atlantic coast of Norway, calling in at all the little coastal towns. This was with the delightfully named Hurtigruten lines. The ship itself was comfortable enough but, if you wanted to spend any time on deck, you had to dress as though for a ram-raid, covering as much of your face as possible.

I was travelling in the winter for the best chance of seeing the Northern Lights (spoiler alert: I didn't see a damned thing).

Even though I missed the Lights there was one polar stratospheric phenomenon I did manage to catch. We were five hundred miles into the Arctic Circle and I saw what looked like a rainbow-coloured lozenge up in the sky. Unlike in the long arc of a rainbow, the boundaries between the colours were so sharp they almost cut my eyes.

These lozenges are supposed to be due to the refractory effects of small clouds of ice crystals at 70,000 feet, but I'm pretty sure it has something to do with the trolls.

A lot of Norwegians still believe in trolls. Not the cute kind of troll you get as toys; the word actually means demon, fiend or even werewolf.

One can see how this land might spawn such phantasms for there is nothing blacker than the overcast Arctic night. Black water, black air, you feel you're crossing the Styx to the Land of the Dead. Sometimes out of the blackness swims the nightmarish bulk and flames of an oil terminal mining the black gold that has made Norway so rich. Its roar fills the Arctic silence.

Mordor made real.

The oil has made them so rich that in some ways the Norwegians have tamed this hostile land. I'd liked the sound of adventuring to the Arctic Circle, what with the polar bears and the trolls. However, it's difficult to sustain the illusion of being a fearless explorer when, several hundred miles into the Arctic Circle, you come across a florists.

Even so, adaptions have had to be made. In this hostile but managed environment the legs and little wheels of old people's Zimmer frames have been replaced by sled runners. No child looks thin or small because of all the furs and clothing which bulk them up into Teletubbies. Parallel lines of buttressing across the mountainsides above the little towns are there to slow down any avalanches that otherwise might sweep them away into the deep, dark water.

Alcohol is eye-wateringly expensive due to taxation and anything stronger than beer can only be bought at certain government outlets. It's understandable because when it's very dark and very cold for six months of the year, alcohol might become too much of a comfort.

Reindeer also feature large in this Arctic world and it's difficult to get by without eating them as it's the one animal they have in plenty. It has the texture of steak but tastes more like horse though without the grassy aftertaste of that meat. Braised in Marsala wine it can be delicious, though eating it can be a trial as any young children present will look at you with tearful eyes full of hurt and betrayal.

Which is pretty rich considering what other things Arctic dwellers get up to with the animals. Reindeer castration is something of a hot topic in the Norwegian Arctic. Castration makes the creatures easier to handle for herding or for pulling sleds. It also allows them to keep their antlers longer, making it easier to dig for grass and lichen under the snow.

Santa's reindeer must all be males and castrated as they still have their antlers, which normally get broken off in fights between un-neutered males.

The traditional Sami reindeer herders' method of castration involves biting the creatures' testicles with their teeth. I hope you'll forgive me if I get a little pedantic here, but it's really semi-castration because the testicles are pulverised without actually breaking the skin or cutting them off. The reindeer is held down while the herder chews the contents of the testicles to pulp.

However, the heavy hand of the government in Oslo has stepped in and criminalised this traditional technique. It is considered a Health and Safety issue because it can lead to the reindeer, quite reasonably, kicking the herder in the teeth.

Instead, the castrators must now use a special device and must receive training in its use. Sadly, the Sami herders live hundreds of kilometres out in the tundra and away from the training centres, so they are no longer able to castrate their reindeer at all.

Health and Safety gone mad!

Before we shift elsewhere in the Arctic, let's talk about Norwegian snow hotels (sometimes they're more accurately called ice hotels). These are constructed every winter out of blocks of ice 70 cm thick. They have rooms where the beds are made from ice blocks and the ice walls have been intricately, though impermanently, carved with bas reliefs. The hotel I visited had one of Marilyn Monroe, skirts blown up from an entirely imaginary steam vent (actual steam vents are frowned on in ice hotels). Some reliefs show the winged horse Pegasus or spacemen or hermit crabs or dolphins.

Similar designs decorated the bar area where the bar itself is an ice block and drinks are served in cored-out chunks of ice. Full sized carvings of huskies pranced up a curved ice shelf spiralling up behind the bar. Wall carvings were styled like the interleaving branches of trees and in some nestled exquisitely detailed little owls. Lights inside or behind the ice made the ice carvings glow blue or purple or red.

It all looks very lovely but there are downsides. For example, there you are trudging through the Arctic in winter but when you step into the hotel the temperature plunges brutally. I had on multiple layers of clothes, including industrial strength thermals, but I was shocked at the inside temperature.

To prevent their guests freezing to death overnight, the hotel dispenses 7000 Tog sleeping bags, polar explorer socks and balaclavas.

You can't keep your luggage and clothing in the hotel because obviously they would freeze stiff as a board overnight. There are also no ensuites as no plumbing could withstand the cold, so if you want to go for a wee in the small hours you somehow have to make your way down a thirty-metre-long ice tunnel to an actual brick and wood hotel annex. You have to do this in your night clothes.

As we were leaving the hotel to go back to the ship, a minibus pulled up and a sleek-looking Indian couple emerged. The taxi driver unloaded a score of upmarket suitcases. A chain of porters formed to pass the cases hand to hand into the hotel.

The woman was breathtakingly beautiful, and although the man was rather less remarkable he was clearly very rich (you pay through the nose to be frozen to death in these hotels).

I reflected that no matter how beautiful his companion, and no matter how rich he was, this was one man who would not be getting laid that night. I'll go further and suggest that these are the only hotels on the planet where nobody has ever had sex.

The thing is, that whether you are trying to have sex or even just trying to sleep in one of those fortress-wall thick sleeping bags, some bit of you will have to be exposed to the outside air, whether it is the back of your head in the former, or your mouth in the latter. Whatever it is will freeze.

The cold will also make you want to pee, requiring that whole Scott of the Antarctic trek to the annex.

I suspect that if I'd had to make that trek even once, I would never have gone back. I'd have bedded down in that warm brick-built annex. But, then again, I'm not masochistic enough to have stayed there in the first place.

Another cold and dark place is Iceland, but it adds another little wrinkle to Arctic life in the form of extreme vulcanism. It's only about the size of Ireland but it has around a hundred volcanoes and thirty or so of these have erupted in recent history.

This happens because Iceland is where the mid-Atlantic ridge comes ashore. The North Atlantic and Eurasian plates emerge here from the molten depths of the planet and spread away from each other. Usually this all happens nine kilometres down on the floor of the Atlantic but in Iceland you can see it happening on land.

In fact, you can bestride two continental plates like a mighty colossus. Everything from pretty much Vladivostok to Vancouver was created along this line, and the plates are still moving apart today. Don't do your bestriding for long, however, because otherwise you will find yourself doing the full splits in barely ten years' time.

Though the movement of the plates may only be by a few centimetres a year, not far beneath an inferno of molten rock is trying to emerge through points of weakness. This activity so near the surface is why Iceland's volcanoes produce almost a third of the world's lava.

The world, of course, hardly noticed this except when a volcano called Eyjafjallajokull erupted in 2010. Even then the absurdly difficult pronunciation of the name would have kept the eyes of the media away, had not the plume of ash shut down air travel in northern and western Europe for six days. Around 100,000 flights were cancelled.

And we'll hear more from Iceland because Eyjafjallajokull is actually a tiddler in their terms. A much bigger volcano called Katla is in another league altogether.

Katla has accounted for as much as 4% of global carbon dioxide emissions. In its last eruption in 1918 it produced so much lava it extended the southern coast by five kilometres. Its lava production in 1755 was similar to the combined flows of the Amazon, Nile, Yangtze and Mississippi rivers.

In the past this monster has erupted at intervals of between twenty and ninety years, and on average every fifty years. However, it's been 103 years since it last went off. Hold on to your hats!

Katla is the volcano that most worries Icelanders ever since Iceland was settled a thousand years ago. When it does pop, lava can flow out of its 10 km wide caldera and reach as far as 50 km.

What's worse is that it is also an abrupt event. To try to minimise loss of life, if the seismometers festooned across Katla get jiggy then every mobile phone in the region, including your own, will ring simultaneously. I don't know the exact recorded message you'll hear but, bearing in mind that from first little seismometric jiggle to Armageddon takes less than an hour, I'm guessing it's along the lines off 'Run like fuck!'

Not being of especially sound mind I like to 'bag' volcanoes and these have included Mauna Loa in Hawaii, Mount St. Helens in the States and Vesuvius in Italy. Katla seemed to be asking for it.

So, I took a hired 4WD and tried to get near Katla by driving over the cindery lava fields that came from the last eruption. Off-road stuff wasn't covered in the rental agreement but that's just how I roll.

It was a long drive over black lava with lots of ups and downs over little hills which had been almost submerged by the flow. Surrounding mountains loomed through the mist and cloud.

We were getting close and I could see the mass of Katla rising to the clouds. I'd come so far I was two hours from the nearest road leading out that might have sped me to safety.

Just then my phone rang.

And that's when the part of my brain controlling bladder function went on strike.

Cleaning myself as best I could, I patiently explained to the caller back in the UK that I wasn't currently interested in mis-sold insurance policies.

Iceland's vulcanism both powers and heats the country. That's why you can luxuriate in the almost-but-not-quite too hot waters of its world-famous Blue Lagoon while looking out over miles and miles of lava field desolation.

Most of the fields look just like broken up rock, as though a Deep South chain gang with pick-axes had been let loose on boulders. Some of the terrain, however, is covered with what is called pahoehoe which means 'smooth unbroken lava' but which Hawaiians refer to as 'chicken guts' because that's just what they look like—lumps of stuff sheathed in smooth membranes.

Cheap heat and power came in handy when Iceland took a big hit in the 2008 financial crisis. Like fiscal Vikings, their banks had gone marauding and all three of the country's biggest banks found themselves defaulting on their loans. Relative to its size, Iceland suffered the biggest banking collapse of any country in history. People didn't like it and police had to use tear gas for the first time in sixty years.

And Iceland still isn't out of the woods. Prices in Iceland are sky high, especially for food, with almost all vegetables having to be imported. Many Icelanders survive by taking three jobs. Luckily, a big boost was given to the economy by the notion of breaking long transatlantic flights for a few days of layover in Reykjavik. Pre-pandemic the place was full of wealthy American tourists doing just that.

When I travel, I suffer from an overwhelming compulsion to eat strange local delicacies and Iceland delivered big time. Edging the Arctic Circle, the rough winters stop them growing stuff like chickens, pigs or cows. That means, traditionally, they have had to find their sustenance where they could. At the risk of some of you never speaking to me again, I'll give some examples.

There was smoked puffin with mustard sauce which I would describe as gamey but redolent of the ocean. The raw whale sashimi was no gastronomic treat and the horse was okay, like steak but with an aftertaste of grass.

One delicacy did give me pause for thought, however. Hakarl is shark which has been buried for three months to allow it to decay and ferment before being dug up and eaten. I'd seen it every night on the menus but just couldn't bring myself to order some.

As the days passed, and despite my gorge rising, I steeled myself and decided to try it on my last night in Iceland.

When I got to the restaurant I was told, without irony, that rotten shark was 'off'.

# *A helpful miscellany*

## Various times, various places

We're coming to the end now so I'll finish with some of the more basic tips which may help you get into trouble if you so wish (or what to avoid if you don't).

### Hitchhiking

It was 1974, I was twenty years old and I knew it all. I was hitching across the States from one coast to the other and back again. In those long-gone days it was easy to get enough money from casual jobs to keep you going.

Hitching was common but, in those days, not for the faint-hearted. I'd never hitched in my life before when I first flagged a car down in Maryland. Nervously, I hauled myself and my luggage into the back seat of one of those already ancient, mammoth-sized American cars with fins. The driver turned to me, his eyes yellow and bloodshot, and asked, "Hey, man, have you got any uppers?"

Welcome to the world of 70s US hitchhiking!

I've never understood why people pick up hitchhikers, though I'm very grateful that they do. Especially in those days when America was so much more violent than it is now.

Another wild card in the hitchhiking pack were the damaged and unstable soldiers just back from the Vietnam war who drove around the country aimlessly looking for something they probably never found. To say they were volatile is an understatement.

Despite a wealth of possible dangers, I hitched for over 5000 miles and never had to wait more than an hour for someone to give me a lift.

That hour, however, nearly killed me.

I'd hitched a lift from a soldier west of Denver on the I70. He'd received orders to drive to an atomic bomb testing range in the Mojave Desert outside Las Vegas. That was still hundreds of miles away and he was very late.

His motive for picking me up was soon revealed. He'd been driving without sleep for a thousand miles and needed someone to take over. In the early hours of the morning, he stopped the car and asked me to do the driving.

I'm a morning person and I get really sleepy around midnight. I found myself driving a high-powered car through the desert even though I could barely keep my eyes open.

Soon enough my mind wondered and I fell asleep. The sound of the tyres scrabbling across gravel rather than tarmac brought me wide awake.

We were heading straight for a vertical canyon wall. I hit the brakes and hauled the wheel over, slewing us to a stop with only a metre to spare.

The soldier was furious and pushed me back into the passenger seat and started driving again.

I was mortified but fell asleep quickly. Just as quickly I was woken by the sound of tyres on gravel.

We slalomed to a stop just before hitting another canyon wall.

For the next few hours, we did everything we could short of slapping each other to keep ourselves awake. Somehow, we got through Las Vegas and out into the Mojave Desert beyond.

We got to his turnoff at around 11 a.m. Grouchily we parted company and I was left alone on a desert highway, the sun approaching its zenith.

That hour under the blazing sun nearly finished me.

The damned highway was empty. This was in the days long before bottled water was a thing and I was way too stupid to have bought myself a water canteen, assuming I could have found anywhere that sold them. I hadn't drunk anything for twenty hours and was bathing in the Mojave summer temperature of nearly 50 degrees Centigrade.

I was wilting fast. There was nothing to lubricate my tongue so it stuck grimly to the roof of my mouth and I couldn't swallow. The sun began to spin in the sky and I feared my bones would become chew-toys for coyotes.

Suddenly an open-topped red car came zooming towards me along the highway. I stuck out my finger but the car flew by like a rocket ship, its bodywork glinting in the sun.

My heart slumped, hope dashed, but then the driver applied the brakes and the car went into a hundred-metre skid, belching clouds of burnt rubber. It came to a halt then reversed feverishly. As it screeched to a stop beside me, the guy inside threw the door open.

"Just back from a chicken ranch boy those girls were prettiest I've ever seen an' so damned polite must have dropped a couple o' hundred on the tables at Caesars best vacation I've ever had heading back to LA my name is Frank what's yours where are you from..."

This and much else was stuttered out machine gun-like before I could even blink my waterless eyes. This guy was ripped to the tits on amphetamines and was a serious hazard to hitchhikers.

But then again, so was the desert sun.

I got in.

Somehow, we got to LA, zooming by endless strip malls of bars, massage parlours, parking lots and supermarkets. The underside of the Great American Wet Dream. In those days an inverted yellow smog bowl hung over the city and for miles around.

Stuff like this coloured my judgement and I've never warmed to the place since.

There were other hazards to hitching, some quite bizarre. I'd been staying for a couple of days in Monterey with the aunt of a girlfriend. Her beau was a guy who was the spit of Clark Gable.

The hospitality was superb and at the end spit-Clark offered me a lift up to San Francisco which I was going to check out next. I readily accepted and then both of us, drunk as skunks, set off (drinking and driving just weren't much of an issue in those bygone days).

Somehow, we got to San Francisco at which point spit-Clark leaned over and tried to kiss me.

Now I can't deny that both he and the real Clark Cable were fine-looking men, but it just wasn't my thing. I got out of the car as quickly as I could.

The great majority of my rides were very positive experiences; in the conversations over those endless Interstate miles you learn much from your driver about their lives and the country. If they get to like you, Americans can show you limitless kindness.

But… it can also go very badly. I'm glad I did it but I wouldn't want a child of mine to hitch. I know that's hypocritical but I bet there are a lot of old ex-hitchhikers out there who feel the same way.

## Be cavalier with your luggage

In New York at a conference, before 9/11, and heading down Broadway to Times Square, I'd marvel at all the clothes laid out on rows of trestle tables. Though second-hand they looked pretty new and quite upmarket. Where did they come from, I wondered?

When the time came to leave, I caught the coach to Kennedy. Without thinking, I dumped my suitcase in the luggage hold then took a seat at the front and watched some of the crappier and more run-down parts of New York zip by as we left Manhattan. Everything was old and dingy and the antithesis of the gleaming skyscrapers I was leaving behind.

The various terminals at Kennedy are built on a ring and the bus stopped at one after the other. My departure terminal was the last one on the circuit and, you probably guessed it, when I got off and went to the baggage hold, my suitcase was gone.

The scam was blindingly obvious. The bus fare to Kennedy was pretty cheap and all someone had to do was buy a ticket, get on the bus, then get off at one of the first terminals at Kennedy and help themselves to a suitcase in the hold.

Travellers are usually well-heeled, or they were thirty years ago. The stolen clothes may have needed a clean but you'd easily recoup the cost of your coach ticket and laundromat by selling the clothes on... say... the rows of trestle tables on Broadway.

The bottom line is that once you've put your luggage in the hold of a coach, try to get a seat so you can watch to make sure it doesn't make a premature departure.

Some sense of perspective though: in all my travels this is the only thing that's ever been stolen. Just take a little bit of care, that's all.

## Don't think 'In Event of Fire' notices in hotels have nothing to tell you

Toronto isn't exactly the most exciting city in the world but at that time it had a definite frisson. This was a few months after the 2003 outbreak of SARS (severe acute respiratory syndrome) brought to Canada by a visitor from Hong Kong. SARS was the Covid of its day and a portent of things to come. Though it had a higher mortality rate (9% compared to 2% for Covid) it was thankfully far less transmissible. In total the outbreak killed 800 people worldwide, 44 in Canada, of which 33 were in Toronto.

I was attending a conference there and it had been touch-and-go whether it would be cancelled. Had the hotel rooms been properly sterilised, were the little viral particles still circulating in the air conditioning? Even pressing a lift button suddenly held an element of danger.

This is all old hat to everyone nowadays but it was a completely unwelcome novelty in those days. And I needn't have worried about SARS because it would turn out to be the least of my problems.

Being on expenses I was in a nice hotel on the twelfth floor. It was July so walking above ground was pleasant. That's not always the case in Toronto where winters are so fierce that the only way to amble about the city is through the huge network of underground malls. These spread beneath the tall buildings like the roots of an ancient tree. People arrive into an underground station and walk to their offices without ever venturing into the open.

Anyway, when I was there it was summer. That evening a nice meal (Jamaican conch burger as I recall) was accompanied by a fine Chardonnay. All very pleasant and when I got back to my hotel I fell quickly and soundly asleep.

So far so good, but I soon found my dreams turning to nightmare. I dreamed I was back on the merchant ship that caught fire. I heard the alarms and smelled the smoke and felt the same fear that the fire would reach the fuel oil and the whole ship would explode into incandescence; a free fireworks display for the partygoers on the Panama City sea front.

I sat up straight, eyes wide open and ready to find my work boots and fight the fire.

Instead, I found myself in a well-appointed hotel room.

I relaxed back with a sigh. Funny, though, I still smelled smoke. At that moment a fire alarm warbled to life.

Suddenly, getting a room on a high floor for the sake of a good view over Lake Ontario didn't seem such a swell idea.

No fire department has ladders that reach up to the twelfth floor.

I scrambled quickly into my clothes and headed for the door. The emergency lighting was too dim to make out the fire instructions and the little diagram on the back of the hotel room door. You know, the one that shows you the way to the fire exits.

I'd just have to guess.

Cracking open the door made smoke billow in. I couldn't see anyone in the corridor but could hear people coughing, the sound receding as they made their way to the stairs.

I hoped they'd paid more attention to the fire instructions and I followed their coughing.

And it worked. Finding the stairs, I started to descend. To my horror, the smoke and smell of burning got worse.

The fire was between me and the safety of ground level.

I had a simple choice. Go back to my hotel room, wet a towel and put it against the bottom of the door to stop some of the smoke getting in, then hunker down and hope the firemen put out the fire before the fire put me out.

Either that or I could keep going down and hope the fire hadn't reached the stairwell.

Somehow the answer seemed clear and I kept descending but my nerve was tested because the smoke and the smell of burning got so much worse. The visibility became so bad I had to hold onto the stair rail so I knew where I was.

It was becoming difficult to breathe and, for a second, I almost turned back but then, miracle of miracles, the smoke got lighter and I realised I'd passed through the floor that was on fire.

I gambolled like a foal down the next few flights of stairs and emerged exultant onto the sidewalk beside the hotel

Unfortunately, the horror hadn't ended. Clustered around the exit were a large group of rather mature hotel guests in their nightwear. I saw things I wish I could unsee.

After that it could only get better. The fire was put out. Nobody died. Happy ever after.

Except that it put me off shortie nighties for the rest of my life, no matter who was wearing them.

# *Last words*

## Here, now

A lifetime of travel has furnished me with no end of anecdotes. That alone made the journey worthwhile, though my friends and family, and perhaps even you, the reader, may have come to disagree.

Some of the stuff I saw doesn't exist now. South Africa doesn't have apartheid. Chile isn't oppressed by a military dictatorship.

But the point still remains that whenever you travel you see something different and it gives you a better perspective on your life and how it is lived.

You see kindness and you see cruelty and often to a more exaggerated degree than you see at home.

The UK or the US or wherever you live is not the model of how the world should be, no matter what your politicians might tell you. It's just one example of how one society does things. Your country may do some things well but other things not so well. Seeing how other countries work, how the people there live their lives, is always instructive.

So, travel broadens the mind and, with the echo-chamber effect of social media where we only hear from people just like us, that is something we all desperately need.

People are the way they are for reasons we don't have the experience or imagination to understand. When we travel to their countries, we see how they live, see what traditions they are programmed by their society to follow, see the social and economic and financial and climatic pressures they are under. When we experience this for ourselves then suddenly it makes a lot more sense than anything we get from the occasional news item.

Plan trips so you don't set yourself up for something stupid, like arranging a swim in shark-infested seas, but don't be so rigid in your itinerary you miss the magic when it unexpectedly appears.

Life's full of risks but if we never took any then it would be dull, dull, dull.

# *Acknowledgments*

My deepest thanks to Nick Kyle and my old shipmate Paul Owen who were with me on some of my more colourful adventures, yet somehow managed to survive.

Thanks to all the other people who helped me when I got into difficulties on my travels, even when they didn't have to. Don't believe everything you hear on the news- there is a lot of kindness in this world.

I may not say it often enough but I'm always so grateful to my family for letting me away on my travels.

I'd also like to express my profound appreciation to Stephen Cashmore and Jim Campbell and all the staff at Sparsile for their unstinting support.

Finally, in memory of my wild shipmate Dennis Sheehan who sailed over the bar those many years ago.

# *About the Author*

Barrie Condon has travelled the world as a student, sailor, scientist and senior citizen. He did this for the love of it and not just for the purposes of alliteration.

Scottish by birth but brought up in Essex, he served in the Merchant Marine before becoming a clinical physicist. He worked as a consultant scientist for the NHS and was an Honorary Professor at the University of Glasgow.

Nowadays he is retired but still travels extensively and writes both fiction and non-fiction. He lives in Glasgow with his wife and two daughters.

## *Previous books by the author*

*Fiction*:

The Tethered God

The Bamboo Cocoon

*Non-fiction:*

Science for Heretics